TRUE GENTLEMEN

TRUE

GENTLEMEN

THE BROKEN
PLEDGE *of* AMERICA'S
FRATERNITIES

JOHN HECHINGER

PUBLICAFFAIRS

NEW YORK

PublicAffairs
Hachette Book Group
1290 Avenue of the Americas, New York, NY 10104
www.publicaffairsbooks.com
@Public_Affairs

Printed in the United States of America
First Edition: September 2017
Published by PublicAffairs, an imprint of Perseus Books, LLC, a subsidiary of Hachette Book Group, Inc.

The Hachette Speakers Bureau provides a wide range of authors for speaking events. To find out more, go to www.hachettespeakersbureau.com or call (866) 376-6591. The publisher is not responsible for websites (or their content) that are not owned by the publisher.

Print book interior design by Linda Mark

The Library of Congress has cataloged the hardcover edition as follows:
Names: Hechinger, John (John Edward), author.
Title: True gentlemen : the broken pledge of America's fraternities / John Hechinger.
Description: First edition. | New York, NY : PublicAffairs, 2017. | Includes bibliographical references and index.
Identifiers: LCCN 2017008179 (print) | LCCN 2017030026 (ebook) | ISBN 9781610396837 (ebook) | ISBN 9781610396820 (hardback)
Subjects: LCSH: Sigma Alpha Epsilon. | Greek letter societies—United States. | Male college students—United States—Conduct of life. | Racism in higher education—United States. | College students—Alcohol use—United States. | Hazing—United States. | Misogyny—United States. | BISAC: SOCIAL SCIENCE / Men's Studies. | EDUCATION / Students & Student Life.
Classification: LCC LJ75.S25 (ebook) | LCC LJ75.S25 H43 2017 (print) | DDC 371.8/5—dc23
LC record available at https://lccn.loc.gov/2017008179

ISBNs: 978-1-61039-682-0 (hardcover); 978-1-61039-683-7 (ebook)

LSC-C

10 9 8 7 6 5 4 3 2 1

For Ricki and Rachel

CONTENTS

The True Gentleman is the man whose conduct proceeds from good will and an acute sense of propriety, and whose self-control is equal to all emergencies; who does not make the poor man conscious of his poverty, the obscure man of his obscurity, or any man of his inferiority or deformity; who is himself humbled if necessity compels him to humble another; who does not flatter wealth, cringe before power, or boast of his own possessions or achievements; who speaks with frankness but always with sincerity and sympathy; whose deed follows his word; who thinks of the rights and feelings of others, rather than his own; and who appears well in any company, a man with whom honor is sacred and virtue safe.

—Sigma Alpha Epsilon's Creed,
John Walter Wayland, 1899

INTRODUCTION

On a sultry August morning in the Port of Miami, seven hundred fraternity brothers streamed onto the *Majesty of the Seas*, a cruise ship with nine bars and a "Vegas-style Casino Royale." In flip-flops and backward baseball caps, rolling hip-tall suitcases stuffed with blazers and bow ties, they came to learn the ways of "The True Gentleman," the solemn creed of Sigma Alpha Epsilon, one of the largest college fraternities in America. "The True Gentleman," a 123-word passage all members must memorize, amounts to a secular Golden Rule drenched with nostalgia. The creed stresses propriety, self-control, frankness, sincerity, sympathy, humility, and respect for the rights and feelings of others. The True Gentleman is "a man with whom honor is sacred and virtue safe."

This cruise represented the modern incarnation of an eighty-year-old tradition, SAE's annual leadership school. Here, recent initiates would learn how to be social chairmen and chapter presidents—and one day, perhaps, become politicians and chief executive officers. As is often the case with the activities of fraternities, this event might not look good to the outside world. "A booze cruise," a fraternity critic could call it. In reality, SAE has held the school at sea since 2006 because it was easier to control drinking. Once aboard, only those twenty-one and older had bracelets letting them buy alcohol. On the Royal Caribbean excursion, the brothers could also be held captive in conference rooms during daylong classes.

The cruise will long be remembered for its role in violating, in every sense, SAE's own creed. Four years earlier, on this same ship, a few men, perhaps in a hot tub or in hushed voices in their cabins, shared a song, its melody from a childhood sing-along, "If You're Happy and You Know It, Clap Your Hands."

There will never be a nigger in SAE,
There will never be a nigger in SAE,
You can hang him from a tree,
But he can never sign with me,
There will never be a nigger in SAE.

The song traveled from the Caribbean to the University of Oklahoma, where it was repeated behind closed doors at its SAE chapter before going viral in March 2015 when two drunk members on a bus were caught singing it on a cell-phone video that horrified the world.

Just five months later, on the August leadership cruise, members of SAE—including several dozen African Americans—gathered in the ship's Broadway-style main theater to hear Bill Dorfman, a motivational speaker and dentist-to-the-stars known for his on-air makeovers on *The Oprah Winfrey Show*. Dorfman dropped the names of celebrities such as Lindsay Lohan and Jessica Simpson. He showed a picture of his rippling fifty-something physique featured in a men's magazine. He recounted how he turned a knack for self-promotion into a $200-million-a-year business and stormed the *New York Times* best-seller list by buying copies of his own book. "People always say money doesn't make you happy!" he thundered into a microphone. "I say, b.s. It makes you really happy!" The crowd roared, perhaps forgetting that the True Gentleman "does not flatter wealth, cringe before power, or boast of his own possessions or achievements."

Later in the voyage, a thirty-five-year-old father of four daughters took the stage to teach "Etiquette for a True Gentleman." He was known as "Boomer," though his full name was Blaine K. Ayers, and he held the grand title of "Eminent Supreme Recorder of SAE"—what most organizations would call executive director. Ayers, a blond, boyish figure, a former homecoming king who married a sorority girl, wore a crisp gray suit, white shirt, and baby-blue bow tie. "Good manners will open doors that the best education cannot," he said, the soft vowels of his native Kentucky floating like a mist from a bygone era. A gentleman, he said, opens doors for a lady. He rises when a woman approaches a table. He stands to her right on a sidewalk. At parties, he holds a drink in his left hand so the right is free to greet others. No matter how hot, he never loosens his necktie or removes his suit jacket. He pens handwritten thank-you notes. "You should be a better man than you were when you woke up in the morning," Ayers told his protégés.

In another room aboard the vessel, Russell Best faced the challenge of teaching nineteenth-century manners to twenty-first-century bros in the age of Tinder. In a class about preventing sexual assault, Best, a former president of his chapter at the University of Cincinnati, began with the basics, words to avoid: "hitting it," "slut," "ho," "stud," "stallion," and "fraternity slam piece." Words matter, Best told the young men as he strained to reach them in their own language. "The way we talk about sex sounds kind of rapey," said Best, who worked for the fraternity's national office. "How many of you think that drunken hookups are part of college life?" All twenty members of the audience raised their hands. "How many of you have gotten so drunk that you woke up in bed with someone, and you didn't know what happened the night before?" Just about everyone assented. Best urged the men to reconsider such behavior. Colleges—or the police—could accuse them of rape if a woman was too drunk to give consent. A junior from Indiana University complained about what he saw as a double standard in sexual assault: "Why is it always the dude's fault when both people are drunk?"

Another class revealed the unholy trinity of fraternity life: racial insensitivity, dangerous drinking, and misogyny. Brandon Weghorst, the fraternity's communications chief, called it: "PR Nightmare: Our Public Image Exposed." He flashed photos on a screen, a growing collection he kept as a cautionary tale for occasions like these: Strippers in front of a chapter house. A Confederate battle flag. A brother pouring vodka down a young woman's throat. "Rush SAE" painted across naked breasts (a fraternity recruitment phenomenon called "rush boobs"). And a couple of unofficial creeds, painted on rocks and walls, the proud handiwork of the late-teenage mind uncluttered with ideals of honor and virtue: "SAE. Work Hard. Play Hard. Stay Hard." and "SAE: We do bitches!! Pulling hoes since 1856."

FEW AMERICAN INSTITUTIONS face as wide a chasm between high-minded ideals and on-the-ground reality as the college fraternity. It is among the many contradictions of the Greek-letter movement, which is as old as the United States itself. Fraternities once faced near-universal condemnation from college presidents, who viewed the secretive brotherhoods as a threat to morality and scholarship; yet today, fraternities are, more often than not, partners with school administrators who praise them for fostering philanthropy, community, and leadership—even as alcohol-soaked Greek parties generate no end of injuries and embarrassing headlines. Women now dominate higher education in numbers and accomplishment, yet these all-male organizations control social lives with their exclusive parties and face complaints of misogyny and sexual assault. Fraternities profess to judge men solely by their character, yet they have long been criticized for fostering divisions of class and race. Their reputations are in tatters, yet fraternities are more popular than ever. They lash out at critics; yet in private they are often withering in their self-criticism and eager for reform.

Over two years, I traveled across the country, trying to understand the jarring conflict between fraternities' words and deeds. I examined their darkest moments, the brutality hidden in basements and bedrooms, shielded by covered windows and student "lookouts" and denied long after overwhelming evidence had revealed the truth. I visited chapter houses at state colleges with big-time football teams, Ivy League schools with pipelines to Wall Street, and smaller colleges with accomplished alumni who dominate Main Street businesses across America. I joined fraternity men and sorority women as they cruised in the Caribbean and had cocktails with members of Congress at a Capitol Hill hotel. I saw a billionaire fly in and out of a meeting in Southern California on his private jet, addressing members before they debated a contentious plan to make their chapters safer. I witnessed a national president confronting an ugly history of hazing and racism, and I watched an unlikely fraternity man devote what could be the last year of his life to keeping a promise to a troubled chapter he helped transform into a national model.

At many schools, especially the public universities that award most bachelor's degrees, the Greek-letter groups that dominate the physical and social landscape have a greater influence on students' lives than any academic department. Visit a college with a flourishing fraternity scene, and you'll find an "Office of Greek Life," where administrators endorse materials that make fraternity gatherings sound as innocent as a square dance. Stroll along fraternity row, and you'll find jaw-dropping mansions that look like the set of *Gone with the Wind*. Greek organizations own $3 billion in real estate on eight hundred US campuses, offering some of the most expensive and sought-after housing and dividing campuses into haves and have-nots. Their members often form a voting bloc that gives them unrivaled power in student government and, later, a lifelong social network that can catapult them ahead of less-connected classmates. About 40 percent of US presidents have belonged to fraternities, including Gerald Ford (Delta Kappa Epsilon [DKE], University of Michigan), the two Presidents Bush (both DKE, Yale), Ronald Reagan (Tau Kappa Epsilon [TKE], Eureka College), and Bill Clinton (Phi Beta Sigma, honorary member). Donald Trump, though frequently called out for the worst kind of frat-boy behavior, never belonged to a chapter. Thirty-nine percent of senators in the 113th US Congress and one-fourth of US representatives belonged to fraternities. So did one-third of all US Supreme Court justices; and business titans such as Berkshire Hathaway's Warren Buffett (Alpha Sigma Phi) and Walmart's late founder, Sam Walton (Beta Theta Pi). There's even a lobbying arm, the Fraternity and Sorority Political Action Committee known as FratPAC, that opposed national anti-hazing legislation and supported a bill that would make it more difficult for colleges to investigate sexual assault.

Fraternity brothers themselves tend to cherish their experiences, viewing their time in chapter houses as among the most meaningful of their college years. The organizations promote close friendships, no small matter at larger, more impersonal universities. Members learn to govern themselves, electing officers who oversee budgets, plan events, and punish those who break the rules. Joining up can often be a stepping-stone to student government. Like corporate chief executives on the philanthropy circuit, leaders raise more than $20 million a year, often through dances and parties that can be the pinnacle of the social calendar. A 2014 survey of 30,000 undergraduates by Gallup and Purdue University found that members of Greek-letter groups reported higher levels of "well-being," such as having a sense of purpose and community and strong relationships with friends and family. More than other students, they believed their institutions prepared them for life after college, and in an emotional response significant to college presidents hungry for donations, they expressed a closer attachment to their alma maters. The Indiana University Foundation, which raises money for the public college, reported that Greeks, which compose 19 percent of its database of alumni, made 60 percent of all donations.

To a degree not widely understood, fraternities pioneered the American conception of college, a place where extracurricular life can eclipse scholarship. This is a book about what it means for students, parents, universities—and America—that fraternities play such an outsize role in higher education. The historical legacy of fraternities in part shapes our very idea of coming of age, and the matter of how we reform—or abolish—them cuts to the core of higher education's mission. To quote one noted SAE brother, the past is never dead. It's not even past.

Much has been written about fraternities' misbehavior, which seems as inevitable as fall leaves and tuition increases. Insurance companies have rated fraternities just above toxic-waste dumps because of claims related to drinking, hazing, and sexual assault. There have been journalistic exposés, as well as shocking memoirs of fraternity life. Historians, sociologists, and other academics have offered illuminating accounts of the roots and culture of Greek life. But the contradictions of fraternities remain rich territory for exploration. I offer the perspective of an outsider who never belonged to a fraternity; a concerned father of a daughter still in college; a reporter who has examined thousands of pages of court and disciplinary records; and a chapter-house guest who listened to the opinions of scores of members themselves. They often complained that they are stereotyped, blamed for the behavior of the worst among them. In the end, though, it seemed more than fair to measure fraternities against their own standards, their own words, and the highest values they seek to promote.

The current moment represents a turning point for fraternities. Several forces have conspired to challenge Greek-letter organizations: social media and cell-phone videos have pierced their secrecy; litigation has led national offices either to distance themselves to avoid liability or to consider enforcing codes of behavior on disparate chapters that have traditionally operated with little centralized authority; and an increasingly diverse campus has led to more intense questioning of fraternities' exclusivity. Still, the rise of Trump has revealed a deep well of white, male resentment that could provoke a backlash against any change.

The roughly seventy historically white, male, Greek-letter organizations have 4 million living alumni and represent the most venerable and dominant force in the movement. Their chapters, most of which belong to the North-American Interfraternity Conference, have more than 380,000 undergraduate members, a 50 percent increase over the last decade and just short of a 1990 record. One in six men who attend a four-year college full-time belongs to a fraternity. With their campus partners, the traditionally white sororities, fraternities form a bloc that can command more power and resources than any other student group. African Americans, Latinos, Asian Americans, and other minority groups, excluded from fraternities at the movement's inception, have created their own Greek organizations. Although they lack the population, money, and influence of the historically white chapters, these fraternities and sororities further magnify the presence of Greek life. At the University of Alabama, for example, fraternities and sororities make up 36 percent of students. Some of the country's most elite colleges, such as the Massachusetts Institute of Technology (MIT) and Dartmouth, are Greek strongholds, where one-half or more of male students belong to a fraternity.

This book focuses largely on a single fraternity, Sigma Alpha Epsilon, in the hope that the narrative's specificity will yield a richer portrait—that the part will shed greater truths about the whole. As David Stollman, a member of rival Sigma Phi Epsilon, told the men on the SAE leadership cruise, fraternities are more alike than different. Stollman, who has visited hundreds of campuses to hold boot camps on recruitment, mentioned the handshakes, Greek letters, and secret rituals featuring candles and robes. More important, he said, Greeks tend to espouse a similar set of ideals. Sigma Chi's creed begins, "I believe in fairness, decency and good manners." Tau Kappa Epsilon calls for a "life based upon integrity, justice, sincerity, patience, moderation, culture and challenge." The Kappa Alpha Order (KA) tells its initiates that "the manner in which an individual enjoys certain advantages over others is a test of a true gentleman." The creed becomes an organizing principle for a life well lived. When members of SAE die, the fraternity holds a service, replete with religious symbolism, to honor the recently departed, those who now reside in "the chapter eternal."

Using the measure of members initiated over time, SAE claims to be the largest fraternity. Since its founding, SAE counts 336,000 brothers, with two-thirds alive today. At its peak in 2014, almost 15,000 undergraduates belonged to SAE chapters on more than 230 campuses. Like every fraternity, SAE has its own character. At its most populous chapters, it has a regional flavor. SAE claims the distinction of being the only continuously operating general fraternity founded in the antebellum South to survive the Civil War. Its members have included the writers William Faulkner at the University of Mississippi and Walker Percy at the University of North Carolina (UNC). Its chapters have especially strong ties to Wall Street. T. Boone Pickens, the Texas oilman-turned-investor, and Henry Paulson, the former Goldman Sachs CEO and secretary of the US Treasury, are both SAEs. LinkedIn, a networking website for professionals, recently listed almost 3,000 alumni in finance, more than any other industry. SAE holds a prominent place in popular culture. Stephen Colbert's conservative blowhard character on *The Colbert Report* comedy show proclaimed his Dartmouth SAE membership. SAE plays a supporting role in *Animal House*, the sine qua non of frat films. In that 1978 movie, SAE inspired the rich, snobby fraternity that was the nemesis of comedian John Belushi's out-of-control chapter.

Today, SAE is perhaps America's most notorious fraternity. The Oklahoma video and other racial episodes continue to alienate African Americans and trouble some of its own black members. "I couldn't believe it," Devontae Dennis, a black member from the University of Wisconsin, told me on the leadership cruise. "SAEs are like my brothers." Dennis stood by the fraternity, but it hadn't been easy. A month after the video hit the Internet, Dennis, wearing an SAE T-shirt, was on spring break in Panama City, Florida. An African American woman ran up and chided him: "You're a traitor." The same year that the video surfaced, *The Hunting Ground*, a documentary about campus rape, singled out SAE. One section left a lasting impression on viewers. In the movie, a narrator asks women on various campuses what SAE stands for. "Sexual Assault Expected," they say again and again.

For almost a decade, SAE was the deadliest fraternity. From 2005 through 2013, at least ten people died in incidents related to SAE, mostly from drinking and hazing, and more than any other fraternity. (During the same time span, more than sixty died at all fraternities.) As a result, SAE paid the highest costs for liability insurance of any fraternity. Universities have disciplined more than 130 SAE chapters over the past five years, some repeatedly. More than thirty chapters have been shut down since 2013.

The leaders of SAE know they are a legal judgment away from oblivion. "We've faced the greatest challenge since the Civil War," Steven Churchill, its national president, told undergraduates at the start of the leadership cruise. As the members came aboard, he could see the wide-eyed stares of other passengers, especially the parents fearing for the safety of their teenage daughters in a sea of men wearing Greek letters. "When people who are on this ship find out we are a fraternity, they will be alarmed," Churchill, a former state legislator from Iowa, said. "When they hear it's SAE, they will be even more concerned. Be a true gentleman. Be mindful of what you say and do. If you're not careful, it can spread like a cancer."

In other words, no matter its power, influence, and storied history, the American college fraternity faces an existential choice. It can perpetuate the ugliest chapters of American history. Or it can turn the page and once again reflect the country's highest aspirations.

PART ONE

VICE

1

DRINKING GAMES

"Whose Self-Control Is Equal to All Emergencies"

Relaxing after a couple of tough exams on a cold and rainy February night in 2011, George Desdunes and his fraternity buddy drank straight Jameson Irish Whiskey out of plastic cups. Before they knew it, Desdunes and Kyle Morton had polished off the better part of a bottle in half an hour. For most, downing nine ounces of the eighty-proof liquor that fast would be quite a feat. By Morton's accounting, it amounted to the equivalent of six or seven mixed drinks apiece, enough to bring their blood-alcohol level to twice the legal limit for driving. Desdunes and Morton were just warming up. In Morton's bedroom, the brothers from Cornell University were "pre-gaming," a routine practice on an ordinary Thursday night at the Sigma Alpha Epsilon house. At 10:30 p.m., Morton, a junior from Scarsdale, New York, headed downstairs for the night's main event, a beer-pong tournament, a test of alcohol tolerance and hand-eye coordination that would last until the early hours of the next morning. Desdunes skipped beer pong that evening because he had better plans. The nineteen-year-old sophomore, who had a fake ID, was getting ready to hit a bar or two in Collegetown, the nighttime haven for Cornell students in Ithaca, New York. He hoped to meet up with his girlfriend, an outdoorsy young woman who had just graduated in January 2011 and was preparing for a career on Wall Street.

"What are you up to tonight?" Desdunes texted her at 11:00 p.m.

"Dunbar's," she replied, naming a dive bar featuring a $6 "Group Therapy" drink special—a pitcher of beer and a carafe of shots of vodka, triple sec, and lime.

Desdunes said he'd probably hit Dino's, another local hangout. Or maybe Level B, a basement dance club and bar known for its $18 "fishbowl," a half bottle of vodka, or sixteen shots. They'd meet up later. Now, before he headed out, all Desdunes needed was a few more drinks—a second round of pre-gaming. About 11:30 p.m., Desdunes hauled a jug of Captain Morgan into another bedroom, where he and three other SAE brothers mixed rum-and-Pepsis strong enough to knock out a sailor on shore leave. Each plastic cup had two or three shots of liquor. Within half an hour, the brothers knocked back three apiece. They averaged seven drinks per guy, one of them figured.

Desdunes and his Cornell fraternity brothers worked hard and played hard, as college students liked to say—and, by play, they meant drink. On the first floor, the bar and the library sat side by side in their ivy-covered mansion of a frat house. Built in 1915, the SAE chapter house at Cornell had been dubbed "Hillcrest," evoking the grandeur of an English country home with its Tudor-style architecture and view of nearby Cayuga Lake. It was a sprawling residence, able to house ninety men. Among its illustrious members had been Eamon McEneaney, Cornell class of 1977, considered the greatest lacrosse player of his generation, later becoming a senior vice president at Wall Street's Cantor Fitzgerald. He died at the World Trade Center on September 11, 2001, while saving the lives of sixty-three people. More recently, two members had been elected to the Ithaca City Council while undergraduates, and still others belonged to the prestigious Quill and Dagger secret honor society. Nominating the chapter for an award the year before, Travis Apgar, the associate dean overseeing Greek life at Cornell, had called Sigma Alpha Epsilon "an example of what a fraternity and its members can and should be."

The current crop of SAE members, including future financiers at Goldman Sachs and Morgan Stanley, liked to think they were cut from the same cloth. They vied for top grades and summer internships with the same gusto they had for beer pong. Regardless of the damage to their livers and brain cells, many were fine physical specimens and world-class varsity athletes, demonstrating the competitive drive that would also be prized on Wall Street. Eric Barnum, the chapter's "Eminent Archon," or president, played varsity golf; Connor Pardell rode on the polo team; Max Haskin played varsity tennis; and E. J. Williams was a wide receiver on the football team.

Lean and muscular, with a wide, open smile, Desdunes was a natural fit in the chapter. A graduate of Berkeley Carroll, a private school in Brooklyn, he had been on the varsity soccer and swim teams. In one way, though, he was unusual among the brothers and their country-club sports. An African American in a historically white fraternity, he was the child of a single mother, a Haitian immigrant who worked as a hospital aide. Now, he hoped SAE's prestige, along with an Ivy League degree, would ensure his success. With dreams of being a doctor, he was taking the notoriously demanding science and math courses of the pre-med track.

For all his ambition, Desdunes slept with a jug of Jose Cuervo tequila on his dresser. Even at a hard-partying chapter, he stood out. His roommate, Matthew Picket, noticed that Desdunes would drink heavily three or four times a week. By heavily, he didn't mean five drinks in a sitting—as the Centers for Disease Control and Prevention defines binge drinking. Picket meant the kind of bender that ended with the loss of consciousness and, in some cases, dignity. Desdunes had been known to tip over while seated at a bar. "He probably drinks more than he should, but he's usually OK to get home on his own," Picket remembered later. "He would be someone that you would check on in a bar, for example. If he was keeled over, you wanted to make sure he was OK." One time, Desdunes urinated by accident on the door of another brother's room; another time, on a Sony PlayStation 3 system. "I almost expected to hear that George would be in the ER from drinking too much," Picket said. "If you continue habits like that, your luck has to run out."

If his fraternity brothers were alarmed, they didn't do much about it. Maybe it was a matter of glass houses. Who didn't have trouble remembering the previous night? "I mean, I did almost the same thing," said Picket, who later listed single-malt scotch as an interest on his LinkedIn profile. As much as vodka made a screwdriver, drinking defined the Cornell SAE house. That night and into the next morning, pledges—provisional members seeking full acceptance—were on call as "sober drivers." Like chauffeurs tending high-rollers at a casino, they served at the pleasure of older members who could call on newbies for rides at any hour. In 2006, Cornell disciplined the chapter after discovering a written pledge guide that suggested the role alcohol played in a freshman's SAE initiation. Among other things, new members were expected to clean vomit out of cars. Along with their driving duties, they could also be called on as janitors for those who couldn't hold their liquor. Pledges were full-service alcohol enablers, pressed into service by the fraternity.

Members knew firsthand the dangers of bingeing on alcohol. In September, an underage woman who had been drinking at SAE was hospitalized. The campus police had pulled over a car and found her moaning in the back seat, her dress pulled down over one shoulder. The Cornell judicial board sentenced SAE to six weeks of social probation to "educate the chapter of the dangers associated with over-intoxication." After the chapter was busted, Barnum, its president, had promised SAE's general counsel that every member would sign a statement agreeing to abide by the fraternity's policies about drinking. In exchange, the national organization dropped its $100-per-member fine for supplying the alcohol to the underage woman who was hospitalized. Five months later, as Desdunes prepared for Collegetown, much of what the men were doing that night violated SAE's "risk-management" policies, as well as Cornell rules and New York State law. They were playing drinking games, providing alcohol to minors, offering alcohol from a "common source" with no controls, and serving the already drunk. SAE spelled out its expectations in a manual called "Minerva's Shield," named after SAE's patron Roman goddess of wisdom. The manual suggested a deeper meaning to its rules; they existed "so may you through wisdom learn to subdue the baser passions and instincts of your nature."

But if the men had read Minerva's Shield and agreed to honor it, they certainly didn't show it. The familiar tropes of fraternity drinking culture persisted, which meant that their private behavior continued to show little resemblance to their public pronouncements. It was a bit like *Casablanca*; if word got out, all would be shocked, shocked to find out there was underage drinking at SAE. But even a casual visitor would have noticed the first-floor bar and the beer-pong table. SAE brothers were also supposed to be on the lookout for dangerous drinking, referring members to counseling and acting, in the words of the fraternity, as their "brother's keeper."

Instead, the chapter seemed to revel in Desdunes's drinking. Members shared stories about his exploits and challenged him to a beer-chugging contest. One day, perhaps, Desdunes's tolerance for alcohol could become inspiration for the next pledge class, kids still in high school who didn't remember John Belushi in *Animal House* or Will Ferrell in *Old School*. It was all summed up in Desdunes's nickname, one of those signposts of frat culture like beer funnels and hangovers. One pledge was known as "Tuna Tunnel," slang for vagina, because the brothers considered him timid. Another was known as "Cornhole Compressor," a reference to anal sex, a preoccupation of frat life. Desdunes's nickname reflected one of his pastimes. The brothers called him "Blackout George."

At American colleges, particularly elite ones, the drinking and buffoonery of fraternity men can seem mystifying. Why would such ambitious students choose to pursue minors in humiliation, vomit, and semi-consciousness? Each time a chapter house gets busted for underage drinking or worse, a national fraternity will say its chapter has strayed from its values of character and leadership. The explanation rings hollow for good reason. The two seemingly irreconcilable strands—debauchery and ambition—have for two centuries been the key ingredients of Greek life. Even if the guys wanted to be sober—and most don't—disentangling high times and high ideals would require a reimagining of one of America's oldest subcultures. Drinking is so deeply associated with fraternities that many can't conceive of chapter houses without alcohol.

Consider the precursor of the Cornell SAE house and the American fraternity: Phi Beta Kappa. In December 1776, high-minded men at William and Mary, the first public university in America, founded the literary and academic society. Its initials stood for its motto, "Love of learning is the guide of life." It's worth noting, too, that its founders met in a bar, a famous one, the Apollo Room of the Raleigh Tavern in Williamsburg, Virginia. Phi Beta Kappa, of course, developed into an honorary scholarship organization, the epitome of academic achievement.

By the nineteenth century, however, the impulse behind Phi Beta Kappa turned into something that looked more like the modern fraternity. In 1825, students at Union College in Schenectady, New York, were tired of studying theology and the dusty Latin and Greek manuscripts of early nineteenth-century universities. They wanted to become movers and shakers, not preachers and monks. This feeling led some Phi Beta Kappans to band together to form what is considered the first "social fraternity," the Kappa Alpha Society. Members of social fraternities rebelled by reading American literature and poetry. They also sought the friendship and loyalty of their peers, so they could start successful businesses and law firms. Animating hidebound institutions with a kind of adolescent energy, Greek-letter organizations became a linchpin of what Roger L. Geiger, the Pennsylvania State University historian of higher education, called the "collegiate revolution" and its focus on extracurricular activities and the liberal arts. Colleges promoted the social skills and knowledge necessary for entrée into the upper middle class. In that way, fraternities helped create the American-style college experience.

At the same time, these societies immediately attracted men whose heavy drinking overshadowed their other accomplishments. Fraternity members, like college students across the country, were chafing at what they considered tyrannical rules governing their behavior. College presidents imposed curfews and fought against gambling and liquor. Students even rioted.

These conflicts with college administrations intensified fraternities' secrecy and they became places where men could indulge
in their favorite vices. Drinking became central to the identity of the fraternity man. Late nineteenth-century accounts of
Yale's fraternity-dominated social life expressed admiration for
the "well-known drinking bout" and the "the noble and hearty"
souls who enjoy "a little of the fiery flavor of sin." At Ohio's
Miami University, future US president Benjamin Harrison led
the Phi Delta Theta fraternity and complained of the "drinking and spreeing" of two of the fraternity's most popular men,
including his own roommate. In 1851, these two horrified the
community when they arrived drunk at a meeting of the Young
Men's Temperance Society. Phi Delta Theta kicked them out,
but other fraternities quickly welcomed them.

SAE's birth in 1856 reflected this mix of high ideals and low
behavior. Its founder, Noble Leslie DeVotie, was a Phi Beta
Kappa–style scholar. Pale and with brooding gray eyes, weigh-
ing only 120 pounds, he was the University of Alabama's vale-
dictorian and a scholar of French and English literature. After
attending Princeton Theological Seminary, he became a minis-
ter like his father. But DeVotie's fellow founders were mediocre
students and troublemakers. The University of Alabama's president, Landon Garland, hated fraternities and did all he could
to stamp them out. He once told trustees that they "tended only
toward evil" and promoted the drinking, fighting, and vandalism that was scandalizing the college's hometown of Tuscaloosa. Even the symbols DeVotie chose for SAE reflected a
duality: Minerva, the Roman name for Athena, the goddess of
wisdom, represented its respect for the intellect; its other symbol, the lion, reflected an untamed spirit.

Today, SAE undergraduates like to tell a story about DeVotie that speaks volumes about fraternity culture. It begins with
the historical record. On February 12, 1861, a stormy day with

choppy seas, DeVotie, a Confederate chaplain, prepared to board a steamer at Fort Morgan, which guarded Mobile, Alabama. On the dock, he lost his step and fell in the ocean, hitting his head. The current swept him out to sea, leaving behind a shawl, his hat, a handkerchief, and letters he was mailing for some soldiers. His body, still wrapped in a Confederate sash, washed ashore three days later. He was twenty-three years old and, according to SAE, the first Alabamian to die in the Civil War. The elders of SAE celebrate DeVotie's short life as a model for the fraternity's long history of military service. But some undergraduates suspect another tradition played a role in DeVotie's death. They have no evidence from the historical record. And their conclusion says more about them than DeVotie. They like to say he was drunk.

I first heard this interpretation from Andrew Cowie, an Indiana University sophomore who attended the SAE leadership cruise. The next month, I visited Cowie on the campus, which is famous for its fraternity life. Cowie led me into the basement of his new $4.5-million house, where portraits of DeVotie and the seven other founders hung on the walls of the room reserved for both parties and official business, such as initiations. On that Sunday morning, my shoes stuck to the floor and I could smell a sour odor, no doubt from a party the night before. Cowie, who grew up in Nashville, was Hollywood's image of a fraternity man, a six-foot-four former center on his high school basketball team with a deep voice and a taste for seersucker shirts. Soon to become president, Cowie had been helping lead his chapter's revival since it had been shut down for underage drinking in 2002. (At one party, the police found seventy-seven cases of beer, a keg, and eighteen 1.75-liter bottles of rum.) Cowie, the grandson of an SAE chapter president from Louisiana State University, appreciated the resonance of a fraternity's founder dying in a freak drinking accident. "I don't know what it says about us and our history," Cowie told me with a chuckle.

SAE brothers also tell an apocryphal story about one of their most famous members, Eliot Ness, the famed prohibition agent, and his nemesis, the gangster Al Capone. As legend has it, Paddy Murphy, Capone's lieutenant and a member of SAE, refused Capone's command to shoot Ness because he saw the lawman's SAE badge. Capone shot Murphy instead. Every year, members of SAE throw raucous parties and hold a mock Irish wake in honor of the fictional Paddy Murphy. It's a chance to celebrate Ness in true fraternity fashion—with a drink.

A few months after meeting Cowie, I traveled to SAE's headquarters on the campus of Northwestern University, where I discovered a historical contradiction at the heart of the fraternity: its headquarters would not be located in Evanston, Illinois—and it might not even exist—were it not for the temperance movement, America's famous fight against alcohol.

One of the movement's fiercest advocates, William C. Levere, had excelled at oratory as a boy. His precocious speeches on the evils of alcohol drew national attention. At age fourteen, he moved from his native Connecticut to Evanston at the urging of the Woman's Christian Temperance Union. In 1894, Levere entered Northwestern, where, predictably, he attacked fraternities. But then SAE tapped a close friend of Levere's, the most popular man in the freshman class, to start a Northwestern chapter. His friend insisted Levere join, too, and for reasons never fully explained, he became a diehard fraternity man.

After college, Levere became SAE's first "Eminent Supreme Recorder," or executive director. He was among the men who built the fraternity into a powerhouse after it nearly died out following the Civil War. Levere also penned a three-volume, 1,500-page history of SAE, which glossed over the fraternity's drinking. It must have taken some doing. In 1908, as Levere was researching his tome, David Starr Jordan, another teetotaler and Stanford University's first president, was cracking down on "beer busts" on fraternity row, where partially undressed men staggered from house to house, vomiting and urinating. When Stanford banned beer busts that spring, hundreds of undergraduates protested. The demonstration began at the SAE house. Men bearing band instruments joined in as if they were headed to a football game. "Beer! Booze!" they chanted.

SAE's headquarters—named after Levere—struck me as the embodiment of its central contradiction. Completed in 1930 at the equivalent of $6 million today, the Levere Memorial Temple looks like a Gothic cathedral. Inside, rows of priceless Tiffany stained-glass windows bathe a sanctuary with light. The most prominent window rises high above the altar: a white-robed Jesus Christ, arms outstretched to two Civil War soldiers, one in Confederate gray, another in Union blue, each leaning on a rifle. "Pax Vobiscum" (Peace be with you), reads the Latin inscription.

The basement feels earthier. It features a wood-paneled dining hall with oddly kitschy murals of college life painted by the German artist Johannes Waller, a favorite of an SAE president who grew up in Germany. In the murals, students and professors are portrayed as gnomes, complete with white beards and long, pointy noses. In one mural, the gnomes appear to be singing while holding huge steins of beer. Nearby, one fellow with a bright red nose, hands on his head, eyes closed, has passed out next to a huge barrel. By his feet are an overturned mug and a puddle of beer. In the sanctuary that greets most visitors, SAE proclaims heavenly ideals, but the basement reveals a less noble reality. It would be hard to find a place that more perfectly expresses the two sides of the American college fraternity.

IN THE MODERN era, drinking fueled the reemergence of fraternities on college campuses after their decline in the counterculture of the 1960s and early 1970s. The more conservative

Reagan era was tailor-made for fraternities' nostalgic traditions. President Reagan also inadvertently bolstered Greek
life by backing a law that required states to raise the drinking
age from eighteen to twenty-one to remain eligible for federal
highway funding. On campus, the change made it harder for
college students to drink, as dorm parties could no longer feature beer kegs. With the status of private groups, fraternities
seized the opportunity to fill the alcohol void. It helped that in
the 1960s, colleges lost their legal status as organizations that
could act in loco parentis—as if they were parents. As adults,
students now had constitutional rights to assemble, as well as
due process in terms of discipline. This shift made fraternities
tough adversaries for administrators. Sororities still prohibited
alcohol in their chapter houses, and unlike fraternities, most
had house mothers to enforce the rules. But fraternities rejected that kind of adult oversight, and the men gladly hosted
underage women to drink at their parties. Simon Bronner,
a Pennsylvania State University professor who wrote a book
about campus culture, observed that as "colleges cracked down
on drinking in dorms, many Greek houses became underage
drinking clubs."

A consortium of fraternities that studied Greek drinking
noted that the 1980s marked a turning point:

> Kegs, party balls, beer trucks with a dozen taps along the sides,
> kegerators, 55-gallon drums with a mixture of liquor and Kool-
> Aid, ad infinitum. "Tradition" became a common theme for
> parties, ranging from "tiger breakfast" to "heaven and hell,"
> with variations. Most of us in the Greek movement would agree
> that there was a corresponding loss of what makes a men's or
> women's fraternity or sorority special or unique. Values, ideals,
> the Ritual . . . became secondary. Parties and alcohol became
> the primary focus.

Both inspiring and reflecting this culture, the movie *Animal House*, which came out in 1978, became a touchstone for a generation of frat guys.

Today, one fact is undeniable: fraternity men are the heaviest drinkers on college campuses. Sorority women are not far behind. From the 1990s through 2007, researchers at the Harvard School of Public Health conducted a study that became the gold standard for research on university drinking. Its leading researcher, Henry Wechsler, popularized the term "binge drinking," which he defined as downing five or more drinks in a row for men, four for women. From 1992 through 2007, his landmark College Alcohol Study surveyed more than 17,000 students at 140 four-year colleges. The questionnaire asked students how many had engaged in binge drinking within the previous two weeks. Eighty-six percent of men who lived in fraternities and 80 percent of sorority residents reported binge drinking, compared with 45 percent of men not living in fraternities and 36 percent of women. The study also looked at "frequent binge drinkers," those who had binged at least three times in the previous two weeks. Two in five members of Greek organizations were "frequent binge drinkers," compared with one in five non-Greek students. "They are the leaders of the drinking culture," Wechsler told me. "They are the highest consumers of alcohol. Of all the associations, the traits associated with drinking, fraternity membership and, particularly, fraternity residence, are the strongest." Countless other studies have since affirmed the portrait of the hard-drinking fraternity man.

Still, fraternities routinely deny this fact. The website of the Interfraternity Council at the University of Colorado at Boulder was typical, calling the link between Greek chapters and binge drinking "a myth" and adding that "the stereotypical party atmosphere is not a reality, and certainly not the norm." Wechsler, the drinking expert, finds those attitudes frustrating because his research shows that fraternities can change only after they acknowledge the truth. In his view, colleges and fraternities can, in fact, choose to crack down on drinking and save lives.

Such a strategy requires adults to challenge fraternities' cherished tradition of combining adolescent self-government and alcohol. Phi Delta Theta, where President Harrison had fought drinking in the nineteenth century, tried that approach and turned around its safety record. In the 1990s and 2000, three of its members had died because of alcohol: one member had been too drunk to leave his house during a fire, another died in bed after being forced to drink in an initiation ritual, and a third died driving drunk on his motorcycle. The fraternity had been paying out millions of dollars a year in insurance claims. In 2000, Phi Delta Theta banned alcohol in its chapter houses. In the fifteen years since, its claims payments plunged more than 90 percent. The average amount an undergraduate paid for insurance coverage fell by half, to $80 a year. SAE brothers have had to pay as much as $340. Phi Delta Theta has had no alcohol-related deaths and fewer accidents, even as membership surged to 12,000 from 8,000. "We've been able to articulate a message to students," Bob Biggs, its chief executive, told me. "If you want a drinking club experience, go somewhere else." Biggs is the first to admit that the fraternity hasn't eliminated dangerous or underage drinking at its chapters. But Phi Delta Theta has reduced it, or at least its worst consequences. At conventions in both 2011 and 2013, SAE leadership proposed following Phi Delta Theta's lead and banning alcohol at SAE houses. In each case, the measure fell short of the three-fourths vote required to change the fraternity's laws.

The disciplinary records of SAE chapters show why its national office wanted to reduce drinking. At its University of California at San Diego chapter, from 2010 through 2014, the university documented minors drinking themselves unconscious and into detox and the arrests of students for disorderly conduct and for lying to the police about alcohol. In July 2014, one member even posted on social media that the chapter had a goat and party guests could "feed him beers" for their amusement. Then there was the University of Arizona chapter, known for its "Jungle Party," featuring a 65,000-gallon pool, fake waterfall, and tree house—a "wonderful combination of hydration, inebriation and sartorial minimalism," in the words of *Playboy* magazine when it named the University of Arizona one of the country's top party schools. At the pool party—and many other gatherings—the university repeatedly cited SAE for minors in possession of alcohol, drunkenness, and hospitalizations for alcohol poisoning. In September 2012, a young woman had played a drinking game at an SAE event where she had tracked her shots by drawing lines on her arm—twenty-four in all. She vomited in a garbage can and passed out.

Over the last five years, more than 130 chapters have been disciplined, nearly always because of behavior related to drinking. That's a remarkable figure, considering that the number of chapters and provisional outposts, called colonies, peaked at 245 in 2014. There's no way to compare SAE with other fraternities. SAE keeps a running tally of infractions on its website because a legal settlement over an alcohol-poisoning death now requires it to do so; other fraternities have no such requirement. But a yearlong investigation of hundreds of fraternity incidents suggests SAE may, in fact, be representative. In a compelling 2014 *Atlantic* cover story, the journalist Caitlin Flanagan found drinking at the heart of accidents that included, with alarming regularity, falls from windows and porches of fraternity houses. In an unforgettable episode, at the Alpha Tau Omega house in 2011, one drunk guest fell off a deck while filming a cell-phone video of another, who was presumably even more drunk. He had been trying to launch a bottle rocket out of his anus.

In terms of killing people through drink, however, SAE surpassed all others. Alcohol abuse has led to the death of SAE members and their guests in a heartbreaking list of ways: a drunk member killed a party guest after the car he was driving careened off a road (December 2014, Washington and Lee University, Lexington, Virginia); a guest froze to death under a bridge after drinking at an SAE party (January 2012, University of Idaho); a freshman pledge died of alcohol poisoning from drinking margaritas, a dozen beers, and Jack Daniels (March 2009, University of Kansas).

At times, SAE men seem inured to the mayhem, the injuries, and the body count. The excuses pile up. It wasn't an official event; he drank before the party or somewhere else. Then, it happens again. In November 2012, Jack Culolias, a nineteen-year-old freshman pledge at Arizona State University, disappeared after a sorority mixer at a local bar called Cadillac Ranch. He had last been seen so drunk he was urinating on the patio outside the bar. Sixteen days later, searchers found him drowned in the Salt River, his blood alcohol three times the legal limit. Six months later, another SAE member was hospitalized after downing about twenty tequila shots during a drinking contest at an off-campus party. He had turned blue. Even then, Robert Valenza, who was the SAE chapter president before Arizona State shut down the fraternity, told me the chapter shouldn't be blamed for drinking. "People will find alcohol. People will be underage," he said. "It's just part of the college experience."

The victims of fraternity behavior are usually less understanding—and some hire lawyers. Starting in the 1980s and 1990s, as Greek membership boomed, it also became easier to sue. The doctrine of comparative negligence let plaintiffs recover damages even if they were partly to blame. This shift opened the door to lawsuits stemming from drinking at a fraternity party. National fraternities have since faced hundreds of lawsuits alleging negligent supervision, and they have paid out multimillion-dollar settlements. Many more agreements—such as the one SAE reached with the family of Culolias, the Arizona State student—are private. Most local chapters have few assets to protect. But the litigation threatened generations of wealth overseen by the national fraternity organizations, which own or operate some $3 billion worth of real estate and generate at least $170 million in annual revenue. Just as significant, insurers dropped coverage of fraternities, and premiums soared. In 1986, the National Association of Insurance Commissioners ranked fraternities as the sixth-worst risk, behind hazardous-waste disposal companies and asbestos contractors. The risk of fraternity life is so great that only a handful of insurers cover college-age men living together in chapter houses.

The national fraternities came up with a strategy to distance themselves from undergraduates. Fraternities and their insurers crafted plans that limited coverage of members for underage drinking, hazing, and sexual assault. Fraternity alumni leaders argued that they didn't want to provide insurance that, in effect, subsidized bad behavior. Yet this move meant the alumni leaders were asking undergraduates to pay for insurance policies that didn't protect them when they most needed coverage. The national fraternity organizations also sought to shift blame from themselves to the undergraduate men, whose families would be forced to pay for legal defense and settlements or judgments through homeowners' insurance policies. James Ewbank, a lawyer who has represented at least ten national fraternities, told attendees at a July 2012 conference that they should "share the fun." Peter Lake, a professor at Stetson University College of Law in Tampa, Florida, who specializes in higher-education law, said fraternities have developed "a curious business model." Lake observed: "You're establishing a national brand and franchising. And then when your core customers are in a pinch, you're turning away."

This lack of insurance coverage can also threaten fraternity guests. In February 2007, Lee John Mynhardt, a senior at Elon University in North Carolina, was kissing a young woman in a locked bathroom at a Lambda Chi Alpha keg party. This apparently angered a student waiting for the bathroom, who banged on the door. Mynhardt, a six-foot-tall rugby player, stepped out of the bathroom. Two drunk men—one a fraternity member, another a guest from a different college—seized Mynhardt in a full-nelson wrestling move, with hands behind his neck, carried him through the kitchen, and dumped him outside. Mynhardt's neck broke. He became a quadriplegic, unable to move from the chest down, with medical expenses that could exceed $10,000 a month.

Mynhardt sued, and Lambda Chi Alpha convinced a judge it had no duty to supervise the chapter. The fraternity's insurer—Lloyd's of London—successfully argued the fraternity men weren't covered because they had violated the fraternity's "risk-management" policies. Mynhardt reached settlements with six students who were covered under their parents' homeowners' insurance, collecting less than $2 million, one-tenth of what his lawsuit had been seeking. Mynhardt moved to a house in Charlotte, near Carolinas Medical Center, where he had been hospitalized. He had one full-time, live-in aide and another who tended to him part-time. He needed help moving to his wheelchair, showering, and getting dressed. In 2012, he enrolled in Charlotte Law School. Because he couldn't use his fingers, he took notes with a stylus attached to his palm and a touch-pad computer. "As soon as there's an incident, national fraternities start distancing themselves," Mynhardt told David Glovin, my colleague at *Bloomberg News*. "It's irresponsible." Even then, Mynhardt wasn't ready to condemn Greek life. "I believe a lot of positive things can come out of fraternities. But if they're not run correctly, things are going to get out of control."

Teenagers probably don't examine the legal contracts they sign when they are invited to join a fraternity. But new members agree to follow complicated "risk-management" policies; if they don't, they will void their insurance coverage. Take, for example, SAE's Minerva's Shield, the program named after SAE's patron goddess of wisdom. This contract, which is typical of those at many fraternities, prohibits "open parties," which means chapters must establish guest lists. The contract also excludes insurance coverage if chapters offer "common source" containers such as kegs, or punches, or liquor of 100 proof or higher. Members are forbidden from playing drinking games or serving a visibly intoxicated guest or, of course, anyone under age twenty-one.

The last requirement for coverage is the ultimate challenge: how to avoid underage drinking when as many as three-fourths of fraternity members and potential guests are underage. To comply with these rules, members have two choices. They can hire a "third-party" establishment such as a bar or banquet hall with a cash bar and a staff responsible for checking IDs. Or they can try "bring your own bottle," or BYOB, which is more complicated than it sounds. The fraternity must establish a guest list with the birth dates of every member. Those of legal age receive an "event-specific" wristband. Then, legal-age drinkers are allowed to bring in six beers, wine coolers, or malt beverages, which must be deposited at a central distribution center. There, guests must be issued a punch card with six holes corresponding to the drinks they brought, so that each guest's consumption can be tracked through the night.

This setup looks nothing like actual drinking at fraternities. George Desdunes and other members of SAE certainly didn't handle alcohol that way at Cornell on the night of February 24, 2011, and into the early hours of the next morning.

AROUND MIDNIGHT, DESDUNES caught a "sober ride" to Dino's in Collegetown. By then, between the Jameson's whiskey and the rum-and-Pepsis, Desdunes had already had quite a few drinks. On his late-night excursion, Desdunes was the picture of millennial cool in his Cheap Monday designer jeans, gray canvas Vans, and a dark green hoodie. He wore a stud in his right ear and a pink rubber wristband that read: "Preserve the boobies." The wristband promoted breast cancer research, neatly combining a fraternity man's concern for the greater good and his focus on the female anatomy. At Dino's, Desdunes didn't order anything to drink.

At 12:24 a.m., Desdunes's roommate, Matthew Picket, texted him that he was locking his bedroom door and would leave the key in Desdunes's mailbox. Picket wanted to protect himself from a risk all the older fraternity members faced that night: a mock kidnapping. At most chapters, full-fledged members hazed pledges, but at Cornell, the tradition was reversed: Pledges kidnapped full members and quizzed them on their fraternity knowledge, then forced them to drink or do calisthenics if they answered incorrectly. The full members had been chastising freshmen because they hadn't pulled off a kidnapping lately. In fact, the freshmen had recently been summoned to a late-night "lineup," where pledges wearing jackets and ties were berated for failing to measure up. "Come capture us," they were taunted at a lineup. "We're waiting for you to do it." In theory, at least, the older brothers could tell the pledges they didn't want to be captured if, for example, they had a big test the next day. Or they could simply stay inside and lock their doors, which is what Picket told Desdunes he was doing that night.

Meanwhile, Desdunes texted his girlfriend, and they arranged to meet at Collegetown Pizza at 1:00 a.m. after the bars closed. She had been out with friends since 8:00 p.m.—first at Dino's and then at the Royal Palm Tavern, another dive bar, where undergraduates carved their names on wooden booths and tables. She had enjoyed three or four drinks herself. When she met Desdunes, he didn't seem at all drunk to her. Around 1:00 a.m., the two walked a half mile back to her apartment, where they listened to music and had sex. Afterward, Desdunes had to decide whether to call for a ride from the sober drivers. If he did, he might be kidnapped. If he were kidnapped, Desdunes worried that he'd be in no shape for a job interview the next morning. He was looking for a finance-related campus position. By coincidence, his girlfriend herself would be the interviewer. Although she recently graduated, she still had a plum campus position at an undergraduate-run student agency. Desdunes asked her for advice about how he should prepare and what he should wear. In the end, he decided to risk calling for a ride on that cold, windy, and icy night.

Around 2:15 a.m., several pledges pulled up in a Honda Pilot SUV, jumped out of the car, and grabbed Desdunes. He resisted, but the pledges overcame him, holding him on the ground and then binding his wrists and ankles with zip ties and duct tape. The kidnapping had begun. One of the pledges would later describe Desdunes's struggle as half-hearted, a kind of "mock" resistance. It wasn't like an earlier foiled kidnapping, when an upperclassman had fought back fiercely; he had punched a pledge in the face, breaking his nose. For whatever reason—fatigue, resignation, a tendency to be a team player—Desdunes didn't go that far. The driver asked Desdunes about the girl he had been with, while the pledges took Desdunes to a freshman dorm, a townhouse in the northern part of the campus. Because his feet were tied, he hopped into the front door. Before the main event, he exchanged texts with his girlfriend:

"I got kidnapped," Desdunes wrote. "Knew I should've walked. See you tomorrow."

"HaHaHa wow so not surprising, well uh enjoy," she replied.

"I'll try but I doubt it. Still have to prep for that interview."

"Yea, hopefully the person interviewing you will be understanding."

"Yeah, I really hope she is, Heard she has a nice body."

"Well thank you, hope your kidnapping doesn't take to long! See you tomorrow."

Then, the pledges took Desdunes's phone, removing his last avenue for escape; under fraternity rules, a kidnapped member would be released if he called a brother and said, "Phi Alpha," the SAE motto. Desdunes found himself on a couch, next to another fraternity brother, Gregory Wyler, a twenty-year-old sophomore. Wyler had asked for a ride to his girlfriend's apartment and, like Desdunes, found himself tied-up and blindfolded with a black ski mask.

Everyone knew the drill. The questions would keep coming. When the members botched them, they had to drink vodka. Or do sit-ups and crunches. Or eat or drink something mysterious, maybe disgusting. They had to name the members of the pledge class. They had to recite a poem. They had to sing "Seasons of Love" from the musical *Rent*, which wasn't easy while drinking: "Five hundred twenty-five thousand six hundred minutes / How do you measure, measure a year?" Wyler and Desdunes sang together. It no doubt helped that they were both musical; Wyler, an accomplished jazz trombonist; Desdunes, a trumpet player in high school who had taken music lessons since he was five. But the men missed plenty of questions, so they had to drink a lot of liquor. Desdunes and Wyler would open their mouths and hope for the best. Wyler wasn't sure exactly what he was eating, maybe pixie sticks, chocolate powder, strawberry syrup, and pieces of a sandwich. At one point, he felt the sticky, gooey feeling of dishwashing soap on his pants. And there was vodka, cup after cup of vodka. Wyler figured he drank four or five cups—maybe with a shot in each. Then he asked for a pail, so he could vomit. Afterward, the pledges told Wyler to drink two more vodka shots and eat hot sauce. Wyler heaved again. He told his interrogators the eight or nine drinks were enough. He was done.

Wyler felt foggy, and after his blindfold was removed, he saw Desdunes was still being given cups of vodka to drink. One pledge figured Desdunes drank six or seven shots. Finally, Desdunes said he couldn't drink anymore. He stood up from the couch, around which pledges had formed a semicircle.

"We were kidnapped the wrong way," Desdunes said, once on his feet. It wasn't clear what he meant because he was slurring his words. It seemed like he expected more questions about the history of SAE. Then, it looked like he passed out—while standing.

"George, George, are you all right?" Wyler asked. "Can you hear me?"

"Yeah," he heard Desdunes say. Wyler figured he'd be fine. It was now after 3:30 a.m. Desdunes had trouble walking and could barely speak. Arms around his shoulders, several members guided Desdunes, hands still bound, back to the Honda Pilot. They lifted Desdunes into the back seat, where one pledge could hear him mumbling. Around 4:00 a.m., pledges took Desdunes into the SAE house through the back door. The door of Desdunes's room, of course, had been locked by his roommate. So the pledge brothers carried Desdunes into the library, laying him on the leather couch. They made sure he was on his side. It was the least they could do. No one wanted a brother to choke on his own vomit.

AT 6:45 A.M., on Friday, February 25, George Ramstead arrived at Hillcrest, as he did most days, to clean up the sour smell of the morning after. In the dining hall, Ramstead, who worked for a custodial service, found the remains of the beer-pong tournament: a dining room littered with plastic cups, broken furniture, cans of Keystone beer. At first, Ramstead didn't take much notice of the young man lying on the couch in the library. It wasn't unusual at the SAE house, a frat boy sleeping it off, unable to make it back to his room, or maybe a friend crashing there after a long night. Around 7:45 a.m., Ramstead, rounding up all the garbage, took a closer look at the student on the couch. He could tell something was wrong. Desdunes was on his back, one arm hanging off the side, head to the left, vomit or mucous on the side of his mouth, his eyes rolled back. One of his pant legs was rolled up, a zip tie around his ankle. Another zip tie with duct tape around it lay on the floor nearby. His pants were down by his mid-thighs, his shirt halfway to his stomach. Ramstead yelled, trying to wake him. He grabbed Desdunes's feet and gave them a shake. No response. When Ramstead called 911 on his cell phone, the operator asked if he could sense any breathing. Ramstead couldn't tell. He also couldn't feel a pulse, and Desdunes's hand was cool to the touch. Upon arrival, emergency workers tried CPR, then drove Desdunes to the hospital, where he was pronounced dead. The cause was alcohol poisoning; his blood alcohol level was almost .40, or five times the legal limit for driving.

It took five hours to drive Desdunes's body from the medical examiner in Binghamton, New York to his hometown, New York City. Marie Lourdes Andre, Desdunes's mother, was at work. She got a call from the human resources department at Brooklyn's SUNY Downstate Medical Center, where she counseled AIDS patients, according to an account in the *New York Times*. She worried she was about to lose her job. Andre, a former nanny whose husband died of lung cancer, had worked hard to get this far. She had a good job and a son at an Ivy League school, on his way to be like the doctors she saw every day at the hospital. When she arrived at the human resources office, she found a police officer waiting to see her.

"Do you have a son named George at Cornell?"

Andre walked down the hall to an examining room, where her son was lying face up on a gurney. A sheet covered his body, but she could see his face. She screamed.

FOR THE NEXT few days, the Ithaca and Cornell police investigated Desdunes's death, questioning the fraternity's officers, his friends, and all the pledge brothers who drove him, tied him up, and fed him liquor. Ithaca police lieutenant Christopher Townsend noted the uncooperativeness of Desdunes's fraternity brothers. It was a conscious decision, the brotherhood closing ranks against the authorities. Eric Barnum, the president, texted all the members, telling them the chapter had hired an attorney, and no one should talk with police.

One pledge went even further. He tried to cover his tracks. At 1:15 p.m. that day, he sent a panicked text to his roommate.

"I need you to do me a favor. It's extremely urgent. Throw out all zip ties and duct tape in the room, please. ASAP."

"Is everything all right?"

"No, I can't really talk right now. Please, get rid of it."

His roommate reported the text to the police, who collected the duct tape and zip ties as evidence.

Wyler, Desdunes's fellow kidnapping victim, was the most forthright. He described the night in great detail, giving the clearest picture of what it was like to be blindfolded on the couch. "Where do you want me to begin?" he asked a Cornell police investigator. "Hopefully, this won't happen again."

The case was, of course, a national media sensation. It had all the elements: drinking, privilege, the Ivy League, a young promising life cut short. There was also the racial angle, a young African American man kidnapped at a historically white fraternity. Later, after the racist chant in Oklahoma became public, Desdunes's death would be cited as an example of the treatment of blacks at SAE. In this case, though, for all the chapter's other flaws, Desdunes seemed to be welcome in a chapter that prided itself on its diversity. Another member, Svante Myrick, who graduated in 2009, has since become the City of Ithaca's first African American mayor, as well as its youngest.

SAE, which said it had a "zero tolerance policy" for violations of its alcohol and hazing policies, suspended the chapter. In March 2011, Cornell said SAE would lose its recognition for at least five years. The public viewed Desdunes's death as primarily about hazing. In fact, it might not have met the legal definition in most states. Usually, older fraternity brothers haze freshmen, and the younger students risk injury—or worse—as a condition of joining an organization. In this case, the victim was already a member. Some called it reverse hazing. In a way, it more resembled a twisted drinking game—Trivial Pursuit, alcohol edition. But New York State has a broad definition of hazing—conduct that risks injury "in the course of another person's initiation into or affiliation with any organization."

In May, a grand jury charged three pledges with first-degree hazing and an offense related to providing alcohol to a minor: E. J. Williams, the wide receiver; Max Haskin, the varsity tennis player; and Benjamin Mann—who like Desdunes, was from Brooklyn. Investigators said Haskin, Mann, and Williams had been among those in the Honda Pilot who picked up Desdunes, tied him up, and took him to the house for the interrogation. The students faced misdemeanor charges, carrying a maximum penalty of a year in jail. A fourth student—the pledge who sent his roommate the message asking him to dispose of the zip ties—was charged with evidence tampering, as well as hazing.

The court sealed the proceeding because that student was eighteen at the time and considered a juvenile. The grand jury indicted SAE, as an organization, too. A month later, Desdunes's mother, seeking $25 million in damages, sued the fraternity and many of its members. Her civil suit attacked the entire culture of the chapter, including its underage alcohol bingeing and hazing.

On May 21, 2012, fifteen months after Desdunes died, the pledges faced the criminal charges at the Tompkins County Courthouse, just half a mile from Cornell. The men waived their right to a jury trial and put their fates in the hands of a judge. Whereas the prosecutor argued that the events met New York State's broad definition of hazing, Raymond Schlather, one of the defense lawyers, said the pledges themselves were a kind of victim, bullied into kidnapping: "These seniors, juniors and sophomore brothers of SAE were adamant, and, in fact, called these young pledges sissies, and what have you, for not having engaged in what they considered a time-honored ritual." In fact, he said, the grand jury indicted the entire fraternity not only for underage drinking, but for hazing because the "entire chapter is an accomplice in this case."

The defense focused on how much Desdunes drank from 10:00 p.m. until 1:00 a.m.—by Schlather's count, twelve to eighteen ounces of liquor, equivalent to eight to twelve 1.5-ounce shots. The lawyers said that's likely why Desdunes died. They also said the drinking was voluntary. Testifying for the prosecution, Desdunes's girlfriend said he didn't show evidence of impairment when they were together: "I mean the text messages I was receiving afterwards, which were perfectly coherent, better than most I receive sometimes, not really a sign of a very drunk person." Many of the fraternity brothers who appeared in court were vague in their recollections or said they couldn't recall key moments, exasperating the prosecutor, who told the judge: "I am asking the Court at this point to allow me to treat them as a hostile witness on the basis that these questions and answers are evasive. These are college-educated students, and they cannot remember anything about this night."

The judge found the three fraternity pledges not guilty of all charges; after the acquittals, the court sealed the proceeding, and the judge's reasoning is no longer public. Schlather told a reporter that the court had "determined without any hesitation or equivocation that these guys are innocent." But, he added: "Having said that, I emphasize that there are no winners, because someone is dead and the family is in pain, and frankly, the lives of three young men are irrevocably harmed." SAE didn't defend itself, so it was found guilty of misdemeanor hazing-related charges and levied a $12,000 fine.

The civil case, which was close to a confidential settlement in 2017, has undoubtedly exacted a heavier toll. Desdunes's mother had hired Doug Fierberg, a Washington, DC, lawyer who has made his career suing fraternities and extracting multimillion-dollar settlements. Fierberg sees himself as an activist intent on improving the safety of fraternities. Because three-fourths of men living in frat houses are underage, he said, national fraternities need to require an adult living on-site—as sororities typically do. Instead, at the Cornell chapter, Fierberg told me, "Anything goes inside of that house."

Fierberg was skeptical of fellow members' accounts of Desdunes's heavy drinking. In his view, to absolve themselves of blame, they were impugning the memory of a brother who could no longer defend himself. Testimony in the civil case revealed how undergraduate members hid their infractions by assigning "lookouts" when they knew they were breaking the rules. The adults overseeing SAE relied on the honor system, or after-the-fact punishment. SAE's volunteer adviser, Ron Demer, who was in his seventies, rarely visited the house after early evening. Cornell administrators, while praising the benefits of Greek life, viewed their own role as largely educational. Even though the college devoted substantial sums to supporting fraternities and sororities, deans considered themselves more as partners than regulators. Travis Apgar, the associate dean overseeing fraternities, commanded a staff of eight and a $700,000 annual budget. In the Desdunes case, lawyers asked him why the school didn't make use of these resources to monitor chapters by showing up at parties. Apgar replied that such policing would violate the spirit of fraternities as a "self-governance community."

In making that comment, Apgar sounded like a fraternity man. That wasn't surprising, because he was. In the same way the Federal Reserve draws on bankers for their expertise, colleges tend to pick fraternity and sorority alumni to oversee Greek life. Apgar belonged to the Tau Kappa Epsilon fraternity when he was an undergraduate at the State University of New York at Albany in the 1990s. He was also a popular paid speaker and consultant to colleges and Greek organizations across the country, offering his own cautionary story of being hazed as a pledge. In an interview with the *Cornell Alumni Magazine*, Apgar made the common fraternity argument that flies in the face of all the facts, suggesting fraternities didn't drink any more than other students on campus. "There's a lot of underage drinking in our student body, period—it's not unique to fraternities," he said in November 2010, three months before Desdunes's death. Still, he acknowledged that the "fraternity community" had, at least tacitly, endorsed underage drinking: "We've inadvertently turned a blind eye to it to a large extent. And by doing that, we've unintentionally sent our students a message that they have interpreted as, 'New York State law doesn't apply to you.'"

Fierberg also maintains that fraternities' strategies protect the organizations financially, rather than eradicating dangerous behavior among their members. After the Desdunes case, he said SAE reorganized to try to keep its wealth out of the hands of the Desdunes family and others who sue the fraternity. At its 2015 national convention, the fraternity changed its bylaws, separating the national organization from the fraternity's charitable foundation—which has $15 million in land and investments—and its housing corporation, which oversees more than $400 million in real-estate holdings. (Clark Brown, SAE's general counsel, said the move was unrelated to the case.)

As is now standard after drinking deaths, SAE's lawyers argued the young men violated SAE's risk-management policies, so they had voided their insurance coverage. In April 2015, Barnum, the president of the chapter, and his parents sued Lloyd's of London, SAE's insurer, seeking coverage. A judge ruled against them. That means Barnum, a project manager at citizenM, a boutique hotel chain, and his parents must rely on their State Farm homeowner's policy.

I reached out to members who were named in the court case. Picket, Desdunes's roommate, was the only one who responded in any detail. "His death is a tragedy I'll probably never fully get over," Picket wrote to me in an e-mail. The buddies had a long-standing arrangement to lock their door, then text the key's location, if either one needed a good night's sleep. He said his decision to take that step to avoid being kidnapped still haunted him. Each year, as many as fifty chapter members visit Desdunes's grave on the anniversary of his death. "There's a culture in Greek Life, and our fraternity was no exception, where kids are on their own for the first time and we're all drinking too much," wrote Picket, who now worked as a real-estate analyst at a money manager in New York. "I wish I would have done more to help George."

After SAE lost its recognition at Cornell, another fraternity opened its doors to the now houseless pledges who had belonged during the kidnapping. Sixteen of the twenty-two joined Tau Kappa Epsilon. Cornell administrators expressed concern the men would transfer SAE's culture to TKE. They were reassured the men had learned their lesson. SAE and TKE both had long and illustrious traditions at Cornell and across the country. Both had stately Tudor-style mansions with names evoking English country estates—Hillcrest at SAE, Westbourne Manor at TKE. President William McKinley had been an SAE; Ronald Reagan, a TKE. Like SAE, TKE's national organization forbids underage drinking in its "risk-management" policies.

In November 2011, TKE held a recruitment event at a Chinese restaurant and offered beer and hard liquor. A freshman ended up so drunk that the brothers took him to his dorm and handed him over to his roommates. He later had to be hospitalized. Ari Fine, a student from suburban Boston, had been there that night. Fine had also driven the Honda Pilot that picked up Desdunes at the SAE kidnapping. He had become TKE's treasurer. In a deposition, Fine later recalled that neither he nor anyone else did anything to stop the underage drinking at the event. Cornell revoked TKE's recognition because of "repeated high-risk behavior around alcohol." The school faulted the fraternity for failing to take the freshman directly to the hospital. The brothers had learned little, if anything, since that night in February when drinking games turned deadly for George Desdunes.

2

BROKEN PLEDGES

"Whose Conduct Proceeds from Good Will"

Following orders, Justin Stuart handed over his phone and wallet. He walked down the stairs to a dark basement, its windows covered with blankets and old clothes. Suddenly, earsplitting music assaulted him. From speakers perched on a washing machine, he heard German lyrics, guttural, threatening, and incomprehensible.

"DU, DU HAST. DU HAST MICH! . . . DU, DU HAST. DU HAST MICH!"

Stuart, a nineteen-year-old college freshman, didn't recognize the song. He had not yet entered kindergarten when the German metal group Rammstein released it. If he had understood the lyrics, he wouldn't have been reassured. It was a sinister soundtrack, playing on the words "have" and "hate," by a band whose concerts featured eerie white masks and flamethrowers.

"DU, DU HAST. DU HAST MICH! . . . DU, DU HAST. DU HAST MICH!"

Stuart had come to this basement, which smelled of mold and stale beer, to begin his initiation into the Sigma Alpha Epsilon fraternity at Salisbury University in Maryland. In a brown wood-shingled home about a mile from campus, a de facto fraternity house, a Salisbury senior named William Espinoza stood in front of Stuart and eight other pledges on that Thursday evening in February 2012 and gave them a hint of what might come next. Stuart and Espinoza had graduated from the same Maryland high school in a Washington, DC, suburb, but now Espinoza held all the power. He was the SAE "pledge educator." Like a US Marines drill sergeant, he controlled the lives and futures of the new provisional members, the pledges. The pledge term of instruction, designed to teach them about the fraternity and test their commitment, had just begun. It would last eight weeks. "Get ready," Espinoza told the recruits. "This will be your favorite song by the end of the night."

Stuart had descended into the basement about 4:00 p.m., when fingers of winter light still reached in through cracks in the window coverings. The aural pounding lasted hour after hour, an endless loop punctuated by a few seconds of silence. As the sun fell and the rest of the light faded away, the pledges withstood the noise, the uncertainty, and many hours later, the hunger. Like prisoners, they wore a uniform—jeans and white shirts. They leaned against the walls, their shoes sticking to the cement floor, which was coated with what seemed like the tacky residue of rancid beer.

"DU, DU HAST. DU HAST MICH! . . . DU, DU HAST. DU HAST MICH!"

At 9:00 p.m., the older brothers, loud, drunk, and menacing, ran down the stairs.

"Backs against the wall!"

"Heads down!"

Stuart and the other pledges complied, their eyes downcast. What followed seemed like a demented version of a pop quiz. The older members asked detailed questions about the history of SAE and the lyrics of a fraternity song. If a pledge answered incorrectly, things got ugly. First came insults, screamed in ears at close range, old-school basic-training style.

"You're a worthless piece of shit!"

"I'll make you suck a dick!"

"You're a good-for-nothing faggot!"

Then, some of the older members got physical. They shattered liquor bottles against the wall and ripped the shirt off one of the students. One spat in a pledge's face. Afterward, when that test was over, the music continued, the repetition incessant, broken by the few blessed seconds of silence.

"DU, DU HAST. DU HAST MICH. DU, DU HAST. DU HAST MICH."

Stuart thought of the American war on terror, the prisoners subjected to the worst the psychologists had to offer, the military torturers playing Eminem and Metallica to weaken defenses and prevent sleep. After eight or nine hours in the basement, as Thursday night turned into early Friday morning, members led pledges, who were blindfolded with old shirts, upstairs to continue their education.

One by one, they arrived on the second floor, where their blindfolds were removed. They were told to kneel before a table draped with a purple-and-gold fraternity flag. Six candles flickered on the table. Behind them sat Espinoza and the chapter president, a burly six-foot-two physical-education major, Sam Kaubin. The pledges had passed the first hurdle. As a reward, they were taught the secret SAE handshake of interlocking pinkies. Like potential new employees, they also received a sheaf of documents, including a nondisclosure agreement. "Shut up and sign," someone said.

The brothers bestowed each pledge with a nickname: Pootie, Slappy, Meat, Semen, and Landfill. Stuart was referred to as "Drop," suggesting he was likely to quit. Afterward, each initiate was ordered to chug a pitcher of beer. Stuart and his fellow recruits were then taken to another house, where, urged on by SAE members, Stuart downed seven or eight drinks and a mystery punch, a fraternity favorite called "jungle juice," often Kool-Aid and vodka or grain alcohol. Stuart, who hadn't eaten for ten hours, had never been that drunk before. He returned to his dorm at 3:00 a.m. and slept through history class.

Stuart hadn't signed up for this kind of treatment. In fact, Salisbury University only a few days before had led him to believe his initiation would be entirely different. When he was first invited to join SAE, he had visited the student affairs office, where he had been asked to sign a document. It noted that hazing violated school policy and is, under Maryland law, a misdemeanor punishable by as much as six months in prison and a $500 fine. "Consent of a student is not a defense," the document said.

SAE's national office took a hard line, too. Minerva's Shield, the same safety rules ignored at the Cornell chapter, couldn't be clearer: "Hazing in any form is not acceptable. Chapters are to be hazing-free at all times. If you have to ask if an activity is hazing, then it probably is." The fraternity's headquarters sought to undermine the common rationale for the practice. "You may have heard the expression 'Break them down to build them up,'" the manual said. "The concept may work for the military, but it has no place in an organization like Sigma Alpha Epsilon that promotes ideals such as friendship and scholarship." It also noted that hazing violated the spirit of its True Gentleman creed.

During pledgeship, members didn't quiz Stuart on that section of Minerva's Shield. But he was required to display a flawless recall of the words of the True Gentleman creed. The brothers ordered Stuart to recite them on a chilly March night in the backyard of the same house where he had been held captive in the basement.

"The True Gentleman," Stuart said, shivering, "is the man whose conduct proceeds from good will and an acute sense of propriety, and whose self-control is equal to all emergencies."

It wasn't easy to get the words out. As he said them, fraternity members sprayed him with a hose and poured buckets of water over his head. It was no wonder he was shivering: Naked except for his underwear, he stood in a trashcan filled waist-deep with ice.

HAZING FLOURISHED LONG before fraternities; it was a venerable tradition with roots in medieval Europe and even ancient Greece. In England, the finest boarding schools featured "fagging," the forced servitude of underclassmen by their elders. In the American colonies, Harvard and its successors gleefully imported the practice. In seventeenth- and eighteenth-century America, colleges enforced "freshman laws," which required first-year students to run errands for, and tip their hats to, upperclassmen. When the Civil War ended, returning soldiers brought military-style hazing to college campuses, especially Greek-letter organizations. Fraternities then made their own enduring contribution to hazing. They institutionalized it within a defining tradition of the college fraternity and called it "pledging." In the word itself, and in the official literature, the practice has the ring of promise, of fealty to a sacred tradition of honor and brotherhood. A teenager earns his way into the group by learning its history and traditions, as well as respect for his elders. After the Civil War, when pledging took hold at fraternities, its duration could be as short as a day. The pledge period soon grew to weeks or months, devolving into the orgy of abuse so familiar today.

Early hazers doled out beatings, force-fed vile substances, and staged kidnappings. In 1873, a Cornell student named Mortimer Leggett was blindfolded, taken into the countryside at night, and left to find his way home in the darkness. He was pledging the Kappa Alpha Society, the first "social" fraternity. Leggett, son of the US commissioner for internal revenue, lost his way, fell off a cliff, and died, thereby becoming one of the first high-profile fraternity hazing deaths. Like medieval torturers, fraternities' hazing pioneers sought to terrify with the primal elements of water and fire. At early twentieth-century Stanford, fraternities favored "tubbing." This practice entailed stripping a pledge naked, then submerging him in cold water until he "strangled," or nearly drowned. In the 1920s at Dartmouth, Delta Kappa Epsilon branded its Greek letters onto the forearms of the pledges. Hazing would reach its apotheosis at the end of the pledge term, a terrifying time often dubbed "hell week."

In his essential history of college fraternities, Nicholas Syrett documents how hazing sought to enforce a vision of "manliness" that fraternities prized. "Manly" men were winners asserting their dominance over the weak. They were sturdy, able to hold their liquor, unintimidated by their peers or societal rules. As universities became co-ed, all-male organizations inevitably raised suspicions about members' sexual orientation, so demonstrations of toughness became especially valued. Because manliness afforded social status—success with careers and attractive women—initiates were willing to put up with abuse to join the club. Fraternities "believed that their membership should be composed only of men who were able to withstand particular tests of manhood," wrote Syrett, a professor at the University of Northern Colorado.

Early American educators and specialists in child development endorsed fraternity hazing as a natural, even beneficial, part of a boy's growing up and a way of establishing his independence from his mother. In 1904, the American psychologist G. Stanley Hall, author of an influential book on adolescence, said Greek organizations were helping men prepare for battle, both in the military and, presumably, in business and politics. "The practical joke is war, cruelty, torture reduced to the level of intensity of play," he wrote. "A good course of rough and roistering treatment" helped free a man of what he called the "petticoat control" of women. Reflecting this view, Thomas Arkle Clark, dean of men at the University of Illinois and a founder of its Alpha Tau Omega chapter, described fraternity hazing as a kind of "horseplay" or "rough house" that "determines what a man possesses, whether he has a streak of 'yellow' or whether he has stamina."

By the 1930s and 1940s, however, the alumni running national fraternity organizations tried to rein in hazing. Many, including SAE, banned "hell week," to little effect. More than a generation later, SAE's national leaders again took aim at hazing. In 1978, it dominated an entire issue of the *Record*, SAE's official magazine. An unsigned essay explained why the abuse continued: "The popular American macho image, the incredible terror of being thought a pansy, or worse, a faggot, impels many men to support hazing activities as consistent with masculinity." The author seemed sympathetic to the impulse behind hazing: "There is something of a bully in all of us. It is momentarily ego-satisfying to mistreat and humiliate another person, even if he's helpless to respond. This is not to suggest that all hazers are sadomasochistic monsters. They aren't. But the few who do derive great pleasure from the enterprise give the rest of us a bad name." This view walked a fine line. Hazing was understandable, natural, a male birthright; it just shouldn't be *too* brutal and you shouldn't enjoy it *too* much. You could imagine a reckless teenager, or a closet sadist, seizing on that muddled message as he shoved a freshman's head into a toilet.

In a related roundtable discussion, which was published in the same issue of the *Record*, some of the men suggested that pledges enjoy the challenge and the excitement of hazing—or, at least, grow to understand its value in retrospect.

Tony Becker, a member of the Stanford chapter, considered that suggestion ludicrous. In his view, hazing reflected a grim view of humanity straight out of Joseph Conrad's *Heart of Darkness* and William Golding's *Lord of the Flies*.

"Do you like to drink liquor until you throw up and eat your vomit?" Becker asked. "I don't either, and I don't think any self-respecting human would."

Robert Arnot, an undergraduate with the University of Texas SAE chapter, said hazing was an absolute necessity.

"On our campus, most of the major, *strong* fraternities have a traditional physical pledgeship," he said.

Arnot was asked why.

"Because it works, and it has worked for decades. Our chapter is powerful on its campus and always has been. Some fraternities in Texas have abandoned hazing only to find that chapter unity deteriorates."

Later, Arnot added: "It builds character, without a doubt. It takes a kid from the country club who's never had to tie his shoes and humiliates him. It takes a green ol' country boy and exposes him to things he's never seen before."

This view, expressed by a generation of fathers whose sons are now in fraternities, has no doubt been passed down, like the lines of wooden paddles hanging on the wall of a chapter house. I saw this legacy celebrated on another wall, as well, at the Levere Memorial Temple, SAE's national headquarters near Chicago. It was that mural in the basement—the one painted by the German artist that depicts students as bearded gnomes. In one scene, a blindfolded gnome is bending over, clutching his huge, green-booted feet, while one of his compatriots rears up to whack the unfortunate creature on his behind with a paddle. On the first floor, in the Levere Temple's extensive library, I also flipped through editions of the *Phoenix*, the manual given to all new members that passes down SAE's history and tradition. The pledge manual often seemed to endorse hazing. "The life of the pledge is not easy," the *Phoenix* read in 1968. "He is often placed in situations which may cause him embarrassment, sometimes even resentment." In 1972: "Your physical endurance and willingness to endure some humiliation might be called into question." In the 1980 and 1988 editions: "Your pledgeship will test 'your enthusiasm and perseverance' and 'your ability to bear up under stress.'" Finally, in 1995, the *Phoenix* condemned hazing, as it does in the current edition. "No organization is worth sacrificing your human dignity just for you to belong," the pledge manual now said.

As the SAE manual affirms, fraternities have shifted from condemning the excesses of hazing at "hell week" to advocating its abolition. But the ban proved challenging to enforce in part because of the fluid definition of hazing. If a fraternity brother asks a pledge to strip and submerges him in ice, is that hazing? Sure. What about drinking games? Can members ask pledges to clean the house? Or wear a costume? Like con men and hustlers who woo their marks with good-natured requests, hazers often start small to win trust, then slowly raise the stakes. The fraternities' "zero-tolerance" approach hasn't worked. That failure has led a handful of fraternities, including SAE, as well as colleges such as Dartmouth, to try a once-unthinkable solution: ban pledging. Even though pledging has long been one of the defining features of the fraternity experience, advocates of a ban say any program for new members, no matter how benign, can function as a cover for hazing because initiates find themselves so powerless.

Fraternity traditionalists are horrified, in part because they downplay the prevalence and seriousness of hazing. As with drinking, contrary to all evidence, fraternities and their campus supporters suggest they are being unfairly blamed for a common behavior. College Greek-life offices often feature the following statement, which is taken from the Hofstra University website: "Myth #1: Hazing is a problem for fraternities and sororities primarily. Fact: Hazing is a societal problem." Such statements are misleading. Hazing is everywhere, the argument goes, so it's alarmist to worry about it at fraternities: by implication, this line of reasoning suggests that a freshman is just as likely to get paddled on the debate team, the literary magazine, or the student-government spirit committee.

When boosters downplay hazing at fraternities, they are citing the results of a 2008 University of Maine survey of more than 11,000 undergraduates at fifty-three colleges. The research, which received funding from Greek groups, found that hazing was widespread at student organizations other than fraternities. Half or more of the members of performing-arts groups, as well as clubs and intramural sports teams, reported being subject to abuse that met the definition of hazing. But the study also found that hazing was far more common at fraternities and sororities. Three-fourths of members of Greek organizations reported that they had been hazed. Among members of other campus groups, only varsity athletes reported a similar level of abuse. In other words, this research shouldn't reassure freshmen wondering about whether to pledge: fraternity members—and varsity athletes—are more likely to be hazed than anyone else on campus.

In the Greek world, hazing has spread beyond the historically white fraternities that pioneered it. Kappa Alpha Psi, a historically black fraternity, has a decades-long history of hazing that has sent pledges to the hospital and, on occasion, the morgue. In his 2014 memoir, Charles Blow, the *New York Times* columnist, wrote about his brutal beatings at the fraternity's

Grambling State University chapter in the late 1980s and early 1990s. Blow, who is African American and became president of his chapter, described assaults with two-by-fours and paddling bearing no resemblance to a childhood spanking: "In response to the paddling, we each developed 'pledge ass'—inch-thick, saucer-sized pads of damaged tissue and damaged nerves that formed just beneath the skin of each butt cheek." An Asian American fraternity developed an equally dangerous form of physical torment. In December 2013, Chun Hsien Deng, a freshman pledge at Baruch College in New York, was blind-folded and forced to wear a backpack weighed down with more than twenty pounds of sand. As he ran a gauntlet, called "the glass ceiling," which symbolized limited opportunities for Asian Americans, brothers of Pi Delta Psi repeatedly tackled him on a frozen yard in the Pocono Mountains. He later died from head injuries after members delayed taking him to the hospital.

Hank Nuwer, a prominent anti-hazing activist who has kept a running total of its casualties, counts at least one death a year at fraternities in the United States from 1969 through 2016. By far, the most common—and most dangerous—hazing involves forced drinking. More than half of fraternity and sorority members in the University of Maine survey reported hazing related to drinking games. One-fourth of them said they had been forced to drink alcohol until they got sick or passed out. Almost all of the more than sixty fraternity-related deaths from 2005 through 2013 resulted from alcohol, hazing, or a combination of the two. (Sorority women do report hazing, but deaths are rare.)

SAE has a particularly brutal history of hazing. At its University of Texas chapter, a sleep-deprived eighteen-year-old freshman pledge named Tyler Cross fell from a fifth-floor dormitory balcony in 2006 after pledges had been given half-gallon liquor bottles to drink. Earlier, "pledge trainers" had touched a hot clothes iron to pledges' faces, shocked them with a cattle prod, and forced them to eat Crisco and cat food. At the University of Kansas, Jason Wren, a nineteen-year-old freshman died from alcohol poisoning during a "Man Challenge" ritual that included drinking margaritas, beer, vodka, and Jack Daniels. The drinking at California Polytechnic State University in San Luis Obispo illustrated the danger. In December 2008, SAE members summoned sixteen pledges to an off-campus house for what they called "Brown Bag Night." Tarps covered couches to protect them from vomit. Pledges sat in a circle, with a trash can at the center. At 10:30 p.m., each pledge was given a brown bag filled with cans and bottles of alcohol. "Drink up," an upperclassman told them. "Finish by midnight."

Carson Starkey, an eighteen-year-old from Austin, Texas, was one of those pledges. He had a bag with two twenty-four-ounce cans of Steel Reserve beer, a sixteen-ounce can of Sparks alcoholic energy drink, and a fifth of rum he would split with another pledge. The initiates also shared a bottle of 151-proof Everclear, which is 75.5 percent alcohol. As members chanted "puke and rally," Starkey emptied his bag in twenty minutes. After he passed out, fraternity brothers debated whether to drive him to a hospital less than a mile away. They placed Starkey in a car and removed his Sigma Alpha Epsilon pin so that doctors wouldn't know he was at a fraternity event. Then they changed their minds. Rather than go to the hospital, they brought him back in the house and left him on a dirty mattress. He never woke up. Four fraternity brothers pleaded no contest to misdemeanor charges related to hazing. They were sentenced to jail terms ranging from thirty to 120 days. Starkey's family sued Sigma Alpha Epsilon and several members for negligence, and settled for at least $2.45 million. As part of that 2011 settlement, SAE must now disclose disciplinary actions on its website. From 2011 through 2013, SAE chapters received twenty sanctions related to hazing, about one-fourth of all violations. It was the second most commonly specified offense, after illegal or dangerous drinking.

Colleges find hazing allegations difficult to prove. Absent a death or serious injury, police rarely file charges. In most states, as in California, hazing offenses are misdemeanors. After the University of Texas SAE death, two "pledge trainers" were sentenced to four days in jail. Six states— Alaska, Hawaii, Montana, New Mexico, South Dakota, and Wyoming—have no laws against hazing. When young men come forward to detail the abuse, their experiences are often categorically denied. In 2010, John Burford, a former SAE pledge at Princeton, recounted a litany of hazing: chugging a twenty-ounce bottle of tobacco spit, getting whipped and bitten at a strip club, swimming naked in a frozen pond, and drinking dangerous amounts of alcohol. SAE's national organization denied the allegations, though they helped prompt a review of Greek life that led Princeton to prohibit fraternities from recruiting freshmen.

Another brother-turned-whistle-blower drew national attention to hazing at Dartmouth's SAE chapter, the model for the preppy frat in *Animal House*. In 2012, a former pledge, Andrew Lohse, wrote a column for the student newspaper about what he called a "systematic culture of abuse." He said pledges were forced to swim in a kiddie pool full of vomit, urine, feces, semen, and rotted food; chug vinegar; and "drink beers poured down fellow pledges' ass cracks." *Rolling Stone* magazine later ran a story based on his account, and Lohse wrote a book. Dartmouth placed the chapter on three terms of social probation for hazing, disorderly conduct, and serving alcohol to minors. The college accused twenty-seven individual members of hazing but later dropped the charges, citing contradictory evidence. Many at Dartmouth then disputed Lohse's account.

Lohse later won a measure of vindication. In February 2016, responding to reports of hazing, SAE's national office suspended the chapter for at least five years, saying such behavior "absolutely will not be tolerated." SAE headquarters reported the hazing to the university, which withdrew the chapter's recognition. Lohse said a Dartmouth administrator let him know that the hazing resembled what he had described years earlier. "It was textbook, just as I had described," Lohse told me. I spoke with an SAE pledge who had been interviewed by investigators. Clark Brown, SAE's general counsel, confirmed much of his account. The pledge told me Lohse's book, *Confessions of an Ivy League Frat Boy*, had inspired the older brothers. Instead of a cautionary tale, it had become an unauthorized pledge manual. "It was kind of a running joke," the former member said. The pledges met on a golf course at night, bringing a strange assortment of items such as women's underwear, condoms, and vegetables, he told me. They were each baptized in a kiddie pool, though he didn't think it held the kinds of noxious materials that Lohse described. They were forced to drink until they vomited and to repeat a mantra recounted in Lohse's book: "What happens in the house stays in the house."

BEFORE HE FOUND himself submerged in ice, Justin Stuart knew nothing about SAE's hazing traditions. He had arrived at Salisbury University, a public institution of 8,600 on the Maryland shore, hoping to network, make friends, and build on his success in high school. Stuart grew up in Potomac, Maryland, a suburb of Washington, DC, and attended Montgomery County's highly rated public schools. In high school, Stuart worked as a lifeguard at a community pool and built houses for Habitat for Humanity. The lanky six-foot-two teenager played varsity lacrosse and golf. "He was the ultimate team player," said Colin Thomson, head lacrosse coach at Thomas S. Wootton

High School in nearby Rockville. "Justin has a good head on his shoulders."

Like many drawn to SAE, Stuart was ambitious and saw himself working in finance. The success of former SAE members impressed him. He had his first interview at the Scarborough Student Leadership Center, a Greek hub on campus named after the SAE chapter's founder. Stuart stood before ten fraternity brothers seated at a table as if they were corporate executives in a boardroom. They asked about his major, his grade-point average, and why he wanted to join. They even videotaped the encounter. His pledge invitation, delivered by members in suits and ties, arrived soon after. Like a college acceptance letter, it was inscribed with an SAE seal. "They made it seem like it was super exclusive and that only the brightest are invited," Stuart told me. He wasn't naïve about fraternities; he anticipated some unpleasantness in pledging such as cleaning up after older brothers, but nothing like what he experienced when his "education" began.

After the first night in the basement with the German music, the SAE pledge program continued on Tuesdays in a science hall. Brothers covered a window with white paper, and, as pledges tried to learn SAE history, they were barraged with insults, including anti-gay slurs. Stuart considered quitting. Members assured him that they had all gone through the same crucible, and the worst was over. He weighed the benefits of SAE membership: entrée to parties, where freshmen could meet sorority women, and access to its alumni network of Wall Street and Fortune 500 companies. Perhaps just as important, he worried that if he left, he would end up shunned and alone.

So Stuart accepted the tasks of the fraternity pledge—the "personal servitude" that had been a tradition for generations. On weekends, just as at Cornell, the pledges were on call to "sober drive" drunken brothers deep into the early morning hours. The recruits' social lives and grades suffered, as did their moods. Like a symphony, the pledge term often builds to a crescendo of pain and humiliation. The anticipation can be as frightening as the abuse itself. As spring break approached, pledges texted each other, dreading what would come next.

"They want to get us drunk to fuck us up," one of the pledges texted in March.

A day after that text, the recruits found themselves again confined in a basement, this time for a ritual known as "family night." Members divided pledges into "families" with names such as Thunderbird and Red Lady. As before, the German song blared in their ears. Stuart was then led upstairs, where he was blindfolded and tossed into a car without a seatbelt. Tires screeching, the driver sped around curves and made quick stops. Stuart thought he was going to die. Back at the house, a brother asked him to bend over. Still blindfolded, he heard clapping, thumping, and chanting—the animalistic rhythm of ritual. A member took a running start and hit him in the buttocks—once, twice, three times. Paddling might sound innocuous, but it can be a cruel assault, a punishment remembered for its mix of lasting pain and embarrassment. Each blow sounded like a punch to Stuart, as if his skin were cracking. He held back a scream, while his back seized up, leaving him briefly unable to walk. (For a day or so, it would hurt to sit down.) Members then told pledges to dress in women's clothing and makeup, or diapers. Stuart wore a skirt, a leotard top, and a platinum-blonde wig. Then he had to chug four or five shots of a "secret drink," made up of various liquors, before being driven to an off-campus party, so his humiliation could be more public. There, members handed pledges yet more alcohol. "If you don't drink this, you're out," they said. Stuart figured he had ten drinks, fewer than some others. He saw one pledge dry-heaving for hours; another was vomiting blood. After the party, the recruits commiserated in text messages.

"They fed me a pint of Jack and Jose," one pledge wrote. "Not to mention sake is the grossest drink I've ever drank but I'm going to try to get used to it." He said he "got carried out and woke up with a burn on my forehead."

Another pledge added: "I woke up in throw up and with a black eye and my knuckles were all bruised and I was limping."

In a text, William Espinoza, the pledge educator, berated the younger students: "You raged at my house and some of you thought it was cool to punch holes in my wall, and you will be patching those fuckers up."

After that night, Stuart decided to quit SAE and alert the authorities. He sent an anonymous e-mail detailing what had happened to the campus police's "silent-witness" website. By then, the late nights at the fraternity had been exacting a toll. Stuart's grades fell from As to Cs. He often couldn't sleep because he worried about his safety. He had heard dark rumors about what was to come: a nighttime obstacle course, milk chugging, eating cat food, or worse, human waste.

Other pledges were also anxious and exchanged frantic texts later that month:

"We will be in the basement tonight. Just prepare mentally."

"Damn . . . Let's go guys at least they can't kill us."

"Or rape us."

FOR STUART, LEAVING the brotherhood wasn't easy. When he missed events, members called, texted, and visited his room. Stuart felt intimidated. His father, Henry "Hal" Stuart, a real estate developer, grew angry and protective. A six-foot-one, 260-pound former high school football player, he drove to the school.

"If they don't leave you alone, things are going to get real," he told his son.

Stuart found news accounts about Georges Desdunes's death at Cornell and decided he had to do more to alert the administration. In May, he sent another report to the "silent-witness" website.

"I was hazed by the SAE (Sigma Alpha Epsilon) fraternity this past semester," he wrote. "It was completely disgusting and you schools should step up your regulation of this."

Although his e-mail was supposed to be anonymous, the campus police tracked him down. At home for summer vacation, Stuart told his story by phone. Lieutenant Brian Waller of the Salisbury University Police called his account "credible and truthful" and referred the matter to the city police department, which has jurisdiction off-campus. Waller also knew SAE had been in trouble before. In 2005, the university cited the SAE chapter for hanging "an obscene banner" outside a house where several sorority sisters lived. In November 2010, two women complained that date rape drugs were slipped into their drinks at an SAE party. The university ultimately found insufficient evidence but cited the chapter for alcohol violations.

"There have been a number of allegations involving this fraternity over the past few years, from hazing to date-rape drugging to harassing a neighbor because of his sexual orientation," Waller wrote in an e-mail, urging the city police to take action. "I fear that sooner or later there is going to be a major incident, and our past efforts will be under the magnifying glass."

The police investigation was brief. Two pledges denied that hazing took place. Stuart's mother, fearing retaliation by fraternity members, told police she wanted her son to drop the case. Stuart decided it would be futile to move forward.

That fall, Salisbury University pressed forward with its own investigation and summoned Stuart before its disciplinary board, which includes faculty and student representatives. A pledge who had dropped out corroborated much of Stuart's account. In all, Salisbury held thirteen hours of hearings over three days.

Stuart had been promised confidentiality, but his name leaked out. On September 28, 2012, Hal Stuart wrote to Salisbury University president Janet Dudley-Eshbach, lamenting the toll the investigation was taking on his son. "He essentially has been blackballed from any social life, eats his meals alone and is miserable," Hal Stuart said. "I commend his courage for even coming back this semester."

The next month, the board determined that the evidence supported Stuart's allegations that SAE fraternity members had submerged pledges in ice, confined them in a basement, verbally abused them, and forced them to drink excessively. "The actions of the members of Sigma Alpha Epsilon fraternity put the members of the pledge class in harm's way both physically and emotionally," the board found. One board member told fraternity leaders at the hearing that their protests of innocence rang hollow. "What you said sounds like Disney Channel, when what I'm thinking [is] more like Quentin Tarantino," the member said.

Another board member observed: "Not all of your members are True Gentlemen."

The chapter appealed the findings on the grounds that members weren't allowed to have lawyers at the hearing. Citing the Tarantino and "True Gentlemen" comments, the chapter contended that board members were biased. In November 2012, the university denied an appeal from the fraternity and suspended SAE through the spring of 2014. The university revoked SAE's recognition as a student organization and barred it from campus. A handful of students were also disciplined. Justin Stuart and his father were far from satisfied. They wanted Salisbury to disclose its findings publicly.

Jen Palancia Shipp, then Salisbury's general counsel, told Stuart she wanted to hear his concerns. He declined, saying he was preparing to transfer to the University of Maryland and needed to put the investigation behind him.

"I just want to not deal with this anymore," Stuart told Shipp in an e-mail. "It's done, ended, the fraternity members can continue to lock people in a basement. It doesn't matter to me. I am just going to move on and work on my degree at UMD."

Shipp said she understood.

"I certainly do not want any other student to endure the same thing as you," she replied.

THE MEMBERS OF the Salisbury chapter never publicly acknowledged what happened. Daryl Spencer, an SAE member and former wide receiver on the Salisbury football team, brushed off questions about hazing. "Are you asking me if that's what happened?" he responded to my colleague, David Glovin. "Maybe you should join a fraternity and find out. My memory is foggy." Espinoza, the pledge educator, referred questions to the fraternity's chapter adviser. "When I was there, none of this came up," he said.

The adviser was Dwight Marshall, who was president of the chapter in the 1980s when he was a Salisbury student. Now in his forties, with a neatly trimmed gray beard, Marshall, known as "Duke," ran a local insurance agency, belonged to the Rotary Club, and during the holidays, wore a Santa Claus tie when he rang the bell at the mall for the local Salvation Army. "It did not happen," Marshall said of Stuart's account. "The quality of guys that are in there—they are outstanding young men." Marshall maintained the college had found the chapter responsible for underage drinking at a non-fraternity event and for what he considered innocent behavior such as requiring pledges to learn the True Gentleman creed, attend study hall, and wear pins, khaki pants, and white shirts. "I could not belong to an organization that promoted hazing or bullying or whatever you want to call it," Marshall said.

Salisbury University said the chapter adviser's description of what happened was inaccurate. Marshall also had to confront questions about his own behavior. Several months after the fraternity was disciplined, he was arrested for drunk driving. He pleaded guilty to driving while impaired and received probation. Marshall said he had been out having several drinks with friends and then used his arrest as a teachable moment for the fraternity, stressing the "importance of not drinking and driving." The university, however, continued tangling with Marshall. Salisbury extended the chapter's suspension for another year after Marshall distributed pledge manuals for recruiting meetings, which had been banned.

As the university cracked down, it antagonized its most fervent supporters. Marshall was a former president of the Salisbury University Alumni Association's board of directors, as well as a donor who had a conference room named after his parents. The sanctions angered an even bigger Salisbury booster and philanthropist: Michael Scarborough, who founded the SAE chapter in the 1970s. As a student, Scarborough had been a leader: secretary of the student government, a resident assistant, and a wide receiver on the football team. Norman Crawford Jr., then president of Salisbury, enlisted Scarborough to help bring fraternity life to the university, which had primarily been a commuter school. Scarborough chose SAE and saw the chapter change lives, particularly for teenagers looking for structure and purpose in college. "The True Gentleman rang true to me, as it did for a lot of people," Scarborough told me.

After college, Scarborough made his fortune as the founder of a Maryland investment firm, Scarborough Capital Management, which rode the boom in 401(k) retirement accounts.

He also rose through the ranks of SAE as a volunteer, serving as SAE's national president, or "Eminent Supreme Archon." Scarborough came up with the idea of holding the national leadership school on a cruise ship, more than doubling its attendance. He also started the Inner Circle, an annual gathering that introduced about twenty-five promising undergraduate SAE members to prominent fraternity alumni, such as General Richard Myers, chairman of the Joint Chiefs of Staff in President George W. Bush's administration. The Inner Circle met at Scarborough's three-hundred-acre Maryland estate, where he managed a vineyard. At Salisbury University, Scarborough joined the university's foundation board and donated $830,000 for the fraternity and sorority center, which opened in 2001 and bore his name. His generosity ended when the chapter was disciplined. He had pledged $2 million for a football stadium, but he canceled the gift. "If they decide that's the hill they want to die on, then let them," Scarborough said.

After Scarborough withdrew the pledge, he decided to invest the money elsewhere—in beer. "Here it is," he said of the $2 million, when I visited him at his new Calvert Brewing Company in Upper Marlboro, Maryland, east of Washington, DC. Scarborough pointed to the giant vats of hops inside the 25,000-square-foot beer factory, as we settled into a booth in the tap room. Still fit in his early sixties, with close-cropped gray hair and intense blue eyes, Scarborough wore a hooded sweatshirt and still looked like the college athlete he once was. Hints of Greek life were everywhere. As I toured the brewery, I noticed that his company's insignia featured a lion and a fleur de lis, two of the most important SAE symbols. Even the motto of the brewery sounded like a fraternity slogan. Delta Sigma Chi, an SAE rival, is committed to "Building Better Men." Scarborough's company is "Building a better beer."

Scarborough was still smarting from what happened at Salisbury. He took no position on whether hazing had occurred, saying he wasn't there so he had no way to know the truth. He said he canceled the $2 million pledge because of a longstanding complaint he has about universities: students are treated unfairly in disciplinary hearings; lawyers can't represent them, and anything they say can be held against them later in criminal court.

"What kind of Communist country are we running here?" he said. "That's crazy. That's a real bone I have to pick with Salisbury. I've told the kids candidly, if it was me, and I'd done something wrong and I was called before a judicial board, I wouldn't go. You're not going to get me to testify against myself."

Scarborough, a fraternity traditionalist who rails against the spoiled children of helicopter parents, would like to see the police, not colleges, punish hazers. "If I found a kid who I could prove beyond a shadow of a doubt was hazing, I would do everything I can to put him in jail," he said. At the same time, Scarborough said colleges and fraternities have started to define hazing too broadly—for example, calling meal runs to McDonald's acts of "personal servitude." Like the SAE undergraduates of his generation who participated in the 1978 roundtable discussion, covered at length in the SAE magazine, he considered some sort of hazing inevitable. "Most of these chapters, whether anybody wants to admit it or not, there's some—quote—hazing, whether it's benign or its pretty darn serious," he said. "That's why part of me says you can't outlaw some of this stuff."

IN THE FALL of 2013, when I first met Justin Stuart, he had already transferred to the University of Maryland, where its fraternity chapters had been doing some hazing of their own. Lambda Phi Epsilon had ordered a pledge to punch a wooden board sixty-four times until his knuckles bled and he fractured the bones in his hand, leaving him unable to drive or type his class assignments. The year before, a pledge at Omega Psi Phi arrived at an emergency room with his buttock muscles so damaged after paddling that a doctor described them as having the consistency of "black leather," resembling third-degree burns. Stuart wouldn't have known about these cases, part of a litany of fraternity hazing at the state's public universities that was later uncovered by the *Baltimore Sun*. He was now a junior and no longer part of that world. He steered clear of fraternity row when he walked across the College Park campus, near Washington, DC, to the student union, which was also home to the university's Department of Fraternity and Sorority Life. There, in the noisy food court, he recounted his hazing publicly for the first time.

"It honestly reminded me of Guantánamo Bay," he said. "It was almost like torture."

Like a police officer testifying on the stand, Stuart, who wore a golf cap from a trip to the Georgia Masters, had a quiet, flat, matter-of-fact way of speaking. His memory was detailed and consistent, both in our initial conversation, and throughout more than five hours of interviews then and later by phone. Stuart could corroborate his account with text messages and provided names of witnesses. It was clear to me why the campus police described him as "credible and truthful" in its report. Stuart's account helped explain a mystery to outsiders: why pledges put up with hazing. Once it started, he said, he didn't want to have suffered for nothing. It was the same reason that investors stick with losing stocks. In pledging, you've already sacrificed some of your dignity. You've already thrown up. You've been beaten. Do you want to give up now? Do you want to admit it was all a waste? "You feel like you have so much to lose—it's worth staying," Stuart said. "I thought it would pay off in the end."

Ultimately, Stuart left in part because he had no interest in abusing pledges when he became a full member. "I didn't want to be known as the ultimate hazer," he said. "It didn't entice me. I didn't want to do it after what happened to me."

The hazing at Salisbury changed the tenor of Stuart's college experience. At the University of Maryland, he lived at home, commuted to the campus, and didn't go out much on weekends. Still hoping for a financial career, he joined the investment club. Sometimes, though, he had trouble trusting other students and had flashbacks to his experience as an SAE pledge. "I have dreams of the basement sometimes," he said. "I hear the yelling. It sounds like they're about to attack me. Then I wake up from my nightmare."

3

SEXUAL ASSAULT EXPECTED

"With Whom Honor Is Sacred and Virtue Safe"

Gabriela Lopez let loose, drinking two beers and sharing a bottle of Ciroc vodka, then moving on to shots. The brothers at the Sigma Alpha Epsilon house, like volunteers distributing water to long-distance runners, passed around the Fireball Cinnamon Whiskey ("Tastes like Heaven, Burns like Hell"). Gabriela downed one shot, then another, before losing track of how many. Her vision blurred, and she could barely walk.

"You need to stop drinking," said her older sister, Maria, who took her into the bathroom to splash water on her face.

The Lopez sisters had arrived about 11:00 p.m., half an hour after the party began. On an overcast night, they walked past the two stone SAE lions flanking the walkway, through the neatly trimmed front yard, by the fraternity brother with the guest list at the front door, and out of the autumn chill. On its corner lot, the fifteen-bedroom chapter house, three stories of

beige masonry and arched windows, towered over the Baltimore
row houses beside it, just as the Johns Hopkins University gates
a couple of blocks away dominated the neighborhood.

Unlike the SAE brothers at the party, Maria and Gabriela
didn't go to Johns Hopkins and, in many other ways, didn't
belong in this world. Their parents had emigrated from Gua-
temala—their mother, a housekeeper and nanny; their father,
a supervisor at a trash transfer station. Maria was nineteen
years old and worked as a teacher's aide for children with au-
tism. Gabriela, the sister with the alcohol wreaking havoc on
her nervous system, was still in high school. She was sixteen,
though, like many teenage girls, she could pass for older, especially in her outfit that night, a green-and-blue flannel shirt
over a white crop top, leggings, and black combat boots, a typical look on a college campus. Legally, both sisters were too
young to be drinking. But on that Saturday night in November
2014, no one asked them, or anyone else, for ID.

In fraternity-speak, it was an "invite-only" party, a misleading term for those outside of Greek life. Only men needed
invitations. All women—all girls, really, it turned out—were
welcome. At the party, which celebrated Halloween a day after the actual holiday, SAE hosted many first-year men, who
were being courted as possible SAE material. It would be an
easy sell, the convenience to campus, the impressive house, the
free-flowing booze, and the "ratio," as it was often called, the
result of the invitation policy guaranteeing that women would
outnumber men, often by a lot. In the spring, the university had
warned the chapter about serving alcohol to minors, but the
message didn't take. By the simple mathematics of undergraduate life, most of the students drinking that night were underage.

Maria and Gabriela came along with three of Maria's friends.
Gabriela had never been to a frat party before. Even though she
was now a high school junior, she had only tasted beer before

that night. Smart and athletic, with long dark hair and large brown eyes, Gabriela was a five-foot-five lacrosse player, as well as a cheerleader, strong enough to stand at the base of a human pyramid and light enough to be the "flyer" who was flung off its peak. She was fearless; after graduation, she planned to join the army. So Gabriela, like so many little sisters, seized the chance to tag along. The sisters weren't crashing the SAE party, not at all. The chapter's social chairman, a Johns Hopkins sophomore named Ivan Booth, had invited Maria, who told him that her sister, Gabriela, would be there, too. Ivan and Maria had met on Instagram five months earlier. Maria had been to an SAE party before, and a romance may have been brewing.

If so, Ivan's Twitter feed might have alarmed Maria's parents. Below the angry-looking grille of a Cadillac sports car was an inset photo of Ivan, wearing ear buds, a blue hoodie, and a backward baseball cap, staring unsmilingly, his lips curled in the faint suggestion of a smirk. He may have been a white suburban boy, but his high school posts sounded tough, as if he were lip-synching off a hip-hop album. "Ass and titties. Ass and titties. Ass and titties," he tweeted, quoting the lyrics from the Memphis rappers Three 6 Mafia. One of his friends referred to him, apparently fondly, as a "fuck boy," slang for a particular mix of privilege and misogyny that would be taken as an endearment only in certain quarters. In the fall of his freshman year at Johns Hopkins, Ivan retweeted comments he found amusing: "the 4 b's of a true party," presumably a reference to "Beer, Bud, Box. Bitches"; a suggested pick-up line, "There's no u in I but if we work together I could be in u"; and, even more emphatically: "PUSSY ALWAYS BEING THE SUBJECT. IN ANY CASE."

There were hints that Ivan was posing. After all, he was an applied mathematics and statistics major enrolled in one of the most selective and academically challenging universities in the country. "Calc AP test tomorrow morning . . . LEGGO," he wrote senior year of high school. He also referred to his time on the lacrosse team and his love of the nerdy television show *The Big Bang Theory*. Ivan worked hard at Hopkins and liked to kick back when he could. "Tonight is my first night of college not having multiple hours of work to do . . . AND it's game night tonight. THIRSTY THURSDAY HERE I COME," he tweeted his freshman year.

As many as one hundred people packed the chapter house that Saturday night for the Halloween party. Although the sisters didn't wear costumes, many guests did. Gabriela saw two women dressed as the pink-striped bags from Victoria's Secret, one guy who looked like a duck and another in military fatigues. The floor pulsed with the hypnotic, repetitive beats of electronic "house music," catchy and wordless, the kind that practically requires you to dance, swaying with your hands held high above your head. Women danced on top of an L-shaped bar. Later, it would be described as something straight out of the movie *Coyote Ugly*, where female bartenders made their names by dancing on top of a bar in front of drunk men. Maria had been with Gabriela for an hour and a half, and she wanted to spend some time alone with Ivan. It was already 12:30 a.m., maybe later. Maria settled her drunk little sister on a couch and walked over to Ivan's apartment, which was just next door. She'd be back soon, she told Gabriela.

After her sister left, Gabriela got up and started dancing—something, maybe the high school cheerleader in her who had studied tap and ballet since she was four years old, made her want to move around, even in her drunken state. The next moments became fuzzy. The time may have speeded up or slowed down, the way it can when you're sufficiently drunk, for the first time in your life, in a strange place, the music enveloping you, so loud that a shout could sound like a whisper.

Gabriela found herself in a dingy bathroom, under harsh fluorescent lights, beer cans littering the floor. Her vision still blurry at times, she saw two skinny men she didn't know. She could make out their bearded faces and hear the menacing tone in their voices. They took off her clothes and cornered her in a shower stall, one of the men showing her his penis and pushing down her head. She tried to turn away. She was so drunk, she couldn't move.

"No," she said. "No."

"Just do it," the man replied.

The man pushed her head down and forced her to perform oral sex and, then, intercourse, leaving her raw and bleeding inside. But it wasn't over, not yet.

The second man took his turn, forcing Gabriela to perform fellatio.

Later, a third man, bearded, heavyset, and wearing a baseball cap, came into the bathroom. Gabriela was slumped on the floor of the shower, leaning against a wall, her leggings stained with semen, her shirt pulled up over her shoulders. Unsteady, she tried to move toward him.

"Why? Why?" she asked.

"Button up your shirt," he told her. Afterward, he urinated and left her on the floor, scared and alone.

FOR YOUNG WOMEN, the fraternity party has an unspoken set of rules: Stay with friends you trust, especially if you're drinking; beware the mystery punch in the cooler; watch as your new buddy, the friendly guy at the bar, pours you a drink; and never let that red Solo cup out of your sight to avoid "date-rape drugs," often reported as slipped into drinks, though rarely proven. It's no wonder that a woman is most likely to be sexually assaulted in her first months at college, before she knows these rules, has a reliable group of friends, and understands her own alcohol tolerance. There are no warning labels for newcomers. Fraternities, and the colleges that host them, don't advertise the special danger of these kinds of parties. If they did, the information might include some of the following facts: at one major insurer of fraternities, sexual assault represented 15 percent of liability losses, the largest category after assault and battery. Female college students who go to frat parties are one and one-half times more likely than women who stay away to become victims of what researchers called "incapacitated sexual assault." Or consider the experience of women living in sorority houses, the population most exposed to frat parties: They run three times the risk of rape.

The danger may have more to do with the binge-drinking of Greek life than fraternity men's attitudes toward sexual consent. Researchers have struggled to disentangle the two. There is an indisputable link between alcohol and the risk of sexual assault. In most attacks, the perpetrator or victim, or both, have been drinking. After assaults, drinking frustrates efforts to prosecute offenders. Cases become mired in controversy—about memory, consent, the characters of the accuser and the accused. Even if members themselves aren't responsible for rape, chapters create an environment where sexual assaults are more likely—even "predictable," in the words of one sociology study—if not by the brothers themselves, then by their guests or a man who slips through the door. In the view of Henry Wechsler, the Harvard drinking researcher, cracking down on fraternity house drinking would no doubt make women safer.

The increasingly fraught debate over campus sexual assault tends to obscure this reality. Members of Greek organizations, law professors—and even some feminists—are asking whether men, and fraternities, are now presumed guilty in campus disciplinary hearings and the court of public opinion. *Rolling Stone* magazine, most infamously, reported on an alleged gang rape at a University of Virginia fraternity—a story that was later thoroughly discredited. There is concern that the definition of sexual assault has broadened to include behavior, such as clumsy advances, that may not qualify. There is debate over the accuracy of the statistic, widely cited by activists and the federal government, that one in five women reports being assaulted over four years of college. No matter the precise number, campus rapes remain more common than previously believed, and the vast majority aren't reported. The relative handful of criminal prosecutions of attacks at fraternity houses have demonstrated why survivors often don't come forward. In January 2015, a twenty-three-year-old woman was sexually assaulted after drinking at a party at Stanford University's Kappa Alpha Order fraternity house; passersby caught a Stanford student named Brock Allen Turner, behind a Dumpster, on top of the unconscious woman, who was only partially dressed. Turner, a champion swimmer who was not a member of Kappa Alpha, was convicted of three counts of felony sexual assault. His lenient sentence—six months in the county jail—and his father's complaint that his life had been ruined for "20 minutes of action" sparked national outrage over the minimization of sexual assault.

Time and again, the language of fraternity members has made light of, or even seemed to promote, violence against women. At Yale, pledges of the Delta Kappa Epsilon fraternity in 2010 were led through the main freshman quad, chanting, "No means yes, yes means anal." At Georgia Tech, a member of Phi Kappa Tau sent an e-mail in 2013 with the subject line, "luring your rape bait," and advising brothers to target "hammered [drunk] women" for sex. At SAE's Stanford chapter, members cheered on pledges in 2014 as they told the following jokes during a toga party, according to the account of a female student who attended: "What do you tell a woman with two black eyes? Nothing, you've already told her twice" and "What do you call the useless skin around a vagina? A woman." At Old Dominion University in Virginia, members of Sigma Nu hung banners at the beginning of the 2015 school year that told parents: "Hope your baby girl is ready for a good time," "Freshman daughter drop off," and "Go ahead and drop off mom too." Later that same year, North Carolina State University suspended its chapter of Pi Kappa Phi after the discovery of a "pledge book" with comments such as "It will be short and painful, just like when I rape you," and "If she's hot enough, she doesn't need a pulse."

Undergraduate fraternity members often dismiss such statements as anomalies or bad jokes. The North-American Interfraternity Conference, the main organization representing historically white fraternities, has long noted that it is the nation's largest sponsor of rape-awareness programs. In 2014, eight major fraternities, including SAE, formed an education initiative on sexual assault, as well as hazing and binge drinking. After each episode, the national fraternities take pains to call the mistreatment of women a violation of their values. SAE, of course, has the True Gentleman creed, which describes a brother as someone "with whom honor is sacred and virtue safe." Sigma Nu's creed celebrates "the chivalrous deeds of courtesy, and sealing not our hearts against the touch of tenderness, to win the love and care of some incorruptible woman."

By stressing traditions of chivalry, fraternities gloss over their long history of demeaning women. In the late nineteenth century, when female students began to be admitted to American colleges in larger numbers, fraternity members, like many male students, excluded and demeaned "co-eds." At Stanford, which had always enrolled women, a member of SAE was expelled in 1908 for writing "grossly obscene, abusive and scurrilous anonymous letters," propositioning female students and the school nurse. "You look kind of used up but you would do," one read. Not surprisingly, in an often hostile environment, female students formed their own sisterhoods, "women's fraternities," or sororities. In a quirk of history, SAE did, in fact, have one female member: Lucie Pattie, an honorary initiate of the chapter at the Kentucky Military Institute. Pattie preserved the secret papers of SAE during the Civil War, or so the story goes. In 1888, an SAE member from Louisiana publicly advocated the admission of women. It inspired "considerable merriment in the fraternity" and no serious consideration, according to an SAE history.

In sexual matters, fraternities fostered a double standard that celebrated their own sexual conquests, while disrespecting women considered "fast" or "loose." Through the early twentieth century, they would engage in chaste, courtly behavior with women they considered social equals and marriage material, while looking for sex with working-class women and prostitutes, according to the historian Nicholas Syrett. After World War II, as premarital sex became more socially acceptable, fraternity men felt increasing pressure to demonstrate their virility with at-times reluctant college women. "Many fraternity men were increasingly forcing themselves on their female classmates," Syrett wrote. In the 1960s, fraternity men at the University of Texas had what they called "fuck dates" with women they hoped would be "easy lays." If successful, they would share names with fraternity brothers, who would then pressure the same women for sex. Yale held "pig nights," where they invited local women into the chapter, so younger members could lose their virginity.

In the most horrifying cases, fraternity members formed groups to prey on vulnerable women. In 1959, eight naked fraternity men from SAE's University of North Carolina chapter were found in a basement with a woman who was an outpatient from a local psychiatric hospital, according to Syrett's review of school disciplinary files. Members said they were playing strip poker.

In 1978, *Esquire* magazine reported, a woman on leave from a mental institution was taken to Dartmouth's fraternity row and passed from house to house for sex. Fraternities have long faced accusations of gang rape. In 1985, the Association of American Colleges identified reports of fifty such campus attacks, mostly at fraternities. In one widely reported case, a woman in 1983 said she was gang raped by five to eight members of the Alpha Tau Omega chapter at the University of Pennsylvania. The men said it was consensual, and no one was charged.

More recently, social scientists sought to document the prevalence of rape by surveying fraternity members themselves. Using questionnaires, psychologists asked men whether they had participated in behavior that amounts to sexual assault without labeling it as a criminal offense. In a variety of surveys, anywhere from 5 percent to 15 percent of college men admitted committing rape. News stories and academic articles often cite two studies in concluding that fraternity members are three times more likely than other male students to commit sexual assault: one in 2007 by researchers from the College of William and Mary; and another, in 2005, at Ohio University. These studies each queried only several hundred undergraduates at a single college; unlike research on excessive drinking at fraternities, the findings are far from conclusive. Other surveys, also based on small samples, have found that fraternity men are more likely to hold what are called "rape-supportive attitudes." These include the belief that women enjoy rough sex or put up token resistance so they won't be considered easy or that a man is entitled to sex if a woman indicated interest, "leading him on."

To fight such attitudes, some colleges are taking aim at all-male organizations. Harvard is challenging single-sex "final clubs." All but one of the elite student societies—the Porcellian Club, Harvard's oldest—began as local branches of national fraternities. A 2016 university task force, led by Harvard's dean, attacked what it called the "sexual entitlement" of final club members. The organizations invite attractive female students to parties, then compete with each other "for sexual conquests," viewing acceptance of an invitation as "an implicit agreement to have sexual encounters with men," according to the task force report, which had similar concerns about Harvard's fraternities. Almost half of senior women who ventured into final clubs—and 40 percent of those participating in fraternities and sororities—reported "nonconsensual sexual contact," compared with 31 percent of all female fourth-year students. Based on the report's recommendations, Harvard president Drew Faust, the first woman to lead the university, announced measures designed to pressure all-male social clubs to accept women, though they also applied to all-female groups such as sororities. Starting with the Class of 2021, members of single-sex clubs will be excluded from leading teams and recognized student groups. The college will no longer endorse members for coveted fellowships such as Rhodes and Marshall scholarships. Greek organizations protested the moves as violations of their constitutional rights to freedom of association. To fight sexual assault, Wesleyan University required student groups to admit women, though one fraternity is waging a court fight. Trinity College, one of Wesleyan's Connecticut neighbors, took the same step, then dropped the idea after opposition from alumni.

At Indiana University, a campus of 38,000 undergraduates known for its Greek life, fraternity parties make sexual assault "a predictable outcome," according to the sociologists Elizabeth Armstrong and Laura Hamilton, who spent nine months following fifty-five first-year women living in college dormitories. The campus police enforce drinking laws in dorms, while generally letting fraternities serve underage students in the privacy of their chapter houses, their research found. Like Hollywood producers—at times, perhaps, more like pornographers—fraternity members cast women into roles guaranteed to make them sex objects. Women were required to wear revealing clothing at parties with themes such as: "Pimps and Hos," "Victoria's Secret," and "Golf Pro/Tennis Ho." Fraternities controlled transportation. Pledges conveyed first-year women in cars from the dorms and then could stall or refuse to drive them back, leaving women to choose between staying longer and being forced to find their way home drunk on their own. Many of the female students the researchers interviewed had heard about rapes or had survived attacks themselves. In fact, two of the first-year women they studied were sexually assaulted at a frat party—during the first week of the study.

Indiana University's own data bolster the sociologists' research. Even though only 12 percent of undergraduate men belong to fraternities, their chapter houses were the locations of 23 percent of sexual-assault reports. One of the accused was John Enochs, a member of Delta Tau Delta, who was charged with rape at an April 2015 chapter house party. (He later pleaded guilty to one count of battery with moderate bodily injury, a misdemeanor.) The college recently disciplined three chapters for creating "an unsafe environment that resulted in an allegation of sexual assault." For its part, Indiana University's administration gives fraternities a wholehearted official endorsement. It promotes Greek organizations as "partners" who help members "lead, serve, build positive relationships and grow intellectually." Indiana Greek organizations themselves stress their own efforts to address sexual assault. Fraternities, for example, launched a "BannerUp" campaign, representing "Men Against Rape and Sexual Assault," hanging banners on fraternity houses with such messages as "Real Hoosier Men Should Respect Women."

Of course, all fraternities aren't alike. Sociologists at Lehigh University found that safer fraternities featured quieter settings that enabled conversations and a balance of men and women interacting in groups; high-risk chapters threw large, loud parties with skewed gender ratios, which transformed them into meat markets, places where men used loud music as a pretext to invite intoxicated women upstairs for sex. Rebecca Leitman Veidlinger, a former sex-crimes prosecutor in Bloomington who consults with universities, reached a similar conclusion. In her view, chapters emphasizing sexual conquest, such as "hooking up" and bragging about it, create an environment ripe for assault. Fraternities can root out that behavior, she said, or "they can be 'that fraternity'—the 'rapey' one, the one that women talk about."

SAE CHAPTERS, IN many parts of the country, have developed just that sort of reputation. The film producer Amy Ziering visited college campuses across the nation, asking women where they felt most threatened. Again and again, she would hear about the local SAE chapter. She also asked about fraternity nicknames. Female undergraduates at the University of North Carolina, the University of Connecticut, the University of California at Berkeley, and the University of Southern California told her that SAE stood for "Sexual Assault Expected," words they would repeat, to chilling effect, in *The Hunting Ground*, her explosive 2015 documentary about campus rape and the failure of colleges to bring perpetrators to justice. The camera panned along dark streets, showing SAE's signature lions and its electrified Greek letters, glowing like a sign in front of an adult movie theater. The movie, hailed for drawing attention to sexual assault at universities, also provoked criticism for a less-than-nuanced presentation of statistics and for relying on some individuals' cases whose facts have since been disputed. Because no one tracks sexual assaults by fraternity—and the crime is so underreported—it's impossible to know whether SAE's houses deserve their nickname. "That acronym is as old as time," Clark Brown, SAE's general counsel, told me. "It was around fifteen years ago. It doesn't mean any more now than it did then. There are a number of acronyms like that for all kinds of fraternities. These are college students being silly. These names aren't based on any facts." To get a sense of the possible roots of its reputation, I examined databases of news articles, court records, and disciplinary files over the five school years that ended in the spring of 2016. Because its 2011 hazing-death legal settlement requires disclosure of all campus infractions, that record provides an unusual window into one fraternity's history of alleged sexual assaults.

During those five years, I found sexual assaults reported at fifteen of 230 SAE chapters. Few resulted in criminal charges. In January 2016, a nineteen-year-old Worcester Polytechnic Institute student said she was raped at the school's SAE chapter and left with bruises on the calves and thighs of both legs, as well as a bite on her lip. The school said fraternity brothers alerted them about the alleged attack, and three months later, a nineteen-year-old by then former SAE member and WPI student, was charged with rape and assault.

Most rape reports later disappeared without charges or any public reckoning. In some cases, fraternity members faced complaints of obstructing investigators. In September 2012, for example, a female student who was drinking at the University of Iowa SAE chapter house reported a sexual assault, was hospitalized, and then dropped out of the school. Later that month, David Grady, the dean of students, said fraternity members had been discouraging potential witnesses from helping investigators and threatened to call the police or expel them if they continued. "I am directing you and members of your chapter not to contact the apparent victim or potential witnesses in any manner at any time for any reason," he wrote in an e-mail to the chapter's president. At nearby Iowa State University, a woman reported a member of SAE had sexually assaulted her during a party at its chapter house in January 2015. An SAE member was handcuffed and arrested after refusing to move out of the way when police were executing a search warrant at the chapter house. Several chapters stood out because they faced so many accusations. SAE's chapters at San Diego State University and California State University at Long Beach were the subject of five separate reports of sexual assault or misconduct in 2014 and 2015. None of the allegations in Iowa and California appear to have resulted in criminal charges. In the ensuing investigations, the universities and the SAE national organization disciplined all the chapters, though primarily for alcohol violations and not sexual assault. Both Iowa chapters and the Long Beach outpost were shut down.

Of all the chapters, the University of New Mexico left the longest trail of sexual-assault reports, which began well before the five-year period I examined. In 2000, the University of New Mexico and SAE settled, for an undisclosed sum, a lawsuit filed by an eighteen-year-old freshman who said she had unwittingly attended a gathering the fraternity dubbed a "cherry-bust party," referring to a place for women to lose their virginity. The woman—an athlete on a swimming scholarship—said members at the party slipped Rohypnol, or a "Roofie," a potent tranquilizer often called a date-rape drug, into her drink. Police accused two members of SAE's El Paso chapter of taking her to a truck in a parking lot and raping her. In a 2001 trial, the two men were acquitted of the rape charges, though one was convicted of criminal sexual contact. Two other rape accusations—in 2003 and 2006—resulted in arrests but no convictions. In 2007, an SAE pledge was charged with rape related to sex with underage girls, including a fifteen-year-old, though the charges were later dismissed. All along, the university repeatedly cited the chapter for out-of-control and underage drinking.

The most recent episode began on a Monday night in April 2013. SAE members held a sorority serenade, an event of long-standing tradition when young men try to impress women with sentimental fraternity songs. Afterward, members from four different sororities visited the SAE chapter house. A nine-teen-year-old freshman who has identified herself by the initials A. O. later gave the following account of what happened next. (In responding to my public-records request, the University of New Mexico, as is typical, redacted the names of students to comply with federal privacy laws.) SAE members invited her and a few other women up to the balcony for a drink, offer-ing each a shot of liquor—brandy, or maybe rum. Then, they headed to the basement, where A. O. drank beer and vodka. One fraternity member—I'll call him Sam—talked with A. O. for a while. It was the first time the two had met. Sam invited A. O. up to his room for a drink, tequila and orange juice. A man and a woman came into the room to join them.

"This is where my memory stops," A. O. wrote in an e-mail to the university. As for what came next, "I remember it like a dream."

A. O. described a series of moments, like movie flashbacks she couldn't place in any particular order: getting sick in a bucket of ice, going to the bathroom, visiting the balcony. She woke up on Sam's couch at 9:00 a.m., then spent much of the day there because she had lost her phone, keys, and shoes. Later, Sam drove her back to her dorm. On Wednesday morning, she told her parents what had happened. Her mother, believing she had been drugged and assaulted, took her to the hospital, where both pregnancy and rape-drug tests came out negative. A sexual-assault examination found signs of penetration, and she filed a report with the University of New Mexico police.

The next month, the university found the chapter responsible for holding an unregistered party and providing liquor to minors. In the harshest punishment available, the school revoked SAE's charter. The university noted six years of misbehavior: drinking, fighting, hazing, and the incident involving sex with underage girls.

The University of New Mexico chapter fought against the punishment, saying it was being held accountable for unsubstantiated accusations against past members. "No member of the SAE chapter at UNM has ever been convicted of any sexual misconduct," it said in its twelve-page appeal to the vice president for student affairs. The chapter said the school's investigation hadn't proven that members, rather than guests, gave alcohol to minors and ridiculed the idea that SAE should have kept underage students from drinking: "Neither did SAE check identification or papers, or strip search people as they entered the house." The chapter complained that SAE was being targeted because of anti-fraternity bias. The university, the chapter said, lacked an appreciation of its ideals and the success of its alumni, "including a recent state governor, a recent U.S. senator, UNM regents, UNM foundation board members, donors and boosters." They were invoking SAE's considerable political power. The "recent U.S. senator" was none other than Pete Domenici, the influential Republican who retired in 2008 after the longest tenure in the history of New Mexico; the "recent state governor," Gary Johnson, who became the 2016 Libertarian candidate for president. It could have been read as a not-so-veiled threat. The university rejected the appeal, saying the fraternity had "failed to learn from its past mistakes."

Bryan Ruddy, SAE's volunteer chapter adviser, told me the national organization and alumni supported the university's action, noting that the undergraduates shouldn't have served liquor at all because fraternity houses are supposed to be dry. "We as alumni came down very hard on them," said Ruddy, an IBM software engineer who had joined the chapter in the 1990s. "It was time to pull the plug there."

In deciding whether to punish Sam, the university found witnesses who had seen A. O. stumbling downstairs, slurring her words and staggering. Sam denied giving A. O. any liquor, saying he would have been "too greedy" to share the alcohol. A. O., he said, had voluntarily given him oral sex but stopped because she got sick. A. O. offered a vague memory of perhaps kissing Sam. A member representing the chapter told the university there had been "plenty of alcohol" in the house and confirmed that A. O. had been given shots of liquor, according to an e-mail from a University of New Mexico Greek Life adviser summing up the chapter's account of the evening. The fraternity member also said A. O. had been "open to sexual activity, 'sending mixed signals,'" was making out with [Sam, presumably], "giving the green light," and "acting like a 'whore.'" In the classic double standard, he denigrated a woman for showing sexual interest, while exonerating a man for his own participation. The fraternity brother suggested, wrongly, that drunken kissing and flirting implied sexual consent and that once a woman gives a "green light" that men can drive through it without stopping, even if a woman is no longer capable of giving consent. The comments represent the "rape-supportive attitudes" described in social-science literature. "I was horrified he had said anything like that," Ruddy told me. "Knowing this gentleman personally, I just think he was speaking emotionally. He was trying to defend his friend, essentially. It's never something we would condone or support."

The university, citing witnesses, concluded Sam had violated the student-conduct code: He had given A. O. a tequila and orange juice, when she was already so drunk she had trouble walking, and then lied about it at his disciplinary hearing. But Sam wasn't found responsible for sexual assault, in part because A. O. couldn't remember the episode. Despite his ruling, Rob Burford, the student conduct officer, condemned Sam's behavior: Sam himself acknowledged oral sex with "an intoxicated underage female" and had supplied the alcohol that "caused her not to remember every detail of what occurred." It sounded at least close to what researchers described as "incapacitated sexual assault." The school put Sam on probation for the rest of his time at the university and prohibited him from contact with A. O. on penalty of suspension or expulsion. It required him to go to a class on "respectful relationships" and pay $50 to attend a two and one-half-hour alcohol and drug awareness program. In his ruling, Buford indicated that A. O. paid a higher price. She had withdrawn from the school that spring "as a result of this incident, which interfered with continuing her education at the University of New Mexico." In January 2014, the woman, using the initials A. O., sued SAE and the University of New Mexico for negligent supervision, citing "a dangerous culture" documented in police reports, student complaints, and disciplinary actions dating to 2001. SAE and the university denied the allegations and said they had no legal duty to supervise the operations of the chapter. In April 2015, the university and the fraternity reached an undisclosed settlement with the woman.

If a single chapter created a dangerous environment for women, so could a single holiday. Over one weekend in 2014, rapes were reported at SAE Halloween parties on both coasts, in Georgia, Maryland, and California. At 10:30 p.m. Friday, October 31, a female student said she was raped in the SAE chapter house at Emory University in Atlanta. The school suspended Greek activities for a month and later said the woman had declined to pursue criminal charges. About two hours later, at 12:40 a.m. on Saturday, November 1, a student at Loyola Marymount University in Los Angeles said she was raped in the garage of an off-campus SAE house where she had been mistakenly looking for a bathroom. No one called 911 after she ran out of the garage, bruises all over her body, and said she had been raped, according to her parents. The woman left with her friends, who later took her to the hospital. She offered police a detailed description: a white man, six feet tall, 170 pounds, with shoulder-length hair, wearing a white top hat, white shirt, and dark pants. Almost six months after the attack, her parents begged for help. "SAE members claimed it was not one of them, but the party was invite-only," the parents wrote in the school paper. "It is our understanding that not one person came forward, just like no one helped the night it happened."

Of the three Halloween parties—and, in fact, of all fifteen reported sexual assaults—I found only one offering the possibility of a full public accounting. It was the third rape reported that weekend, at the party overseen by Ivan Booth, the Johns Hopkins sophomore and SAE social chairman who had invited his friend Maria Lopez and her sixteen-year-old sister, Gabriela. That was the party where Gabriela was attacked and left in the bathroom of the chapter house in the early morning of November 2, 2014.

As the Halloween party was winding down, about ten stragglers relaxed in the basement of the Johns Hopkins SAE house. Evan Krumheuer, a junior who belonged to the fraternity, saw someone inside the bathroom. It was a girl, huddled in a corner, just behind the door frame, trembling, so drunk and scared that she could come up with only a few words.

"I need help," Gabriela said. "I was raped."

Gabriela had managed to put most of her clothes back on. She reached over to collect her white tank top, which lay on the other side of the bathroom. Evan, a champion wrestler on the Johns Hopkins team, put his arm around Gabriela's back and helped her up the stairs to the first floor. Steven Pearlman, a graduate student, called Gabriela's sister because Gabriela herself was too drunk to dial. Maria and Ivan rushed back to the house and saw Gabriela, who was crying hysterically. Steven—who didn't belong to SAE but was renting a room while working as a teaching assistant—noticed no one had called the police, so he dialed 911.

After Gabriela left in an ambulance, the police investigation moved quickly. She had described her two attackers as skinny African American men with beards. In the historically white fraternity, only a handful of the one hundred guests were black men. Evan, the wrestler who had helped Gabriela up the stairs, offered a lead. He had seen someone he knew near the bathroom before the attack—an African American named Chaz Haggins. When he was organizing the Halloween party, Ivan had invited Chaz. They had gone to high school together in suburban Maryland, and they were friends who shared an appreciation of hip-hop music and muscle cars. Chaz had arrived late that evening with another friend, Ethan Turner, who had graduated from the same high school. They had initially been turned away by the brother at the door. Once the SAE member figured out the connection with Ivan, Chaz and Ethan joined the party.

Like the two sisters, Chaz and Ethan were unusual that night in the crowd of future Silicon Valley coders and Wall Street bankers. Chaz, who was twenty years old, was a stocker at Walmart, where his mother was a manager. Ethan, who was nineteen, held down two jobs, busing tables at a banquet hall and stocking shelves at a Food Lion supermarket. Six-foot-two, outgoing, and charismatic, Chaz cut the larger figure, and he knew the chapter house pretty well. He had spun albums as a DJ in the basement, sitting in a booth emblazoned with the fraternity's letters. Ethan was quieter. His family considered him a born "follower," a five-foot-five video-game enthusiast who loved to play board games with his family.

As social chairman, Ivan would clearly have been in the best position to help police figure out who was at the party. But during his interview with detectives, just after 5:00 a.m., he volunteered nothing. Detectives asked about African Americans at the party. Ivan told them he had seen one, someone he didn't know, and there were none on the guest list. Ivan suggested that someone could have slipped into the party. After the first couple of hours, he told the police, control of the door broke down.

"Tell us about Chaz," one of the detectives said, finally.

"He's a good friend of mine," Ivan said. "He's a very genuine person. It would be very uncharacteristic to perform an act like that, to be involved in something like this."

"So, possibly, couldn't he have done this tonight?"

"You know. I know his character."

"So you're saying he was there, then?"

Ivan told the detective he had heard Chaz was there when he returned to the chapter house with Maria and saw Gabriela crying.

"So doesn't this kind of go against what you said earlier that there was only one African American male there that you knew?" the detective asked.

"I was answering in terms of what I had seen and, like, people, I had seen at the party."

"But you knew he was there. He's a good friend of yours."

"I heard he was there."

The detective pushed harder. Had he been in contact with Chaz? Ivan said he had texted Chaz earlier in the week.

"Was it in reference to the party?"

"Just seeing if he was free, and if he wanted to come down. He was going to try to, but he wasn't positive if he could come down or not."

"So you texted him about the party?" the detective asked. "So he was invited to the party?"

"If he were to have shown up when I was there, yes," Ivan said. "He would have been invited. He was technically invited by me. However, I was unaware of the fact that he was in attendance."

Since Chaz had said he might come, why wasn't he on the list?

"I'm not going to put his name on the list because he says he's going to try. I need like actual physical evidence."

At the end of the interview, Ivan was asked if there was anything else he could say that could be helpful.

"No," Ivan said. "Besides the fact that I would add that Chaz's apparent presence at the party was completely unannounced to me, and the situation itself transpired while I wasn't present at the house. So we can't offer too many details about the situation itself but the prerequisites, and I have the list and everything, and I do have the pertinent information."

Ivan sounded more like a lawyer defending a corporation than a college sophomore answering questions about the rape of his friend's little sister. His language was bureaucratic, stilted, and passive. He elaborated on process and gave answers to direct questions as necessary, offering nothing more. Chaz had been "technically invited by me." Ivan required "actual physical evidence" before putting a good friend on the guest list, a good friend whose character he vouched for, yet whose "apparent presence at the party was completely unannounced to me." The state's attorney's office would later call on many of the people who were there the night of Gabriela's rape to give testimony for the prosecution: Gabriela's sister, Maria; Evan, the fraternity brother who found Gabriela in the bathroom; and the graduate student, Steven Pearlman, who called 911. Ivan Booth was the most notable omission. No doubt, the prosecution watched this interview and came to a simple conclusion: the SAE social chairman wouldn't be much help.

Later that morning, Gabriela's sister showed her pictures of Chaz and Ethan from her Instagram account. "That's him," she said, after looking at each one, before bursting into tears. She later identified each of them at a police photo array. The next month, Chaz and Ethan were charged with rape and sexual assault in Gabriela's attack. For its role, SAE was punished, too. Johns Hopkins suspended the SAE chapter for one year because it served alcohol to minors and failed to monitor its guests. "It is beyond just alcohol; it's the overall management of the event and the evening, with alcohol being a big factor," Kevin G. Shollenberger, vice provost for student affairs, told the *Johns Hopkins News-Letter*, the student paper. "From what I hear from students, it's a big part of the culture there."

The Johns Hopkins campus never found out what had really happened that night. The newspaper accounts made it sound like strangers had somehow found their way into the SAE house. Other fraternities rallied around SAE, as did the *News-Letter*. In a March 2015 editorial, the paper called the chapter's suspension "draconian" and "absurd on its face" because the accused weren't affiliated with SAE and "the brothers immediately called the police and worked with law enforcement." The article didn't seem aware that Chaz was, in fact, a close friend of the chapter's social chairman, who had invited him—at least, "technically," to use Ivan's own word. Chaz may not have been a member, but he had been a DJ for SAE. It could be argued that he was, in fact, "affiliated" with the fraternity. The brothers didn't call police; a graduate student living in the house did. Ivan's cooperation with the authorities had been grudging, at best. The editorial objected that the Johns Hopkins chapter of Pi Kappa Alpha, often known as "Pike," had also received a one-year suspension after its own members in 2013 had been accused of gang rape. In fact, Pike hadn't been punished for that accusation. The police investigated the alleged attack but didn't file charges; the suspension, like SAE's, was primarily for underage drinking. More broadly, the editorial conveyed resignation, a sense that such episodes were inevitable on a college campus. "We all know this could have happened to anyone," the editors said. The punishment didn't chasten the SAE chapter. Members ignored their suspension and held another party. As a result, that April, Hopkins terminated the chapter's recognition. It would be years until SAE could even consider coming back—2019, at the earliest.

Sorting out who was responsible for what happened would take years, too, and it would be costly. Johns Hopkins requires each fraternity chapter to take out a $2 million insurance policy that covers host liquor liability, sexual misconduct, and sexual assault. The coverage must protect the university, as well as the fraternity. That July, Gabriela's family filed a lawsuit against Sigma Alpha Epsilon, Johns Hopkins, Ethan Turner, and Chaz Haggins. Along with alleging battery against the two criminal defendants, the complaint accused SAE and Hopkins of negligence for allowing "untrained, underage members" to throw "regular and notorious parties that involved provision of alcoholic beverages to minors and inebriates that, by virtue of their promotion, creates an environment that made sexual assault and rape likely." The lawsuit, which Hopkins later settled for an undisclosed sum, sought $30 million in damages. The case against SAE was still pending.

In February 2016, Ethan Turner's criminal trial unfolded on the fifth floor of the Baltimore City Circuit courthouse, a grand marble landmark of a building with soaring columns and brass doors. This particular courtroom, at the end of a long hallway and behind a nondescript wooden door, was easy to miss. It was the size of a small chapel, cramped and dreary, paint peeling off the radiators. Inside, on long wooden benches lined up like church pews, Ethan's friends and family, a dozen or more at a time, made up most of the spectators. During breaks, they expressed their support for Ethan and disparaged Gabriela.

Ethan's defense attorney, Matthew Fraling, never disputed that Gabriela had been raped. Gabriela's medical exam had shown she was bleeding hours after the attack and that she had been drunk and incapacitated. The state's DNA expert said two men had attacked her: Chaz, and another man whose identity couldn't be determined. Fraling maintained that Chaz was the rapist, but not Ethan, and that alcohol had clouded Gabriela's recollection. Often, Fraling focused on a kind of unindicted co-conspirator: Sigma Alpha Epsilon itself.

Fraling cross-examined Evan, who had helped Gabriela out of the bathroom. He zeroed in on what he called "overindulgence" at the party.

"Yes, people were drunk," Evan said.

"How many bars did you have up and running?"

Evan said that there was one in the basement and another to the left of the front door, the one where women were dancing on the bar.

"It's like *Coyote Ugly*," Fraling said, to a sustained objection.

"Was it standard practice for the fraternity to distribute alcohol to sixteen-year-olds?" Fraling asked.

"No."

Fraling leveled his toughest questions at Gabriela's older sister, suggesting she had left Gabriela on the couch so she could "hook up" with Ivan.

"This is a frat house, this is a guys' fraternity—right?—for college guys," Fraling said. "And you left your sister, inebriated, with more than seventy-five people, and you felt that she would be safe?"

"I didn't think anything would happen to her," Maria said, her voice breaking.

The two sisters, once close, were now estranged, Maria struggling with guilt, confronting a relationship that could be beyond repair. How could she have known? Her mother didn't even know what a fraternity was until she heard her daughter had been raped at a chapter house.

Soon after Maria testified, Gabriela herself walked to the witness stand, passing within several feet of Ethan, who sat behind a long table with Fraling. Unlike the day of his arrest, Ethan, now twenty, was clean-shaven and wore wire-rimmed glasses, a bow tie, and a boxy, dark suit that looked a couple of sizes too big, as if he were a child wearing his father's Sunday best. Gabriela looked older. For her day in court, like an office worker on a lunch break, she was dressed in a khaki blazer and black pants, and her hair was neatly coiffed. But she was still only seventeen, and terrified. After the attacks, she had been so shaken that she didn't return to high school. Instead, she took classes on her own and finished early. She put her plans for the army on hold. To keep busy, she worked three jobs—at a pizzeria, a shop selling honey, and a breakfast restaurant. She didn't socialize much anymore, and she avoided parties with alcohol. She had nightmares and flashbacks about the attack.

Gently insisting on explicit detail, the prosecutor walked Gabriela through what happened that night. She spoke softly, her voice barely above a whisper. In his cross-examination, Ethan's defense attorney suggested that her family's $30 million lawsuit gave her a motive to lie. He asked Gabriela to list all she drank that night: the two beers, the vodka, the Fireball shots; and he highlighted the moments she couldn't remember. Still, Gabriela was never shaken from her account.

The prosecutor asked Gabriela how sure she was that Ethan had attacked her.

"One hundred percent," she said.

After spending more than an hour on the stand, Gabriela was excused. She stepped outside, then broke down for the first time, her sobbing slowly growing fainter as she walked away from the courtroom.

The defense called only one witness, Alex Stiffler, who had driven Chaz to the house that night. Alex said he was Ethan's best friend. He answered a question hanging over the trial. Gabriela had said she saw three men in the bathroom, the two who attacked her and a third who told her to get dressed and then left. Who was the third man? Gabriela had seen a heavyset man, Hispanic with a beard. It was Alex, a community-college student. On the stand, he said he had headed down the stairs to the basement that night to smoke pot, when he saw a slender young Hispanic woman pulling Chaz into the bathroom. Later, Alex said, he needed to relieve himself. So he entered the bathroom and saw the same young woman slumped in the shower, unclothed and motioning toward him.

"Why? Why?" he quoted Gabriela as saying.

Alex said he was repulsed.

"I didn't want to touch her," he said. "I got out of there."

In a withering cross examination, the prosecutor, Robert M. Perkins III, who worked with the special-victims unit, suggested Alex was covering up for his friend. He focused on inconsistencies in his testimony when compared with his statement to the police. The prosecutor asked if Alex had spoken with Gabriela's sister that night. Alex said no. Perkins produced cell-phone records showing calls between their cell phones.

Then Perkins asked the toughest question.

"You see a girl lying on the floor, and you don't do anything?" Perkins asked.

Alex said he thought the young woman was coming on to him, and he wasn't interested. It was a curious reaction, especially since Evan, the SAE member who arrived shortly afterward, had immediately realized something terrible had happened to her. Alex's account was consistent with another possibility: He knew about what his friends were doing in the bathroom with the intoxicated Gabriela. Perhaps it was now his turn, but he thought better of it and left?

As Perkins's questions became more pointed, Alex grew combative. Like a class clown mouthing off to a teacher, he resisted answers and smiled at the crowd of Ethan's friends in court. "You said you entered the bathroom to urinate," Perkins said, as he began to ask a question.

"I said I went in to take a piss," Alex interrupted.

Did he speak with Chaz after what happened?

"I might have spoken to him. I might not."

Finally, Perkins read from Alex's statement to a Baltimore police detective on the morning after Gabriela was attacked.

"Anything to get me out of this," Alex had said.

Why would he say that? It sounded like someone who might have feared being charged as an accomplice.

"I was scared," Alex said, "even though I wasn't involved with this."

Although he was only in his early thirties, Perkins had prosecuted many sexual-assault cases. He knew he had about as much evidence as any assistant state's attorney could hope for. Having a DNA match, as the state had for Chaz, would have been helpful, but it wasn't unusual that such tests were inconclusive. Perkins viewed Gabriela as an especially articulate and credible witness. After her cross-examination, the jury saw her videotaped statement to police on the day of the crime, and it was exactly the same as what she had said on the stand. Her civil lawsuit wouldn't have been filed until months later. The jury saw a sixteen-year-old girl who vomited into a wastebasket after talking with the police, not someone who was considering her strategy for civil litigation. Still, all prosecutors knew that nothing can spell "reasonable doubt" more than a drunk witness, and no matter the legal standard for consent, many jurors are apt to blame the victim. Before the trial, Perkins had asked prospective jurors if they would be biased against a woman who had been attacked after she had become drunk voluntarily. A female juror stood up and said she would. A male juror, in his twenties or early thirties, also had qualms. "My fraternity was kicked off campus for the same thing," he said, gesturing toward Ethan. "I don't know if I could be impartial because it could have been me standing there." Both jurors were excused. Still, Perkins couldn't be sure that others didn't secretly harbor those views, even if they couldn't admit it to themselves.

In his closing argument, Fraling, the defense attorney, returned to the environment of the fraternity house and Maria's responsibility for what happened.

"She left her sister alone at a frat party with more than one hundred people," he said, pausing for emphasis. "At a frat party."

Fraling gave special emphasis to the word "frat party," lingering on it, like a kind of epithet. It was as if Fraling were saying "whorehouse," not the setting of an "invite-only" Halloween celebration at the elegant home of the Johns Hopkins chapter of Sigma Alpha Epsilon. Fraling didn't have to explain to the jury what he meant. He considered it common knowledge, the fate of a defenseless girl at a fraternity house: Sexual Assault Expected.

IN HER JEANS, plaid shirt, and purple Ugg boots, the forewoman on the jury didn't look much older than Gabriela. The judge asked her, separately, about the first three of five counts in the indictment, which accused Ethan of being an accomplice to Chaz.

"Not guilty."

"Not guilty."

"Not guilty."

Ethan's family looked overjoyed. But the verdict wasn't complete. The judge asked about the other two other charges.

Second-degree assault?

"Guilty."

Second-degree sexual assault?

"Guilty."

The judge ordered two sheriff's deputies to take Ethan into custody. He was handcuffed, his arms behind him. His mother collapsed on the courtroom floor.

The jury hadn't been told something else because it might have strongly predisposed them against the defendant. The week before, Chaz had pleaded guilty to raping and assaulting Gabriela, and neither side called him as a witness. In his deal, he accepted a twenty-year sentence—though all but five years were suspended. Unlike Ethan, he had been in jail since his arrest, so he was likely to be released in eighteen months, with credits for good behavior and time served. He would have had much to lose in a trial and far less to gain, unless he could have won an acquittal, which was unlikely because the prosecution had matched his DNA to the evidence collected from Gabriela's rape kit.

Now, Ethan faced the prospect of far harsher punishment. At Ethan's sentencing in April, the prosecutor asked for twenty years, ten years suspended, or twice the length of Chaz's sentence. Ethan's family begged the judge to give him a second chance, saying he had been a quiet child—a "follower" with no criminal record who came from a close-knit family that would look after him if he could stay at home during his sentence. His lawyer said he was less culpable than Chaz.

"I would never hurt a woman or anybody else," Ethan, now in his prison jumpsuit, told the judge, his voice barely audible. "It's not in my character."

"I'm not the same person I was a month ago."

The prosecutor read a short statement from Gabriela about her terror since the attack. She wasn't there. She didn't want to take time off from work—or perhaps to see her attacker again. Her mother, who hadn't planned to say anything, changed her mind.

"My heart is broken," she told the judge. "Who is going to give a second chance to my daughter?"

Judge Melissa Phinn, a former public defender who had been on the bench since 2013, said she believed Ethan was a follower and hoped his family could help him turn his life around. But she wanted him in prison.

"I didn't see any remorse from you," Phinn said, describing his behavior in the courtroom with his friends and family. "I saw laughing. . . . One night of drinking and partying. It's not so funny now. It's going to cost you."

Phinn gave Ethan the same sentence as Chaz: twenty years, all but five suspended. To Ethan's family, it was an eternity; to Gabriela's, not anywhere close to enough.

After the trial, Fraling, the defense lawyer, told me Steven Pearlman was the only one in the house he considered to have offered wholehearted cooperation with the authorities. If the non-SAE graduate student hadn't called the police, Fraling, who had worked twenty-three years as a Baltimore prosecutor, doubted the fraternity members would have done it themselves. "They circled the wagons," Fraling said. Responding by e-mail to my questions about Ivan Booth's role, his attorney, Garrett Brierley, called the information I related "greatly inaccurate" but said his client wouldn't comment because of the pending civil litigation. Pearlman told me he felt sure that one of the fraternity brothers would eventually have called the police. In part, Fraling blamed the alcohol-soaked fraternity environment for the events in the chapter. A year before Gabriela was attacked, SAE's membership had voted down a proposal that would have prohibited drinking in chapter houses. Doug Fierberg, the plaintiff's lawyer who has sued many fraternities after deaths and assaults, said alcohol-free houses, along with a responsible adult living on-site, could reduce both drinking and rape. At Johns Hopkins, Pearlman's presence had, at least, ensured a successful investigation. But he had been living there only by chance, and it hadn't been his job to supervise the undergraduates.

Almost a year after the trial, when Gabriela was ready to speak with me, she was still struggling with memories of the assaults. Therapy helped, as did frequent visits to the gym. She held on to her childhood dream. Once the civil case was resolved, the former "flyer" on the cheer squad planned to join the US Marines and become a paratrooper. She was already gathering weekly with other recruits for physical training, running for miles, and practicing pull-ups. "I love travel and adventure," she told me. "I think it will help me physically and mentally, help me become stronger. I'm hoping it will guide my life in the right direction." She was still distant from her older sister, who was having trouble forgiving herself for leaving Gabriela on her own at the party. "I don't blame her at all for what happened," Gabriela said. "I never would want her to feel it was her fault. It wasn't."

After watching the trial, speaking with Gabriela and her parents, and poring over evidence that had never fully been disclosed, I saw how the realities of race and class influenced its outcome. Although Gabriela's family found her attackers' punishment less severe than they had hoped, it far surpassed the punishment after a similar assault the next year. At Stanford, Brock Turner, the white star swimmer who assaulted the unconscious woman outside the Kappa Alpha fraternity house, was sentenced to six months in county jail; Ethan and Chaz, five years in prison. The California decision sparked outrage from those who said it reflected the privilege of wealthy men and the minimization of sexual assault. The two cases illustrate how white male defendants can pay a lower price than African Americans for similar crimes.

Race and class may have also partly explained why the Johns Hopkins crime, alone among recently reported SAE assaults, resulted in convictions. Gabriela's attackers were easily identified because they were outsiders, working-class African Americans who stood out at the chapter house. That night, they made up nearly all of the black guests at the fraternity. When Gabriela described the suspects as skinny African Americans with beards, the police could quickly zero in on suspects and get warrants for DNA tests. If they had been white college students, narrowing down suspects at a party of one hundred would have been more challenging, especially if fraternity brothers didn't volunteer information. The search for the white attacker at the Los Angeles SAE party that same weekend went nowhere. I had to ask myself: What if the men who attacked Gabriela had been white? What if they had been Johns Hopkins students? What if they had been members of SAE?

4

THE SAE LAW

"Who Does Not Flatter Wealth, Cringe Before Power"

Ian Gove's Sigma Alpha Epsilon chapter was in serious trouble. Gove, the son of a sailor in the Merchant Marine, wasn't about to back away from a fight to save it. On a Tuesday evening in November 2012, he sat in a conference room facing a panel of classmates and faculty at the University of North Carolina at Wilmington. Gove, who was twenty-one years old and chapter president, planned to go to law school to become a litigator. Now, the college senior had the chance to test his mettle. Usually, he drove a pickup truck and chewed tobacco. On this day, he wore a suit and tie as he confronted the student-conduct board hearing. The chapter faced charges of hazing, underage drinking, and violating a ban on social events. Overseeing the prosecution was an assistant dean, an educator with a PhD who administered the school's honor code and wanted SAE shut down.

It looked like an unfair fight, but Gove had a secret weapon: One of the sharper legal minds in the state of North Carolina sat by his side. His associate was a trial lawyer, state senator, and sometime law professor named Thom Goolsby. A leading Wilmington citizen, Goolsby was an SAE alumnus from his days at the University of North Carolina at Chapel Hill. Known for his caustic wit, conservative Republican politics, and dapper style, he was a man who could pull off a purple seersucker suit with white shoes. He didn't think much of the proceeding or the way his fraternity brothers were being treated. "This is a kangaroo court," he sniffed to Gove. The eminently qualified SAE legal adviser whispered in Gove's ear as if they were co-counsel.

"As a reminder, Senator Goolsby, you may not speak or address the board, but you are allowed to talk with the respondents," the student chairing the tribunal had said at the opening of the hearing.

Even in silence, Goolsby's presence spoke volumes to administrators in the room. UNC–Wilmington counted on state funding. Not only had Goolsby chaired the state legislature's judiciary committee, he sat on the finance and higher education panels as well. Outside the hearing room waited another state-capital power broker, Parks Griffin, one of the chapter's founding members. Griffin ran a local insurance agency and also raised money for Pat McCrory, North Carolina's Republican governor.

That evening, during the more than three-hour hearing, Gove did Griffin and Goolsby proud with his aggressive representation of SAE. Every chance he could get, Gove objected to the proceedings as biased against the fraternity. Gove asked members to disregard e-mails from a next-door neighbor who had dutifully chronicled a series of late-night keg parties that fall. He saw it as outrageous that he couldn't cross-examine the neighbor, whose integrity he soundly impugned.

"These are college kids living next to a neighbor who obviously doesn't want college kids living next to him—which is why he fabricated this testimony that he's not here to defend," argued Gove in his low, flat baritone that signaled confidence and command.

At times, Gove had to be nimble, as he was acting as both defense attorney and defendant. A board member asked him why he had lied to the police when the officer had busted a party at an SAE house. Gove had been asked if it was a fraternity party, and he had said no.

"That's actually a form of profiling by police officers," said Gove. "It's like someone asking if I was Jewish when they were out on the scene. Yeah, I said, 'No.' I shouldn't have answered it. That doesn't pertain to the officer's investigation. . . . That also shows a very biased tendency from the officer. We have to be cautious of when, you know, you deal with police profiling."

Gove exuded confidence, even though the dean's evidence seemed overwhelming. The ill-fated evening had begun at the Cape Fear Men's Club, the haunt of generations of politicians and business leaders in Wilmington. The state's oldest private club, known for its extensive collection of maritime memorabilia, faced periodic criticism over its lack of black and female members. On a Wednesday evening that September 2012, the chapter had gathered at the club to initiate eighteen pledges. After the so-called pinning ceremony, the men were still wearing ties and jackets with their fraternity badges when they stopped for slices at Fat Tony's Pizza. They then headed to an off-campus house for a celebration with sorority women. The fraternity leaders directed the young men to drink only from a cooler with strong liquor inside, a pledge later told the university. He suspected it was "PJ," the term often used to describe grain alcohol mixed with Kool-Aid. After a neighbor complained about the party, the police arrived around 11:00 p.m. One eighteen-year-old pledge mistook a police cruiser for a taxi and tried to climb inside, then vomited in nearby bushes. An officer reported seeing men screaming at pledges in coats and ties who were doing push-ups. Later that evening, police found a drunk pledge, who had left the party, passed out in the bathroom of Wilmington's Browncoat Pub. He became the third underage SAE recruit to be hospitalized for drinking after fraternity events that year. Pending an investigation, the college banned the chapter from holding parties.

The next month, SAE was cited for violating the ban by holding a toga party mixer with the Phi Mu sorority. The dean's office asked a Phi Mu member to testify. Before the hearing, SAE's vice president contacted her and told her to deny it was a mixer, even though she had signed a document saying it was. He told her to call it instead an informal "grab-a-date," a category of party where women each pick a man and aren't restricted to a single fraternity.

"This has the potential to completely kick us off campus," the vice president texted her. "We need you to say you just filled it [the form she signed registering the mixer] out too quickly because you didn't think it mattered and that you intended to have a Phi Mu grab a date. There were other organizations there other than SAE. I know this is a lot to ask but our fraternity could potentially hang in the balance of what you say."

The dean's office seemed to have unassailable evidence of fraternity wrongdoing: documentation of witness tampering, police testimony that included a seventeen-minute dash-cam video of the drunken underage pledges, and a signed statement from a pledge about the cooler full of mysterious liquor. Many a defense lawyer would counsel his client to plead guilty. But Gove had no such plan. Neither did Senator Thom Goolsby or Parks Griffin, who would be chairing the governor's inauguration committee. When they were finished, the administration and the college's own president would learn the cost of tangling with SAE.

COLLEGE ADMINISTRATORS WHO try to crack down on fraternities find themselves confronting a determined adversary that
is well financed, politically connected, and capable of frustrating the most dogged investigators. Even college presidents have
reason to fear for their jobs. Both on campus and through their
trade organizations and Washington political-action committee, fraternities have successfully fought measures to curb drinking, hazing, and sexual assault. The battles are so bitter partly
because they reflect America's cultural divide. Decades of studies have found that Greek-letter organizations attract conservative students on college campuses, whereas college professors
are more likely to be liberal. Reflecting this ideological clash,
fraternities chafe at restrictions on individual behavior in the belief that young men are best left to their own devices to govern
themselves. Their mostly white, male members can view themselves as an aggrieved group, oppressed by what they consider to
be the overbearing regulation of "politically correct" universities.

In a country divided so starkly by political orientation—
into Republican "red state" and Democratic "blue state" territory—college administrators and fraternity leaders often find
themselves speaking different languages. Consider how Gove
compared himself to a member of a minority group who had
been the victim of police profiling; as they pressed their case,
Gove and his alumni backers would increasingly employ the vo-
cabulary of the American civil-rights movement that fraternities
once so firmly rejected. The sociologist Arlie Russell Hochschild
has identified a defining characteristic of the American right's
definition of freedom. It focuses on the "freedom to"—such
as the freedom to bear arms or ride without a motorcycle hel-
met. Fraternities often cite this kind of liberty—to choose their
friends and to socialize—without interference from those they
consider to be hostile college authorities. (To an outsider, it

recalled the 1980s Beastie Boys lyrics: "You gotta fight for your right to party.") In Hochschild's view, progressives tend to stress a different view of freedom—the "freedom from," for example, pollution, racial bias, or sexual discrimination and assault. Universities, then, have a bias toward regulation. They are more concerned about students' freedom from the dangerous environment some fraternities create.

The solution, on both sides, would seem obvious: secession. Colleges could ban fraternities or refuse to recognize them. Fraternities could operate as truly private separate organizations, free from disciplinary control. But universities and Greek organizations often need each other. Fraternities are heavily invested in their colleges and communities. Fraternity and sorority alumni are more likely to give to their colleges and are larger lifetime donors than other graduates. Especially at cash-strapped public universities, colleges rely on their housing as quasi-official dorms and would have to come up with an expensive alternative. Fraternities and sororities, which house 250,000 undergraduates, are the second-largest student landlords in the United States after colleges. At the same time, a college's blessing helps a fraternity recruit dues-paying members that keep their houses and national organizations solvent. Chapters benefit financially from colleges' endorsement, their free advertisement on websites, the complimentary office space on campus, support from administrators—and, in places such as Indiana and Alabama, direct taxpayer support, by offering public land for their houses. For all their power, fraternities are often scrambling for funding for their houses because only a relative handful of alumni volunteer or donate money. Like a couple stuck in a bad marriage, fraternities and universities both need—and resent—each other.

The dynamic is even more complex because national fraternity organizations, whose small headquarters can each be responsible for hundreds of chapters, rely on colleges to police members. As a result, the umbrella group often finds itself at odds with undergraduate members and local alumni. On campus, college deans are a national organization's first line of defense against extreme behavior that could kill members, as well as subject a fraternity to years of costly and potentially institution-ending litigation. The year before the three Wilmington SAE pledges were hospitalized for intoxication, George Desdunes, the Cornell University SAE brother, died of alcohol poisoning. Earlier that same year, Jack Culolias, the SAE member at Arizona State University, was found dead in a river after a night of drinking. The next year, Joseph Wiederrick died under a bridge of hypothermia after drinking at an SAE party at the University of Idaho. To prevent such tragedies and protect itself from catastrophic financial losses, the national SAE organization promotes rules against underage drinking. In the UNC–Wilmington hearing, the college was, in effect, trying to enforce SAE's own rules. In fact, Blaine Ayers, SAE's executive director, backed the school's disciplinary efforts, saying the Wilmington members had "tarnished the good name of the fraternity." But the chapter pressed on with its fight anyway.

Local alumni can employ rough tactics. In 2002, David Fiacco, the University of Maine administrator overseeing judicial affairs, suspended its SAE chapter for a year for underage drinking at a party. Citing "high-risk student behavior" and a history of similar violations, Fiacco ordered the chapter to undergo alcohol education, perform 750 hours of community service, and ban drinking in its chapter house. The chapter's prominent alumni decided to fight back. They included Greg Jamison, an insurance executive who chaired the University of Maine Alumni Association, and James Dill, a University of Maine pest-management specialist who later became a state senator. The alumni hired an attorney, Larry Willey Jr., a former Bangor mayor, who retained a private investigator to look into Fiacco's background for evidence of bias against fraternities. The investigator tracked down Fiacco's 1998 conviction for driving while intoxicated in Colorado, as well as a restraining order taken out by a former girlfriend, according to court records. The group, none of whom responded to requests for comment, arranged to have the information mailed in a plain manila envelope from Colorado to the University of Maine System Board of Trustees, the university president, the campus newspaper, and the *Bangor Daily News*. "Is this honestly the best qualified candidate that the University of Maine could find for the Office of Judicial Affairs?" they asked in an unsigned letter. The newspapers didn't print the material, and the university stood by Fiacco. The judicial officer later sued SAE over its tactics, alleging the intentional infliction of emotional distress. In his complaint, Fiacco said he had become depressed and withdrawn and had to receive counseling. A judge dismissed his case because the information was true and Fiacco was a public figure. Fiacco, who retained his role, said the episode reflected poorly on the chapter's values. "If you're going to say it, put your name to it," Fiacco told me. "To have someone mail something anonymously from Colorado back here in Maine, it's pretty shady."

Frustrated with disciplining individual chapters, colleges often target all their fraternities, and, when they do, they run into a powerful roadblock: the North-American Interfraternity Conference, the trade group representing about seventy historically white fraternities. Founded in 1909, it works with the main sorority trade group and other Greek organizations, as well as sympathetic politicians in Washington and state capitals across the country. Its leader was Pete Smithhisler, a bespectacled, gray-haired Midwesterner who choked up when giving a speech about the day he was invited to join Lambda Chi Alpha as an undergraduate at Western Illinois University in the 1980s. "I knew those men, and I knew I wanted to be like them," said Smithhisler, who became the Interfraternity Conference's president in 2007. He spent most of his professional life promoting and defending fraternities, which he called "the premier leadership experience on college campuses."

Smithhisler's Interfraternity Conference fought any college trying to restrict recruitment. Some higher-education leaders and public-health experts promote bans on recruiting freshmen, especially in the first semester. First-year students make up about 40 percent of fraternity-related deaths. It's no mystery why. Fraternity members drink more than any other group on campus, and the youngest students, away from home for the first time, are the most likely to binge drink and be victims of hazing. Aaron White, who directs college and underage drinking prevention research at the National Institute on Alcohol Abuse and Alcoholism, told me: "The first couple of months of school are a particularly vulnerable time for students with regard to heavy drinking. Delaying rush makes a lot of sense."

But Princeton, Duke, and Vanderbilt are among only eighty of eight hundred campuses with fraternities that require the organizations to defer the recruitment of freshmen, typically for a semester or longer. The Interfraternity Conference has successfully opposed deferred recruitment at dozens of other campuses. Fraternities, of course, stand to lose one-fourth of their revenue if freshmen can't join. The conference also argues that restrictions deprive freshmen of opportunities for leadership, career networking, and charitable work. As Smithhisler once said, "It would be a travesty if the fraternity experience were not available for the development of these young men." At the University of Colorado at Boulder, the conference backed fraternities' decision to operate without university recognition, rather than accept deferred recruitment and live-in chapter advisers. The conference threatened to sue the University of Central Florida when it instituted a recruitment moratorium because of excessive drinking. The college lifted the ban.

At times, the pressure can build behind the scenes. In 2010, California Polytechnic State University banned the recruitment of newly arrived freshmen after the alcohol-poisoning death of Carson Starkey, a first-year pledge, during an SAE initiation ritual. Almost immediately, the Interfraternity Conference sprang into action. Conference officials e-mailed and met with administrators. They even paid the $8,000 bill for an assessment of Greek life. The report, prepared by fraternity executives, college administrators, and a social worker, was damning. It called recruitment "dehumanizing and superficial" and said alcohol was "a, and perhaps THE, defining factor" of Greek life. Nevertheless, the report called for an end to deferred recruitment, saying it ran "counter to a student's right to choose." A new president and vice president for student affairs—both fraternity men—supported the argument, even though the student newspaper editorialized that the school was "opening the door to more trouble." Carson Starkey's parents, who ran a nonprofit group to raise awareness about alcohol poisoning, also opposed the move. "I find it troubling that they would be advocating against our efforts to try to save lives," his mother, Julia Starkey, said of fraternities.

More recently, the Interfraternity Conference, along with college alumni, sought to block another way to change fraternities: forcing them to accept women, partly to reduce the risk of excessive drinking and sexual assault. In 2012, Trinity College, a well-regarded liberal arts institution in Hartford, Connecticut, took aim at single-sex fraternities, saying they were part of a "hedonistic" culture that hurt academics and endangered students. In recent years at Trinity, two drunk pledges had suffered spinal cord injuries, and scores of others had been hospitalized for excessive drinking. Under President James Jones, the college cracked down on events with alcohol, banned pledging, and said Greek houses must recruit co-educational pledge classes by 2016. Fraternity alumni revolted by withholding donations and raising money for a lawsuit. Many worked on Wall Street or in influential corporate jobs and had been among the school's most loyal supporters.

"I've been contributing for many years; I'm not going to anymore," said Hans Becherer, a 1957 graduate and former chairman of Deere and Company, the world's largest agricultural-equipment company. "It's a very nice liberal view that Jimmy Jones is pushing—that everybody is going to be happy in a new social organization. I think people like to join with similar-minded kids."

Not long after, Jones announced he would be leaving a year earlier than expected, in 2014. His successor as Trinity's president, Joanne Berger Sweeney, dropped the plan to require co-ed fraternities.

Similarly, Trinity's Connecticut neighbor, Wesleyan University, that same year mandated that its two remaining all-male fraternities accept women by 2017. The school required all undergraduates to live in school-sanctioned housing. Amid concern about sexual assault, the Wesleyan Student Assembly had conducted a survey. It revealed that 47 percent of students felt that fraternity party spaces were less safe than elsewhere on campus—and of those, 81 percent said co-education would make the spaces safer. A student had sued Wesleyan in 2012 after she said she was raped at a fraternity house. Sexual-assault concerns helped convince President Michael Roth to require co-education. He also saw a broader need to remake Greek life for a modern college. "All of these Greek organizations excluded African Americans; all of them excluded Jews; many excluded Catholics, at some point in their history," Roth said. "And then they changed. This seems to me like that kind of change." The fraternity Delta Kappa Epsilon sued, claiming it had been deprived of rights enjoyed by other organizations on campus. With the case pending, the group has been operating without a house. "I think it's a really tragic loss for the campus, but also for my brothers," fraternity vice president Will Croughan told a reporter.

As mentioned in Chapter 3, Harvard University's leaders also want all their campus groups to be co-ed. Along with fraternities, the school is targeting its all-male "final clubs," such as the Porcellian, which counted President Theodore Roosevelt and Supreme Court Justice Oliver Wendell Holmes as members. In 1984, Harvard stopped recognizing final clubs, yet they continue to exert a powerful hold on campus social life, as do fraternities. After complaints about the 2016 decision to forbid members of single-sex clubs from holding leadership positions, Harvard said it would re-examine the policy. But in July 2017, a faculty committee advocated a more decisive step: a ban. The professors' policy would prohibit Harvard students from joining "final clubs, fraternities or sororities, or other similar private, exclusionary social organizations." The school would phase out the organizations, eliminating them entirely by 2022. The groups promote "gender segregation and discrimination" and "go against the educational mission and principles espoused by Harvard University," the committee said. To take effect, Harvard's president would ultimately have to endorse the controversial plan.

As at Trinity and Wesleyan, the school faced a backlash from the Interfraternity Conference and other Greek organizations, as well as many Harvard alumni, professors, and students, who said the college has violated undergraduate rights. "I sincerely hope that the administration will not set the precedent of creating a 'blacklist' of organizations that students cannot join," said Charles Storey, graduate board president of the Porcellian. "Such McCarthyism is a dangerous road that would be a blow to academic freedom, the spirit of tolerance, and the long tradition of free association on campus." He also said that admitting women would increase the risk of sexual assault. He later apologized and resigned his Porcellian post after outrage over that remark.

Fraternities have many allies in this fight. Federal law enshrines Greek life. In 1972, the landmark Title IX civil-rights law endangered single-sex groups. It prohibited sexual discrimination at colleges receiving federal money. Two years later, Senator Birch Bayh, Title IX's author, introduced a law specifically exempting fraternities and sororities. The Indiana Democrat, while fighting for women's rights, was also a fraternity man. He had joined Alpha Tau Omega as an undergraduate at Purdue University. Greek organizations, unknown to most outside their world, hold extraordinary sway in the federal government, as I was to discover during a trip to Washington, DC.

IN THE SHADOW of Capitol Hill, taxis and limousines arrived to drop off guests for cocktails at the elegant Liaison Hotel. Flanked by two American flags, members of Congress posed for photos with fraternity brothers and sorority sisters. The congressmen were the honored guests of the Fraternity and Sorority Political Action Committee, or FratPAC, which bills itself as the largest PAC representing college students and higher education in America. Each spring, hundreds of fresh-faced undergraduates storm Congress to lobby for fraternities and start a lifetime of networking for their own careers. The day culminates with this $500-a-plate cocktail reception and fund-raiser. On this Wednesday evening in April 2016, their host was FratPAC's executive director, Kevin O'Neill, a partner at the Washington law firm Arnold and Porter. O'Neill, a member of

Lambda Chi Alpha who graduated from Syracuse University in 1992, had been the school mascot, Otto the Orange. Now, he name-checked rival schools' teams to get the crowd excited during the cocktail reception as politicians grabbed the microphone and held forth on the power of Greek life. Bradley Byrne, a US congressman from Alabama, proudly recited his fraternity credentials. At Duke University, he had joined Phi Delta Theta. Two of his sons were now members. A third joined the Kappa Alpha Order. His daughter was a Chi Omega and his wife, an SAE "little sister." His chief of staff, Alex Schriver, was a Delta Tau Delta at Auburn University before he took the DC job at twenty-five. "He hired one of our star students," O'Neill bragged to the crowd about Schriver. "He's the youngest chief of staff in the House of Representatives."

Richard Hudson, a congressman from North Carolina, also testified to the power of the fraternity network. He had joined the Kappa Alpha Order at the University of North Carolina at Charlotte, where he became student body president. After college, his KA brothers worked on his political campaign. His chapter treasurer, who became a corporate executive specializing in accounting, handled the finances. "I'm eager to work with you," Hudson told the crowd. "It's important to be here in town and network like you've been doing. Keep those business cards and stay in touch."

FratPAC magnifies the formidable clout of fraternities in Washington. As noted in the introduction to this book, 39 percent of senators in the 113th US Congress, and one-fourth of US representatives, belonged to Greek organizations—as well as one-third of all Supreme Court justices and about 40 percent of US presidents. SAE hasn't had a president since McKinley, but it has had its share of kingmakers. Bill Brock, a 1953 graduate of Washington and Lee University, was a former US senator from Tennessee who became the Republican National

Committee chairman credited as the architect of Ronald Reagan's 1980 victory. In the 1990s, another RNC chairman, Haley Barbour, who had joined SAE at the University of Mississippi, helped engineer the first Republican takeover of the US House and Senate in forty years.

During the FratPAC evening at the Liaison, the conservative Republican bent of Greek life was on full display. The two Southern speakers Byrne and Hudson were both Republicans. Byrne could trace his ancestors in Mobile to the 1780s. The *National Journal* called Hudson the twelfth-most-conservative member of the 113th Congress, and the National Right to Life and the National Rifle Association both gave him top ratings. Since 2005 when it was founded, FratPAC has given almost two-thirds of its more than $1.3 million in campaign contributions to Republican lawmakers.

FratPAC's legislative goals represent the fundamental contradiction at the heart of its agenda: it wants public support without government scrutiny. On the day I visited its annual fund-raiser, FratPAC's priority was passage of the Collegiate Housing and Infrastructure Act, which would let Greek organizations use tax-deductible donations to build and renovate chapter houses, not just for libraries and study halls. Congress has estimated the law would cost taxpayers $148 million over ten years, although fraternities maintain their housing saves public universities from issuing billions of dollars in debt to finance new dorms. Representative Pete Sessions, an alumnus of Pi Kappa Alpha's chapter at Southwestern University, first sponsored the tax proposal. The Texas Republican, who received $42,000 from FratPAC, had more than one hundred co-sponsors. In an early round, its sponsor had been Representative Paul Ryan, the Wisconsin Republican and former vice-presidential candidate who later became Speaker of the House. FratPAC funneled $42,500 to Ryan, who belonged to

Delta Tau Delta as an undergraduate at Miami University in Ohio. Now these politicians were joined by eager, impeccably dressed fraternity men and sorority women who stormed their local members of Congress to beg for a tax break.

Two of the fraternity lobby's other priorities include ensuring the survival of single-sex campus organizations and opposing what it considered ill-advised plans to rein in student misbehavior. In 2012, FratPAC bore down on US representative Frederica Wilson, a Florida Democrat and former elementary school principal. Wilson, known for her flamboyant cowboy hats, called herself the "Haze Buster." She had backed a Florida anti-hazing law in the state legislature and had proposed a national anti-hazing law. It would revoke federal financial aid from anyone found responsible by a school disciplinary board for hazing. She appeared in Washington with the mother of Harrison Kowiak, who had been beaten to death during a Theta Chi hazing ritual at Lenoir-Rhyne University in Hickory, North Carolina. O'Neill, the FratPAC executive director, reached out to Wilson, as did some college administrators and members of African American fraternities. The lawmaker had belonged to the historically black Alpha Kappa Alpha sorority, and FratPAC had donated $1,000 to her campaign. O'Neill maintained that hazing was better handled by local police because college disciplinary boards don't offer enough legal protections, such as a right to a lawyer. Wilson never introduced her bill.

The fraternity lobby had been even more worried about the due-process rights of college men in sexual-assault cases. Although others, including prominent law-school professors at Harvard and the University of Pennsylvania, shared its concern, FratPAC took its zealous defense too far for even many of its own undergraduate members. In 2015, three Republican lawmakers introduced the innocuously named "Safe Campus Act." Its most controversial provision would have required the victims of sexual assault to report the allegations to law enforcement before requesting a campus hearing. Two of its sponsors were beneficiaries of FratPAC, Sessions and US representative Kay Granger, a Texas Republican who had received $10,000 in contributions. To make the case, the Greek movement formed the Safe Campus Coalition. It was made up of the two main fraternity trade groups—the Interfraternity Conference and the National Panhellenic Conference, which represents sororities—as well as three national fraternities, Kappa Alpha Order, Alpha Tau Omega, and Sigma Nu. The coalition spent $250,000 lobbying for the bill. It hired FratPAC's O'Neill and Trent Lott, a Sigma Nu member and the former Republican US senator from Mississippi.

The bill provoked a firestorm. US senators Kirsten Gillibrand of New York and Claire McCaskill of Missouri both excoriated Greek organizations for backing the measure. Democrats and prominent advocates for sexual-assault victims, they were also sorority women. Gillibrand had been a member of the Kappa Kappa Gamma sorority at Dartmouth; McCaskill, a member of Kappa Alpha Theta at the University of Missouri. Each had received $2,500 from FratPAC. Many individual members of sororities and fraternities, not to mention groups representing universities, also considered the proposal wrongheaded. Eight national sororities ultimately broke with the trade groups and dropped their support of the bill. "We believe our sisters who are survivors should have choices in how, when and to whom they go for support or to report the crime," Alpha Phi wrote in a letter to its members. The national fraternity groups ultimately abandoned the bill, too. Amid concern over the lobbying campaign and the Interfraternity Conference's overall approach, Smithhisler resigned.

In this case, the Greek organizations met their match. The UNC–Wilmington disciplinary hearing would be a tough fight, too.

As the hours wore on in the Wilmington hearing room, Ian Gove, the SAE chapter president, never really disputed the central accusation against SAE: the fraternity threw a party where many pledges and other underage students were drinking to excess. Instead, he stressed a few sidelights. The police didn't see any "open source" of alcohol that the fraternity provided, and they didn't make any arrests. (They did, in fact, issue a citation for underage drinking.) As for the alleged hazing, Gove maintained that a couple of members, not pledges, were showing off in a push-up competition.

In one stroke of luck for the chapter, one of the pledges at the party recanted his signed statement that said the fraternity had insisted the new members drink from the cooler full of mysterious liquor. (This was the same undergraduate hospitalized after being found in the local bar.) He testified that the university had pressured him to sign a statement he hadn't read completely. That evening, infuriating the assistant dean prosecuting the case, he now said that the liquor at the party had found its way to him through a different route: A "good-looking girl," whose name he didn't remember, had handed him a drink.

What about the pledge who had been so drunk that he mistook the police car for a taxi?

That pledge also sought to shift responsibility from the chapter. While taking a taxi to the pinning ceremony some four hours earlier, he said, he stopped at a store and convinced a stranger to buy him a 23.5-ounce Four Loko, a caffeine-infused malt liquor drink, and a 24-ounce Bud Light Tall Boy. Back in the cab, he said, he had chugged those drinks but had imbibed nothing else at the party. The board was skeptical that the early evening alcohol could have left him so sick and disoriented. He weighed 215 pounds and said he regularly drank three beers in a sitting. And how should the board understand the e-mail begging the sorority member not to describe the toga party as a mixer? Gove and his vice president maintained the gathering had, in fact, always been "grab-a-date," and the message had merely been inelegantly worded.

At the hearing, pledges testified that most of the people attending the party were holding drinks and, of course, many, if not the vast majority, were under age twenty-one. Gove was asked if, as president, he bore some responsibility for underage drinking at the party.

"I mean, to be honest with you, I don't, you know, go around and [check] breath," he replied, then added: "I'm not trying to be smart."

At the end of the hearing, Gove promised that the chapter would undergo alcohol education.

"I don't think it's right that many underage people are drinking," Gove said. "If it was one or if it was all of them, that's not OK. I'd like to take steps as the president to make sure that's understood, and I'd like to reach out and help these members."

Nevertheless, the board found the chapter responsible for alcohol violations based on several underage pledges' admissions they were drinking at the party. The panel also found that the fraternity had held a mixer with Phi Mu, violating the terms of the social-events ban. It didn't find the chapter guilty of hazing.

Chip Phillips, the assistant dean overseeing judicial proceedings, recommended a four-year ban on the chapter, citing a need for "significant change in its culture and behavior" and "a consistent pattern of violations."

"It is only a matter of time before someone becomes seriously hurt or dies as a result of the actions of this organization," Phillips said.

Gove was outraged.

"Four years of suspension is absolutely absurd," he told the board. "I feel like bringing up stuff in the past that we have been found not guilty of is an extreme violation of our student rights.

I feel like we do a lot for the community, the school, through our breast cancer awareness, our philanthropy events and community service."

After the proceeding, Dean Phillips headed out into the hall where, he said, about fifteen members surrounded him like "a gang in a schoolyard." Phillips, who was asked for a copy of SAE's disciplinary file, said he felt so threatened that he asked for a police escort. ("They were there to support me," Gove told me later. "They weren't there to intimidate anyone.") Mike Walker, dean of students, later called out the fraternity for its "potentially intimidating behavior and disrespectful conduct toward university staff." The board ultimately suspended the chapter for two and one-half years. Gary Miller, UNC–Wilmington's chancellor, rejected SAE's appeal.

Gove and his alumni supporters then staged a public campaign to discredit the disciplinary process and the administration. Chancellor Miller, a biologist who had recently arrived from Wichita State University, was hardly an anti-Greek zealot. He had joined the Kappa Sigma fraternity as an undergraduate at William and Mary. Still, the SAE members scoured the record for bias. They challenged the impartiality of a judicial board composed of university employees, non-Greek students, and members of rival fraternities. They noted that Dean Walker was a member of rival Tau Kappa Epsilon, and the school had given a lesser penalty to that fraternity for what SAE considered a more serious infraction.

Tapping the SAE network, Gove reached over the chancellor's head to the state capital in Raleigh. He wrote to John R. Bell IV, a UNC–Wilmington graduate who had belonged to the SAE chapter. Bell was now a Republican state representative, a rising star on his way to becoming House majority leader. Gove convinced Bell to sponsor a bill that would require colleges to permit undergraduates to hire lawyers for disciplinary hearings. As Gove pressed his case for a right-to-counsel law in the capital, he also managed to secure a coveted internship in the governor's office.

"This fraternity is not only dear to me, but also to the other hundreds of alumni and members that it encompasses," Gove wrote to members of the General Assembly. "That is why it was so disheartening to be the active president of Sigma Alpha Epsilon as the UNC–W Dean of Students office stripped us of our right to be a student organization."

Gove bemoaned the "total disregard for due process," lack of legal counsel, and "coercive investigative tactics used by an administrator to seek confessions among the students." SAE had been victimized by "prejudice" from an administrator because the fraternity brothers have "diverse viewpoints, values or beliefs." Gove was referring to an episode from 2008 that he believed had poisoned the administration against SAE. Late one September evening, SAE members had been playing seven-on-seven flag football against the Kappa Alpha Order. The two were natural rivals, both proud of their Southern roots. After SAE scored a touchdown, a member ran down the field, past the other team's sidelines, holding an SAE banner that included a Confederate battle flag. Horrified, the referee told the student to stop. "Heritage, not hate," the SAE member replied. The college suspended the chapter from the intramural program until the next school year, citing taunting and unsportsmanlike conduct. The chapter suspected it was for flying the rebel flag. "It was just two Southern fraternities playing football," Gove told me later. "But the university considered it a hate crime, even though it was free speech. After what happened, the university targeted us."

The higher-education establishment fought against Gove. A national group representing student-conduct boards warned that a law could give an edge to those who could afford to hire lawyers. "Whoever's able to hire the best and most expensive attorney is likely to win the day," said Chris Loschiavo, the group's president, who directed judicial proceedings at the University of Florida. The University of North Carolina said the law would make discipline more adversarial, lengthy, and costly. The UNC–Wilmington Student Government Association agreed.

In July 2013, Gove's chapter triumphed. The right-to-counsel bill won nearly unanimous support and was signed into law by Governor McCrory. It was even named in SAE's honor: the Students and Administration Equality Act, or the SAE Act, for short.

The Foundation for Individual Rights in Education, a non-partisan civil-liberties group, pushed to pass similar laws across the country. The group was concerned more about the rights of men facing potential felony charges for rape or drug dealing, not fraternity chapters confronted with the loss of college recognition. Still, Arkansas and North Dakota have passed similar laws and student right-to-counsel bills have been introduced in seven states, including Maryland, South Carolina, and Virginia.

That summer, SAE gained even greater power on the UNC–Wilmington campus. Governor McCrory appointed to the university's Board of Trustees two SAE alumni, including Michael Drummond, owner of a High Point, North Carolina, packaging firm. "My goal in joining the board, my sole purpose, was helping the fraternity," Drummond told me. "I had heard enough. I had had enough. Either get rid of the chancellor or get the chancellor on board with helping the fraternity out." He recalled telling Chancellor Miller as much: "You can do this one of two ways. Do the right thing and put them on campus or do it the hard way. We won't stop till we're done." (Miller confirmed the conversation.) To address the SAE trustees' concerns, the university paid $4,500 for an outside review of the chapter's discipline. Betsy Bunting, a former vice president of legal affairs for the UNC system, backed the college's decision.

"The real problem for the fraternity is that they never disputed the facts establishing their violations of the Student Conduct Code," Bunting concluded in her report. "They attempted to attack the procedures, but these contentions were minor and did not in any way undermine the fairness of the proceeding."

Undaunted, SAE's supporters intensified their attacks. They had a fierce ally in a professor named Mike Adams, a criminologist, sociologist, and free-speech advocate. Adams had defended the chapter in the Confederate flag episode. He also had his own beef with the University of North Carolina at Wilmington, which had denied him tenure. Adams had sued and ultimately won after claiming the tenure denial stemmed from his controversial conservative writings. He specialized in incendiary essays, which he shared with conservative websites and Fox News, with headlines such as "Onward, Christian Pansies" (on the necessity of Christians opposing same-sex marriage) and "Silencing Whitey" (Black Lives Matter as "an anti-white anti-free speech mob"). Adams was also a fraternity man with fond memories of his days at Mississippi State University's Sigma Chi house in the 1980s. In February 2014, Adams wrote a scathing series of articles about what he considered the abuse of power by UNC–Wilmington administrators. "Dictators and Deans," one installment was called. Exhibit A was the investigation of SAE: "The idea of questioning kids about potentially criminal conduct without permitting their attorneys to be present (and while facing university counsel) violated widely accepted values of fundamental fairness. The problem isn't drunken students. The problem is administrators who are drunk on their own power." Adams, who later became the chapter's faculty adviser, told me he wasn't sure what had actually happened. "Whatever the misbehavior was—it was relatively minor," he said.

By the end of the school year, with the board's blessing, Chancellor Miller was publicly looking for another job. Supporters took out full-page ads calling for him to stay and some suggested SAE alumni had run him out of town. After only two years on the job, Miller left in July 2014 to become chancellor at the University of Wisconsin at Green Bay. Former trustees' chairwoman Linda Pearce called Miller "a victim of North Carolina good old boy politics." Some trustees said Miller's supporters had exaggerated the fraternity's power on the board, which had become disenchanted with his leadership. But Drummond, the SAE board member who had given Miller the ultimatum, told me, "If he had made friends with us and helped us, he'd probably still be there." Miller told me he didn't want to rehash what happened, except to say, "Our whole goal was to protect students. We made the right decision, and I still feel that way."

Local alumni also took aim at SAE's national office, which had kicked out Gove and other members of the fraternity. They again turned to Goolsby, the state senator and trial lawyer who had sat by Gove's side at the disciplinary hearing. "I have been in the practice of law for twenty years and have conducted hundreds of trials," Goolsby wrote. "Never have I appeared before a more ridiculous, kangaroo court. The ability to present a fair rebuttal and evidence was virtually nonexistent. Your chapter did not get a fair hearing." In February 2015, SAE's Supreme Council reversed itself. It reinstated the chapter and reactivated all the members. The next year, the local alumni won an SAE award, recognizing them "for giving outstanding assistance and guidance to their chapter."

Now, it was just a matter of returning to campus. Here, the chapter ran into another barrier: William Sederburg, the interim chancellor. Sederburg, a former college president in Utah and Michigan, was skeptical that the chapter had learned its lesson. Bell, the state legislator and SAE alumnus, invited Sederburg for a meeting. It would be at the Cape Fear Men's Club, where SAE had held its pinning ceremony. Sederburg, a former

Michigan Republican state senator, knew a thing or two about optics. "You didn't want to be seen as a public official in the Cape Fear Men's Club," he told me. "It's known as a bastion of ultraconservatism. It doesn't have blacks, Jews or women as members." The chancellor refused the meeting, and SAE just waited him out. In July, the university appointed a permanent chancellor, and the administration agreed to let SAE back on campus.

Even then, the chapter remained defiant. SAE insisted that all communications between the fraternity and the university be in writing—and include a representative of both the alumni and the national staff. SAE declined to submit to the rules of the Fraternity and Sorority Life Office because members considered them undue scrutiny based on "misleading statistics about Greek life." As a result, the chapter couldn't join the campus Interfraternity Council like other fully sanctioned fraternities.

Sederburg, now a senior scholar with the American Association of State Colleges and Universities, said the university shouldn't have agreed to the chapter's return because it hadn't accepted responsibility for its behavior. "When you do this sort of agreement with a student group, we want them to tell us. 'We really want to clean up our act.' That hasn't happened," he told me. "The attitude here is, 'We've been wronged, and we want to fight politically.'"

On its website, the chapter now boasts of its victory in "the fight to end discriminatory practices against fraternities." A chapter with a member who had displayed a Confederate flag and had met in a club that had excluded blacks was now using the language of Martin Luther King Jr. to defend its cause. An online history of the SAE Act quoted King's famed letter from the Birmingham jail: "Injustice anywhere is a threat to justice everywhere."

In April 2016, I flew to Wilmington to meet the members of the victorious chapter, men who had defeated two college presidents and inspired their own law. Gove looked the part of a former fraternity chapter president: neatly pressed khaki shorts, a long-sleeved button-down shirt, and loafers with no socks. But Gove was no preppy legacy. He was born in Key West, Florida, but grew up in Raleigh, where his mother worked as a lab technician at North Carolina State University. His father, a former lobsterman, worked as a pilot who guided vessels through the currents of New York harbor. When Gove rushed SAE as a freshman, he wasn't sure he would fit in. But he immediately felt comfortable with the low-key men he met at the chapter. "Everybody thinks fraternity guys are rich and privileged, and they like to get drunk," he told me. "But you have to know, it's more than that." At Wilmington, dues were $450 a semester; and unlike the grand Southern chapters, this one doesn't have a house. "This isn't Alabama," he said. "We have surfers and fishermen." He was impressed that the older guys took the time to have conversations about his interests and weren't just looking to sign up as many students as they could. Gove saw members making a lifelong commitment. "These would be my best friends in years to come," he said.

When I met him, Gove had graduated from UNC–Wilmington and had enrolled at Campbell University's law school in Raleigh. Not surprisingly, he wrote his law-school-application essay about the SAE Act. "I learned more through the alumni and the fraternity because of what we went through than I did studying at UNC–W as far as life lessons go," he told me. "If you truly believe, don't give up even if it looks like the odds are against you." Gove said his chapter may not always have followed the rules but had nevertheless been unfairly treated. "I'm not going to say we're all angels and that no one ever drinks," he said. "But it's unfair to hold the entire chapter accountable for the actions of a few bad apples."

His benefactors awaited us at a fish restaurant, where we sat on a deck in the eighty-degree sunshine overlooking yachts and a drawbridge on the Intracoastal Waterway. Parks Griffin, the governor's fund-raiser, and Dennis Burgard, owner of a real-estate company and one of the two SAE UNC–Wilmington trustees, were both in their fifties, graying and distinguished. Griffin grew up in Durham, North Carolina, the son of a dentist and City Council member. In 1977, he helped found the chapter just as Greek organizations began their campus revival. Griffin was now the kind of civic-minded businessman at the heart of many a small city. He had been on the boards of the UNC–Wilmington athletic booster club and the North Carolina Azalea Festival, one of Wilmington's biggest attractions, as well as the Cape Fear Museum and the Wilmington Airport Authority.

As we sipped iced tea and ate chowder, it became clear to me that the alumni had paid little mind to what had happened on the night the pledge was hospitalized.

"The members said we're angels, the university said we're devils," Burgard said. "I knew the truth was somewhere in between."

In their view, modern universities were overrun with a growing cadre of bureaucrats eager to justify their own existence by targeting fraternities, even though young men drink elsewhere on campus.

"The amount of rules placed on fraternities is crazy," said Burgard, citing forty pages from the dean's office. "Any group of nineteen- to twenty-year-old guys are going to drink."

Griffin continued along that vein: "The chess club doesn't have to go to sexual-assault training. The chess club doesn't have to go to a class about alcohol. The university is saying, 'You fraternity guys are the problem.' It stigmatizes them."

The SAE alumni were making a common fraternity argument; their prominence on campus made them a convenient target, a scapegoat for typical male behavior. It relied on the assumption, disproved by decades of public-health research: that everyone drank as heavily as Greek men.

Later that day, I met five members of the newest crew of SAE members for a tour of the university. The chapter had recently raised $1,000 for breast-cancer patients. Members also volunteered at a children's hospital, helping them secure $10,000 in donations by staffing one of its charitable events. But because they no longer belonged to the Interfraternity Council, they couldn't compete in intramural sports or join Greek-wide philanthropy events. For a while, they couldn't have mixers with sororities, though the rules had since been relaxed.

"The campus isn't on our side," said Austin Bates, a senior. "The university was very reluctant to welcome us back."

It was already dark when we walked inside the student union, the site of the chapter's disciplinary hearing with the administration. It was a bright, airy building, its lobby lined with flags, each bearing the colors and symbols of a fraternity: garnet and gold for Pi Kappa Alpha; azure, crimson, and gold for Delta Kappa Epsilon; purple, green, and gold for Lambda Chi Alpha. The flags' grandeur and air of permanence made the Greek-letter groups seem more like members of the United Nations Security Council than social clubs for adolescents and young men. One flag was conspicuously missing—SAE's. The purple-and-gold banner no longer adorned the entryway because the chapter wouldn't agree to university regulations. It stung, but members weren't backing down, not even to display their colors. "It would be nice, to say the least," said Derek Linder, the twenty-one-year-old chapter president. "But we know who we are."

PART TWO

LEGACY

5

SING, BROTHERS, SING

"Who Thinks of the Rights and Feelings of Others"

More than forty freshman fraternity pledges gathered in the cavernous dance hall of their University of Oklahoma chapter house as upperclassmen stood on a balcony. When the pledges looked up, they could see a Sigma Alpha Epsilon crest and its symbols of honor: a knight, a shield, and a phoenix rising from the ashes, representing the fraternity's post–Civil War revival. The students knew they were lucky to be part of such an august institution. On the glorious fall days when the Oklahoma Sooners played home football games, alumni would gather to drink beer and whiskey, listen to live music, reminisce about their days in the chapter, and exchange stories of boom and bust in the oil patch. When the chapter house opened in 1965, the beige brick split-level residence, built in the Frank Lloyd Wright Prairie Style, had inspired wonder and envy on Oklahoma's leafy fraternity row. Relying on wealthy alumni and financial backing from the university, it

had cost the equivalent of $4 million today. A high wall ringed
the house, reinforcing a sense of exclusivity and secrecy, as if it
were a diplomatic compound in some faraway capital. Almost
twice the size of the Oklahoma governor's mansion, the house
boasted air-conditioning, a poolroom, and a multiplex stereo
system. It slept eighty, including suites for its president, treasurer, and house mother.

The setting reflected the chapter's prestige and influence,
which rivaled the grandest Southern houses. To a degree not
fully appreciated by outsiders, members of SAE had helped
build the state's flagship campus in Norman, about twenty
miles south of Oklahoma City. The university's art museum
was named after Fred Jones Jr., an SAE member who died
in a plane crash in 1950 during his senior year. His parents,
who made a fortune running one of the nation's largest networks of Ford auto dealerships, donated the money for the
building. Two members of the chapter belonged to the family
that founded Love's Travel Stops and Country Stores, a main
sponsor of Sooners athletics and a major donor to the university. Another SAE alumnus used his private jet to fly football
coaches on scouting trips. SAE members sat on the board of
the university's charitable foundation, and many others could be
counted among the university's most loyal donors. The young
men on the dance floor that evening in February 2015 knew
they were now part of a tradition that could take them as far as
they wished to go in Oklahoma—and beyond.

The pledges were there to learn a tradition essential to
SAE, which is often called the "Singing Fraternity" because
it treasures its songbook almost as much as its True Gentleman creed. The upperclassmen began the songfest with the
standards that had long defined what it means to be a member
of SAE. They belted out a feisty fight song featuring the SAE
motto, Phi Alpha.

I'm Phi Alpha born,
and I'm Phi Alpha bred.
And when I die,
I'll be Phi Alpha dead.

They sang melodies for sorority serenades such as "Violets," which members have been crooning on bended knee for generations.

Violet, Violet,
You're the fairest flower to me.
Violet, Violet,
Emblem of fraternity.
With your perfume memories come,
Of Sigma Alpha Epsilon,
Dearest flower beneath the sun,
My Violet.

And they sang "Friends," perhaps SAE's defining song, its lyrics gracing all manner of celebrations, inspiring men to reach their arms around each other and express a sentimentality not usually seen among modern college students.

Friends, friends, friends,
You and I will be,
Whether in fair or in dark stormy weather,
We'll stand or we'll fall together,
For SAE.

After the pledges practiced the favorites, they heard muffled conversation high above them from the upperclassmen leaders on the balcony. It sounded like an argument about the song they would teach next. Then, they heard an instruction.

"Make sure you don't sing this song outside of these walls."

The tune, "If You're Happy and You Know it, Clap Your Hands," may have evoked their childhoods. But the lyrics reached farther back into history with raw and toxic words that flowed downward, like the currents of a polluted river from the 1950s.

> *There will never be a nigger in SAE,*
> *There will never be a nigger in SAE,*
> *You can hang him from a tree,*
> *But he can never sign with me,*
> *There will never be a nigger in SAE.*

The song had traveled an unusual route. Members of this chapter had first heard it in 2011 at their annual Caribbean leadership cruise. It wasn't part of the official curriculum, and it wasn't in any SAE songbook. Members from another chapter, likely from Texas or Louisiana, had taught it to the University of Oklahoma students. No doubt, the members learned it furtively on that cruise ship, whose passengers included African American tourists, as well as black members of SAE. By the winter of 2015, the song had become part of the chapter's underground ritual. Just about every member had heard it at least once before in a session just like this one. The chapter didn't have a single African American member, a student whose very presence might have killed that song or perhaps driven racist students away.

The next month, SAE's Founders Day, March 9, fell on a Monday. One of the most important dates on the fraternity's calendar, it celebrated SAE's birthday in 1856 at the University of Alabama. On the Saturday evening before Founders Day, members of the University of Oklahoma chapter and their guests "pre-gamed"—or loaded up on liquor—at the house before setting off for an Oklahoma City country club for their celebration. The members dressed in black tie, and their dates wore formal dresses and heels, as they boarded charter buses parked near the house. Before the event, upperclassmen told pledges to impress their dates with singing. Don't let anyone look like a jerk when he stands up to lead the bus in song, the leaders warned. On board one of those buses, twenty-five members sitting with their dates launched into the old standards, just as they had in the dance hall the month before. Then, they added some raunchy favorites, including songs making fun of rival fraternities. After a while, the men seemed to be losing steam. A twenty-year-old sophomore named Levi Pettit stepped into the void.

Pettit, who had been a top golfer at the Highland Park High School in Dallas, was a fraternity leader, its rush chairman, and the person responsible for recruitment. Unsteady, clearly drunk, he let loose the song that was supposed to stay inside the house. One of the freshmen, Parker Rice, who had graduated from a Jesuit prep school in Dallas, stood to join him. They began lustily: "There will never be a nigger . . ."

Some members—it wasn't clear how many—joined in or clapped rhythmically. Sitting toward the back of the bus, Corina Hernandez was horrified. A Mexican American student from Oklahoma State University, she was visiting her friend Garrett Parkhurst, a freshman member of SAE. They had gone to high school together, and the two had just begun to date. A high school beauty queen who now belonged to the historically white Kappa Delta sorority, Hernandez was comfortable in Greek life. But she had never heard such ugly language before, and now she felt threatened as she looked around the bus and saw only white faces. "I'm so sorry," Parkhurst told her, again and again. It wasn't clear how many people had joined the singing. Parkhurst hadn't. Neither had several of his friends, who had been more focused on their dates than the singing.

Still, no one said anything. No one stopped the song; no one objected. The moment passed. They put it behind them, just as they had moved on from the song in the balcony the month before. The members and their dates enjoyed a night of dancing at the country club.

The next morning, Sunday, a cell-phone video appeared online. It wasn't clear who had taken the video and then posted it, but Unheard, a group of black University of Oklahoma students, distributed it on Twitter. Nine seconds long and shaky, the video showed Pettit and Rice, drunk and tuxedo-clad, leading the bus in the song. It quickly went viral, bringing national outrage to the campus of the University of Oklahoma. There were protest marches, television trucks on campus, and international news coverage. By Sunday evening, SAE's national board, calling the video "disgusting," voted to close the chapter and expel all members, saying its behavior wasn't consistent with the values of the True Gentleman.

College leaders have often been criticized for tepid, slow responses in crises. Not University of Oklahoma president David Boren, who had a politician's understanding of what had happened and the damage it could do to the university. Boren, the college's president since 1994, was a former Oklahoma governor and senator, a powerful Democratic figure in the state and in Washington. On Monday, he said he was severing all ties with the SAE chapter. Because the university had helped finance the house and leased the land to the chapter, Boren could take even more decisive action. He shut the house and ordered all students to remove their belongings by midnight the next day. Boren said he would expel Pettit and Rice for creating a hostile environment under federal civil-rights law. "To those who have misused their free speech in such a reprehensible way, I have a message for you," Boren said. "You are disgraceful. You have violated all that we stand for. You should not have the privilege of calling yourselves 'Sooners.' Real Sooners are not racist. Real Sooners are not bigots."

Members of SAE received death threats, and some were afraid to go to classes. Vandals ran their keys along the exteriors of cars belonging to a fraternity with similar letters. The University of Oklahoma football team canceled practice, dressed in black, and took to the field, standing arm in arm, for a moment of silence.

SAE alumni had hoped their past backing of the university would temper Boren's response to the video. But Boren went further than most college presidents who condemn a chapter's behavior, making an extraordinary repudiation of the once-powerful fraternity. In his seventies, Boren was nearing the end of his tenure. While he held office, he didn't see SAE returning to the University of Oklahoma.

THE RACIST SONG captured in that nine-second video has come to define SAE's image. It has proved more damaging to its reputation than deadly alcohol poisonings, hazing rituals that include cattle prods, burning with irons, and force-feeding of cat food, or even the re-designation of the SAE acronym as "Sexual Assault Expected." Like the footage documenting police killings of unarmed black suspects after traffic stops, the video revealed something raw and real about race that couldn't be dismissed. It resonated because it reflected a truth about fraternities' failure to confront their own histories as white-only organizations.

Such behavior flourishes in part because Greek life remains so segregated. Although fraternities generally aren't required to disclose demographic data, studies show that traditional fraternities skew white. At Princeton University, three-fourths of the members of fraternities and sororities in 2009 were white, compared with half of the overall student body. Matthew Hughey, a sociologist now at the University of Connecticut, studied Greek life at three unnamed East Coast colleges and found rigid segregation. The few minority students who entered white fraternities confronted persistent racial stereotyping, which they tolerated because they valued the superior resources and networking opportunities of membership. On average, 4 percent of members of the historically white fraternities he studied were minorities—or roughly two in a chapter of sixty-three, according to his study, published in 2010. Hughey called the system "a form of American apartheid."

These divisions promote intolerance. Traditional fraternities are among the most "racially isolating environments for white students," according to a 2014 study of twenty-eight selective colleges. Ninety-seven percent of the students said their Greek organizations were predominantly white. Those who joined were less likely to have at least one close friend from another race or ethnicity. "Campus educators need to ask serious questions about whether Greek life in its current form is counterproductive to the university's commitments to preparing students for engagement in a diverse democracy," wrote Julie Park, an assistant professor of education at the University of Maryland.

An earlier study that tracked more than 2,000 University of California at Los Angeles students over four years of college came to a similar conclusion. The authors, including psychology professors from UCLA and Claremont McKenna College, found a campus where student organizations fostered racial divisions. Minority students joined minority organizations, including African American fraternities, whereas white students flocked to traditional Greek organizations. Fraternities and sororities attracted men and women with both a sense of white racial identity and opposition to affirmative action and other policies promoting diversity. Fraternities and sororities "in part function as ethnic clubs for White students" the researchers found. "Our results suggest that Greek student organizations also appear to be nurseries for the sense of White victimization." By contrast, racial prejudice decreased with exposure to ethnically diverse roommates, friends, and romantic partners. The study proposed that colleges promote random roommate assignments or the intentional mixing of races in living arrangements—precisely the opposite of what happens at most Greek organizations. Colleges, by their own account, exist to promote the free exchange of ideas; the US Supreme Court has repeatedly hailed diversity among students as essential for the education of a workforce that will survive in a global marketplace. Yet fraternities, by custom and structure, often work to undermine racial understanding.

In the most extreme cases, these racial divisions provoke violence. A 2014 study of FBI hate-crime statistics from 349 colleges concluded that campuses with large populations of historically white fraternities are more likely to report verbal and physical assaults involving bias against blacks and other underrepresented groups. "The presence of fraternities is associated with a campus climate that is more dangerous for minority group members," concluded the sociologists Nella Van Dyke at the University of California at Merced and Griff Tester, now at Central Washington University. "A large Greek system may be both a contributor and a product of a campus culture marked by in-group/out-group animosity."

SAE itself could be considered ground zero for this kind of animosity. Immediately after the video became public, news accounts could find many previous episodes that pointed to a tolerance of racist behavior at SAE. In 1982, the University of Cincinnati chapter held a Martin Luther King "trash party," where guests were asked to bring items such as a Ku Klux Klan hood, fried chicken, and a canceled welfare check. An SAE chapter at Texas A&M in 1992 had a "Jungle Fever" party featuring blackface, grass skirts, and "slave hunts." In December 2014, the SAE chapter at Clemson University threw a "Cripmas party," one of many "ghetto"-themed parties at historically white fraternities that have angered black students. At Oklahoma State University, until the bus video became public, SAE had long held a "Plantation Ball" to commemorate the fraternity's founding. These theme parties suggest a broad acceptance of offensive attitudes.

In other cases, fraternity members targeted individual black students. In 1990, a drunk member of the Kansas University chapter of SAE harassed a black sophomore who was delivering pizzas to the house. He allegedly pushed her down the stairs and called her a "nigger bitch." After campus protests, the member, who resigned from SAE, was charged with disorderly conduct and battery and pleaded guilty to a misdemeanor. In 2006, an African American graduate of the University of Memphis said she attended an SAE party with her white SAE boyfriend, where they were both called "fucking niggers." Her boyfriend quit the fraternity after the chapter told him only to date white women, according to her account. This episode attracted far less attention than the video in Oklahoma because it lacked visual documentation. But it sounded most similar in its echo of what many would have thought a bygone era.

Even after the Oklahoma video surfaced and SAE members across the country pledged to fight racism, accusations mounted. Eight months later, an African American student from Columbia University said she was turned away from a Halloween party at Yale's SAE chapter after she was told it was "white girls only." The chapter, noting it had black members, denied her account, and Yale said its own investigation found no evidence of systematic discrimination against minorities at the party. Still, the episode became part of a broad debate that dominated the news about insensitivity toward minorities on the Yale campus, political correctness, and free speech. At the same time as the

SAE controversy, a lecturer in early childhood education, who oversaw one of Yale's residence halls with her husband, a Yale professor, sent an e-mail questioning administrators' advice about avoiding culturally insensitive Halloween costumes. After a firestorm, the couple resigned from their positions.

While the facts of the SAE situation at Yale may have been muddy, two other episodes appeared more clear-cut. In February 2016, two white SAE members at the University of Texas at Austin were charged with public intoxication and deadly conduct and expelled from the chapter after they allegedly threw glass bottles and yelled, "Fuck you, nigger," at a black student. Later that year, the University of Wisconsin at Madison suspended its SAE chapter after a black member said he had been subjected to eighteen months of harassment, including being called racial epithets. (He also reported that members used homophobic and anti-Semitic slurs.) In one case, he said, a white member at a Halloween party addressed him with a racial slur and choked him until other members intervened. Members seemed to enjoy making racially insensitive statements, according to the black student's account. They would often use a racial or homophobic slur, then try to absolve themselves by saying: "No offense." The Wisconsin case reflected the blurring of the line between "politically incorrect" behavior and racism that the 2016 presidential campaign revealed.

SAE was by no means alone in this kind of behavior. Consider just two episodes from 2014. That year, three members of the Sigma Phi Epsilon chapter at the University of Mississippi plotted to tie a noose around the neck of a statue of James Meredith, the school's first black student. At Lehigh University, Sigma Chi members spray-painted racial slurs and threw eggs at a multicultural residence hall. Yet these cases obscure a more nuanced picture of the racial reality of historically white fraternities, which have accepted some minority members and

instituted programs promoting diversity. In fact, two years before the Oklahoma incident, the SAE national organization
surveyed its chapters about their racial composition—strong evidence of the fraternity's concern. SAE found that 3 percent of
its members were African Americans, a cohort that makes up 14
percent of the four-year college population. SAE had signed up
far more Latino and Asian American members. Overall, about
20 percent were members of minority groups, which compose
38 percent of the college population. These figures showed SAE
had plenty of work to do, as did many liberal arts colleges with
similar demographics. Chapters showed significant variation.
Some major outposts in the South reported no black members.
Others, especially those on the West Coast, such as California
State University at San Marco and Occidental College in Los
Angeles, were much more diverse. Amid all the condemnation
of SAE at Oklahoma, it was rarely noted that the national organization itself shut down the chapter hours after leaders heard
about the video—and the day before the University of Oklahoma took action.

I was particularly interested in the experiences of black SAE
members, many of whom stood by the fraternity after the video.
Most had joined because of their network of friends and paid
little attention to SAE's history. Their comments suggested how
much a fraternity's culture depended on the campus equivalent
of retail politics—face-to-face meetings and hanging around
together. McHenry Ternier, a freshman at the University of
Rhode Island's chapter, where half of its members belonged to
minority groups, went on television to defend the chapter. "The
campus supported us. They knew who we were," Ternier, who
is African American, told me. Will Davis, a senior from Illinois
State, found himself in a tough position when the Oklahoma
video hit the Internet. He was one of three black students who
were about to start a new Illinois State chapter just as the video

became infamous. "Why would you want to join a racist fraternity?" he remembered a friend asking. "I spent three or four days asking myself if I wanted to be part of SAE." For Davis, the answer was yes; he had many friends among the sixty members of the new chapter, which took part in a demonstration called "Not on Our Campus," that pledged "our fraternal community's commitment to creating a safe, diverse, supportive and inclusive environment." Davis had many qualities that would make him a good fit for SAE. He grew up in Wheaton, Illinois, where he was comfortable living in a predominantly white community. SAE respects athleticism, ambition, and military service. A six-foot-two linebacker for the Illinois State Redbirds, Davis was planning to join the US Air Force and then apply to medical school. Still, Davis harbored no illusions about the challenges SAE faced. "Greek life is very segregated," he said. "It's always been that way. It's part of their history."

In June 2015, I met Davis at the biennial SAE national convention, where hundreds of students and alumni gathered to chart the fraternity's future. Held at a Newport Beach, California, resort, the proceedings were uneasy at times because of the Oklahoma video's release three months earlier. I watched an alumnus of the University of Oklahoma chapter screen another video—in a sense, a sequel. He was the father of one of the members on the bus, and he hoped this new video would quell the accusations of racism. The video's lighting was harsh and unforgiving, as if the students were confessing to a crime. In effect, they were. They admitted their silence when confronted with racism.

"Any type of discrimination is not OK."

"It's not OK to stand idly by."

"We embarrassed ourselves and our families."

"We should have stopped the chant before it got to the bus."

"Our biggest failure was not stopping it from being shared."

"The chant does not represent our values."

"Even though I only heard the chant once before, I knew it was wrong."

"There's not a racist culture in our house. We regularly opened the house to African Americans."

The video, expected to make the rounds of SAE as a cautionary tale, inspired conflicting emotions. The students sounded sincere, their shame as visible as the dark shadows under their eyes. Yet they struck some discordant notes. They had heard the song only "once before." Wasn't once more than enough to sing about lynching black people? What does it mean that they didn't have "a racist culture"? They didn't object to that song being taught at their own chapter house? What else would a "racist culture" entail in 2015? It seemed odd to have to say that "we regularly opened the house to African Americans."

After seeing the students' apologies, I decided to travel to Oklahoma to meet them. What I found there would surprise me.

WITH ITS TURRETS and gargoyles, the Bizzell Memorial Library stands at the center of the University of Oklahoma campus and holds the state's largest collection of books, 5 million volumes, including Melville and Dickens first editions. For all its academic prestige, the library also represents a troubling racial history. In 1948, George McLaurin, a retired professor, applied to the university's doctoral program in education. He was at first denied admission because he was African American. Eventually, he was accepted under court order. Still, the university insisted that he remain apart from the white students. McLaurin was forced to sit in a designated spot in the Bizzell Library, away from the regular reading room. His appeal to the Supreme Court became a central part of the reversal of the "separate but equal" doctrine in higher education.

Today, students of all races and backgrounds mingle in Bizzell Library, but their apparent ease belies the racial tensions that still exist at the university. In November 2015, eight months after SAE's racist song became public, I met a white sophomore named Drew Rader outside the library. Rader, who had been on the bus that fateful evening, wore a faded rose-colored T-shirt emblazoned with SAE's letters and an eight-ball, a memento from a 2014 casino night fund-raiser. No one noticed his clothing as he walked across the campus during a class change as students streamed by in Oklahoma sweatshirts.

Since the chapter had been shut down, Rader was living off campus. To sit down for a talk, he took me instead to Headington Hall, a luxurious new $75 million dorm where he and two other SAE pledges had lived freshman year. With its suites, leather furniture, and wood paneling, as well as an eighty-seat movie theater, it was built as an athletic dorm to lure football players. Under National Collegiate Athletic Association rules, half of its rooms had to house non-athletes, and Rader and his friends lucked out, living here and then winning bids (invitations to join) so they could move to the chapter house sophomore year. This dorm, with its view of the football stadium, represented the powerful nexus of fraternities and football at Oklahoma and most public universities with big-time sports. Not only did an SAE family sponsor the football team, the family of one of Rader's pledge brothers had donated money for Headington Hall and was one of the team's biggest boosters. Now this symbiotic relationship had broken down. The football team, composed of many African Americans, had excoriated SAE after the video. As we settled down in a conference room, team members walked by after workouts while Rader and his pledge brothers gathered to speak with me.

Rader told me about hearing the racist song shouted from the balcony of the dance hall. "I didn't take it seriously," Rader said. "I didn't put any thought into it. It didn't trigger anything in my mind as being a threat. It was taught in a joking manner. It wasn't taught as a serious thing—like we were never going to let in a black person. That would be ridiculous." Rader seemed blasé about what had happened. Although he considered the song offensive, it seemed to have little literal meaning to him beyond a kind of adolescent stupidity. Rader said he and his date, a member of the Delta Gamma sorority who was now his girlfriend, hadn't heard the song on the bus.

Rader belonged to the President's Leadership Class, an elite and diverse group of about one hundred students chosen for their academic and other accomplishments. Its members included J. D. Baker, an African American student who had been Rader's friend since high school, where they had met at a student-government competition. In the view of the UCLA researchers, these kinds of interactions were essential for improving the racial climate on college campuses. After Rader saw the video, he texted Baker and other black friends to apologize, then met with them face-to-face. Rader remembered his black friends as understanding, but when I spoke later with Baker, he had a different recollection.

"You had the opportunity to show leadership on that bus," Baker recalled telling him. "If you had stood up on that bus, everything would have been different. Everything would have been different for your fraternity. Everything would have been different for the entire university."

Still, Baker, a member of the Black Students Association, was far less shocked about the video than the rest of the country. The child of a firefighter and a cosmetologist, he had grown up in a suburb of Oklahoma City and had heard that kind of language before. As one of four African American members of Lambda Chi Alpha, a historically white fraternity with a two-hundred-student chapter, he was open to friendships with white students. It wasn't always easy. Baker was often subjected to stereotyping. He wore black glasses and favored cardigans and neat jeans, so his fraternity brothers often called him an

"Oreo." "'You act white, but you're black,'" they told him. Most of the time, he just laughed it off.

Given Baker's ability to live in both worlds, it was easy to imagine how his friendship with Rader could have deepened throughout college in a way that might have helped Rader take a stand against the song. Instead, the two students came away with nearly opposite lessons. Baker focused on his friend's failure to show leadership and stand up for racial tolerance, while Rader nursed a grievance.

In Rader's view, the university had punished fraternity members excessively, while another privileged group on campus, student athletes, received preferential treatment. Rader noted the lax discipline of star Oklahoma Sooners football player Joe Mixon, who pleaded guilty in 2014 to a misdemeanor charge after punching a female student in the face and fracturing her jaw and cheekbone. The running back, who is African American, was suspended for a year. He returned for the 2015 season and became a top National Football League prospect, though the controversy over the assault continued to dog him. "It seems like there was a double standard," Rader told me. An aspiring lawyer, Rader wrote a paper for his English class that compared Mixon's punishment with the expulsion of his two fraternity brothers for singing the offensive song. Rader argued that President Boren had violated the students' constitutional rights to free speech, a position that a number of legal scholars had taken after the episode. In his view, the university gave an athlete a pass because of his financial value to the university. "When Joe Mixon can be forgiven after brutally assaulting a female, and other students can be expelled for saying unsavory words, there is clearly a problem," Rader wrote. His professor gave him an A. "Personally, I thought it was an overreaction," Rader said of the uproar over the video.

Rader's reasoning typified much of what I heard after fraternities faced censure for their members' behavior. Defenders will often highlight the transgressions of another group, such as athletes, and suggest that in comparison, they are being unfairly punished. In Mixon's case, the comparison implied that a black student had been excused for violence, whereas white students had been expelled for mere words. It also selected another privileged group, star athletes, and suggested white fraternities should be treated with the same leniency. Boren, the University of Oklahoma president, told me he had also shown compassion to the two SAE students by allowing them to withdraw before being expelled, so they could start over at another college. "People want to say you're soft on African Americans but you're tough on whites," Boren said. "Nothing could be further from the truth."

Apart from the debate over punishment, Rader felt Pettit and Rice were taking a fall, when they were no more responsible than anyone else. Rader considered Rice a close friend; Pettit's aunt and Rader's mother had been college classmates. "They were in the wrong place at the wrong time," Rader said of the two expelled students. "It made it sound like they were the only two singing."

Two other SAE members, Garrett Parkhurst and Sam Albert, grew up with Rader in Elk City, Oklahoma, population 12,000. They all played on the high school tennis team. Parkhurst was the student who had apologized to his Mexican American date on the bus. Although he hadn't said anything at the dance hall, Parkhurst said he understood the gravity of the song. He thought it would have come up at the next chapter meeting if the video hadn't surfaced. "I knew immediately this was a terrible thing, and it wasn't going to end well," Parkhurst told me.

Sam Albert was a year older and hadn't been on the bus that night. He could barely keep his emotions in check when he described his shame at what happened. His father, who owns a store that sells outdoor clothing and cowboy boots, had been treasurer of the chapter. Albert first visited the house when he was seven years old; his father had showed him the room he had lived in as a student. "I thought it was the coolest thing ever," Albert said. "I looked up to him so much."

Albert had a special perspective. His great-grandparents were immigrants who had fled Lebanon in the 1900s. He grew up hearing stories about how the Ku Klux Klan had burned a cross on his family's Kansas lawn in the 1930s. Just like his younger friends, Albert, who was now a junior, had heard the song in the dance hall when he was a pledge. "I'm not in a place to do something about it," he recalled thinking at the time. "I'm a freshman, and they probably don't like me and wouldn't listen to me. Once I'm an upperclassman I'm going to step up and say something when I have some power and people know who I am. This has got to stop." He heard about the video at a church breakfast and called his parents. "I was so embarrassed," he said. Albert's account demonstrated how the hierarchical structure of fraternities—especially pledging—can strip recruits of their moral compass. Just as they don't step in when witnessing violent hazing, they remain silent when confronted with racism. I found Albert's account especially affecting because he understood he had abandoned his family's values to win acceptance from his peers.

As we spoke, another student, Jack Counts III, joined the group. At the California SAE convention, his father, a chapter alumnus, had screened the film of Counts and other students apologizing. Like Rader, Counts belonged to the President's Leadership Class. Counts recalled that he and other pledges on the dance floor had noted the bad timing when older students taught the song from the balcony: "People were saying, 'This is bad. It was close to Martin Luther King's birthday. This is something we shouldn't be doing.'" Yet Counts said he felt powerless as a pledge and expressed the same feelings of inferiority that can lead students to accept hazing. "I didn't know a lot of upperclassmen," he said. "I mostly got in because my dad was an SAE. You don't want to say something. You want to stay out of it. Now, if I were in this situation again, I hope I'd step up and say something."

Counts said he realized it was hard to explain everyone's silence and that anything he might say now would ring hollow. After the episode, members had met with a Southern Methodist University professor named Maria Dixon Hall, who had publicly expressed sympathy for the white students in the aftermath of the video. Hall, who is African American, had opposed the expulsion of the two members. She chalked up the incident to the immaturity of adolescent boys unduly shaped by the culture around them. "Since we know we all have said things behind closed doors that would have us vilified if they ever saw the light of day, how about we cut these boys a little slack," she wrote in a piece for a religious website. Young white men are prone to suffer what she called "a full blown cardiac arrest of racism. Rather than give them a defibrillator of God's grace and challenging them to see the worth of all—we pull the plug and do a dance on their graves." In her session with SAE members, Dixon said she knew how difficult it was to stand up to right a wrong, to stop a fight or a crime in progress. She urged them to learn from their silence. Counts's father told me he saw members crying at the meeting.

Some African American community leaders were also forgiving. In a news conference, black civil-rights figures and pastors in Oklahoma appeared with Pettit, who had led the chant. "All the apologies in the world won't change what I have done, so I will spend the rest of my life trying to be the person who heals and brings people of all races together," Pettit said. Rice issued a written apology: "I admit it likely was fueled by alcohol consumed at the house before the bus trip, but that's not an excuse. Yes, the song was taught to us, but that too doesn't work as an

explanation . . . My goal for the long-term is to be a man who
has the heart and the courage to reject racism wherever I see or
experience it in the future."

The other SAE members told me the video didn't reflect the
racial climate at the chapter. Counts said SAE had been recruiting an African American student before the video became public. They recalled that many African American members of the
football team had been regulars at their parties. "We had the entire starting defensive line at the house," Parkhurst said. "I wish
they had stood up for us. It hurts a little bit." Sterling Shepard,
a star wide receiver for Oklahoma who has since joined the New
York Giants, had been friends with white fraternity members,
and Counts's father told me the fraternity had extended Shepard
a bid, which he had declined. Shepard, who is African American, and Counts had graduated from the same Oklahoma City
private school, Heritage Hall. "Football and basketball players
had been friends with people in the house, and they didn't do
anything to defend guys in the house," Counts said.

Given the content of the video, that would have been a lot
to ask. Shepard's comment on Twitter had been muted: "It's
sad that it's 2015 and stuff like this is still happening." Another
high-profile player had been particularly horrified *because* he
knew members; if anything, the betrayal felt more personal.
After the video, Erik Striker, a linebacker and team captain,
texted his mother and called her in tears. He then unleashed
a video on Snapchat that went viral, attacking white fraternities for "telling us racism doesn't exist," chanting the song in
private and, in public, "shaking our hand, giving us hugs and
telling us you love us."

The football players had been shocked in part because they
expected better. I could see why. The members I met seemed
open-minded and reflective. They had friendships that crossed
racial lines. Given the right role models, they might well have

learned to stand up for different values. The fraternity had let them down.

THE DAY AFTER I met with the students, I visited Counts's father, Jack Counts Jr., whose loyalty to SAE has been a defining aspect of his life. Counts greeted me at his photography company, Candid Color Systems, in a nondescript office park in Oklahoma City. The idea for his company, whose bread and butter is photographing fraternity and sorority members, graduations, and sports, began when he was an Oklahoma SAE and made extra money photographing sorority women at pajama parties for 75 cents apiece. In preparation for our meeting, Counts had laid out generations of SAE memorabilia in velvet-covered scrapbooks adorned with gold crests. Counts, who is in his late sixties, flipped through a yearbook and found a picture of his grandfather, a student senate president who had been one of the first presidents of the Oklahoma chapter. His son would have been the fourth generation at the chapter.

"These traditions go back to the founding of the university," Counts told me. "It tears you up inside that this happened. It wasn't supposed to be this way. This wasn't what we were about."

The former SAE social chairman has shown his devotion to the university in many ways. Five months after my visit, President Boren inducted Counts into the Seed Sower Society, meaning he had given at least $1 million to the University of Oklahoma. In his case, he was singled out for support of athletics, including the Headington Hall project and the Sooner Air Program. Counts ferries coaches around on his Cessna jet when they make scouting missions to high schools across the country.

Counts picked up a dog-eared purple volume, entitled the "Songs of Sigma Alpha Epsilon," published in 1921. "I can tell you I took a look through it to try to find that song," he told me. "It wasn't anywhere."

Some of the lyrics have a nostalgic Southern flavor, such as "The Beacon Song": "In the happy, sunny South, SAE first saw the light / And arose to be a beacon in the land." There is also the old standard, "Sing, Brothers, Sing," a rousing work that evokes straw hats and barbershop quartets:

When we came up from Dixie land a score of years ago,
Our rivals met us with a band; They thought we were a show.
But they were very wrong, you know, to do the way they did,
They are just forty times too slow, for we get the men they bid,
I tell you . . .
Sing, brothers, sing; Sing brothers sing;
And let Phi Alpha Ring. Sing, Brothers, Sing.

I asked Counts to play the video of his son and his friends apologizing, so I could look at it more carefully and match names to faces. After we watched it together, Counts, normally upbeat and garrulous, found himself at a loss for words. "It makes me want to cry," he said. "These guys . . ." He couldn't finish the sentence.

On a break for lunch, Counts introduced me to his old friend and SAE fraternity brother, Rusty Johnson, a Vietnam veteran who now owns an oil and gas company with one hundred wells. We met at Earl's Rib Palace, on a commercial strip near his office. With a mostly male clientele, it was the kind of place where the waitress calls you "Baby" and hub caps and license plates decorate the walls. The men reminisced about the annual trips they took to Las Vegas with their 1960s pledge brothers.

"My badge was a big deal for me," said Johnson, who can count a dozen family members who belonged to SAE. "It was a big deal when I pinned my badge on my oldest and youngest sons. Once they earned the badges, it's really special to pin it on them. It was really one of the highlights of my life."

Counts and Johnson are part of a group of SAE alumni who were quietly trying to bring the chapter back to the campus. They needed to strike a delicate balance because they know how precarious their position has become. Although some alumni criticized Boren for what he said after the video became public, Counts was far more measured. "He's been a great president," Counts said. "He needed to take quick action, but I think he painted all SAEs with a broad brush that wasn't fair." Counts said a college wouldn't shut down a football team because of a few players' behavior. "What's the statute of limitations for a nine-second video?" Johnson asked. "I can guarantee you that you get a bunch of eighteen- and nineteen-year-old guys together for a while and somebody is going to do something stupid. What happened at OU could have happened anywhere." It sounded like the rationale I heard about drinking: everybody does it, and fraternities are scapegoats. It was worth asking the question: Would the song have flourished anywhere? Would it have survived at a school without fraternities or pledging?

Johnson and Counts acknowledged how the chapter's recruitment strategy thwarted diversity. "We gave preference to legacies, so a lot of pledges would end up being white guys from large metropolitan areas," Counts said. At times, he sounded like a college admissions officer interested in promoting a class more reflective of the general population. "We would like to see more ethnic diversity," he said. "We would like to see more geographic diversity, too." In Counts's view, that kind of membership would have saved the chapter. "If we had five black guys in the house, would that song have ever existed?" he said. "Nope. It is sort of self-correcting. People aren't going to offend their friends." Counts's point rang true; a diverse membership would certainly have saved the chapter.

SAE was hardly the only segregated fraternity. After the racist video surfaced, the University of Oklahoma's Student Affairs

Office surveyed its Greek Row and discovered that many other traditionally white fraternities had no black members. By 2017, amid a university push for diversity, all but two chapters included some African American members. Still, overall, blacks amounted to less than 3 percent of members. (The chapters had many more Latinos and Native Americans.) President Boren told me African American enrollment at the university had risen since the incident because families appreciated the stand the school had taken. "It was like we declared war on intolerance," Boren said. "We've learned a lot of lessons."

COUNTS HAD INVITED me to a tailgate and home football game, something of a state holiday in Oklahoma. That Saturday, several dozen SAE boosters drank beer and soda on a parking lot under a tent in the colors of the American flag. It was a low-key affair because the fraternity had been banned from the campus, and members were gathering just a few blocks from President Boren's house. Most were alumni, although sorority women and a few undergraduate members showed up, some wearing Game Day polo shirts with subtle SAE logos. Near the tent, Howard Dixon, the former SAE chef, grilled bratwurst. The Jamaican-born Dixon worked for fifteen years at the chapter house, where he was known for his chicken fried steak and chicken and waffles. Dixon wore an SAE lion necklace, a gift from one of the members. Among the tall, athletic guests, the five-foot-tall Dixon stood out. He was also the only black person at the gathering, as he often was in the fraternity house. Dixon lost his job when the university shut the chapter down. Members raised tens of thousands of dollars for him, and another Greek house promptly hired him. In her essay, the Southern Methodist University professor had suggested the members of the chapter, rather than be expelled, meet with their beloved cook, who might ask: "Is this what you really think of me?" I asked

Dixon about the song. Like the pastors and civil-rights leaders, he offered forgiveness. "We all need to love each other," he told me. "When you cut yourself, you bleed red. So do I. Accidents happen. I'm just glad I can be here to help. As long as there is SAE, I'll be here."

After the tailgate, Counts and his wife, Alison, who was a member of the Oklahoma Delta Delta Delta sorority, joined the throngs in Sooners colors of crimson and cream making their way to the sold-out football stadium. The couple, both of whom are avid photographers, had all-access passes, which let them capture the action from the sidelines. They planned to give their photos to the Athletic Department as well as hang them in their offices. Alison Counts pointed out the billboard for Love's Travel Stops and Country Stores, which was bright yellow with a red heart. Billionaires Tom and Judy Love, who built a single gas station into a chain of 380 convenience stores in forty states, spent millions as primary sponsors, alongside Coca-Cola and AT&T. Their grandchildren belonged to the SAE chapter. "They were none too happy when their two kids were kicked out of the house," Alison told me. At that moment, it became especially clear to me just how powerfully SAE had transgressed. University presidents are often cowed by the power of the fraternities; yet Boren had seen the video and shut down the chapter almost immediately.

In the Counts's luxury box, high above the fifty-yard line, family and guests, many SAE alumni, dined on shrimp cocktails and barbecue while watching the Sooners obliterate Iowa State, 52–16. In the front row, Jack Counts III sat next to Lindsay Strunk, a nineteen-year-old sophomore and member of the sorority Pi Beta Phi. Strunk told me about their first date aboard the infamous bus. The younger Counts had apologized to her, and the moment had passed quickly. They had recently enjoyed spending time together at a Halloween party thrown by former

SAE members. Dates tried to match each others' costumes. Counts, with his shock of curly blond hair, and Strunk, with her long, straight blonde hair, already looked like a matched set. But they played along. Counts wore a bear suit and Strunk a gold dress and a sash that read "Honey." Parkhurst, who was also in the luxury box, had his arm around Corina Hernandez, the Mexican American former beauty queen and sorority sister from Oklahoma State. Their first date on the bus had also blossomed into a long-term relationship. Hernandez told me that online commenters had been calling for the expulsion of the women on the bus, too. At the time, she worried her name would get out. "When it happened, I was just dumbfounded," she said. "I felt there wasn't time to do anything. I also remember all those white faces. I'm thinking, 'I'm the only person who isn't white.'"

Colleges purport to encourage interactions across the silos of class, race, and ethnicity; here, a fraternity thwarted its own members' natural inclination to learn from other students. Hernandez made Parkhurst more sensitive to the perils of bigotry. Parkhurst told me he had planned to bring up the song in the next chapter meeting. I imagined how SAE's Oklahoma chapter could have gone in another direction. It could have promoted its members' tolerance and respect. Instead, it brought out the worst in them.

IN DOWNTOWN OKLAHOMA City, the Elemental Café offers "micro-lot" beans from farms in Ethiopia and Costa Rica and "single-origin" cocoa powder. From its floor-to-ceiling windows, you can see the Oklahoma City federal courthouse, site of one of the nation's worst terrorist attacks, inspired in part by the *Turner Diaries*, a book revered by white supremacists. This juxtaposition of multiculturalism and racism seemed like a fitting place to meet the last African American member to have joined the University of Oklahoma chapter of SAE.

William Bruce James II, who graduated in 2005 and was now a lawyer, grew up in Ada, Oklahoma, population 17,000, where his father was a senior vice president of a bank. A National Merit Scholar at a math and science magnet school, he had considered historically black Howard University and Dartmouth but chose Oklahoma because he was offered a full scholarship and it was close to home. When he enrolled in 2001, James wanted to join Omega Psi, a historically black fraternity whose members included the poet Langston Hughes and civil-rights leader Jesse Jackson. His mother told him to steer clear because she worried about hazing.

James felt comfortable joining a historically white fraternity. His earliest memories had been of his role in integrating white environments. He was the first African American boy in his preschool; his sister, the first African American girl. He checked out the various houses at the University of Oklahoma. Some held no appeal. To him, they seemed "cookie cutter," populated with preppies in pastel shorts or Wall Street types with slicked-back hair. James visited SAE with a white childhood friend whose grandfather had been a member. He liked that they weren't selling a "hedonistic fantasy," though he did lose his way in the enormous house and stumbled on a pool table and big-screen TV. He noticed one Native American member and another from Venezuela. He liked the variety and joined the fraternity. James loved Greek life at Oklahoma. He became a "new-member educator" and "song chair" and also led homecoming rallies. During freshman year, James met the person he would end up marrying: a young white woman from the Delta Gamma sorority. They had been in a play together and fell in love. After college, his SAE friendships continued. Five of the groomsmen at his wedding were fraternity brothers. When his son was a year old, James took him to the Oklahoma SAE house and showed him his picture hanging on a wall. James dreamed of his son joining one day. Then, the morning after the chant on the bus, his wife, a therapist, showed him the video.

"I was shocked," James told me over a cup of herbal tea. "It was something that never should have happened. I felt like I had accomplished something at the fraternity. I thought of all the conversations I had with my pledge brothers. The whole idea of we'll trust each other because we're brothers. We've taken a giant fall."

James appeared on television amid the uproar over the video with another SAE member named Jonathan Davis, who had joined the chapter in 1999 and been its first black member. Heartbroken and angry, both men nevertheless came to the defense of their housemother, who had been vilified on social media for another video that came out just as the chapter was shutting down. Beauton Gilbow, a seventy-nine-year-old white woman who grew up in Arkansas, was known as Mom B. She was much beloved by members who remembered how she taught them manners and helped decorate the house with her own antique furniture. A newspaper unearthed a 2013 video that gave life to the scandal. In it, Gilbow, white haired with bright-pink lipstick, sang along with the lyrics from a rap song by Trinidad James and gleefully repeated the "N-word." "I wouldn't even hesitate for a split second to say Mom B. is undoubtedly not a racist," Davis, a medical-sales representative in Colorado, told CNN at the time. "I see her being caught up in the moment. She does like to mix it up socially, and likes to have fun with the guys and their dates that they bring over to the house." James recalled how much Gilbow cared for him and his family, and how she displayed pictures of him, his wife, and their family in the fraternity house entryway. "Mom B. means a lot to me," he said. He called to tell her, "Hey, don't ever use that word again, even in a song. But from me, you're forgiven."

Fifty SAE brothers called and e-mailed James, asking if he was OK. He also received what he called "random" Facebook friend requests from SAEs across the country. He wondered if the senders, worried about being considered racists, wanted to prove they had a black friend. The national office invited him to teach at the leadership school, but he couldn't bring himself to do it. He still has close friends from SAE, but something changed after the video. At some point—he doesn't remember when—he and his fraternity brothers stopped offering each other the secret handshake with the interlocking pinkie fingers. He may have stopped. Or maybe they did. Out of respect, he thought. "I feel like a part of my past has been destroyed," he said, "the part where I was an SAE."

James remembered some powerful moments as the chapter's only black member. Some were uncomfortable. At times, brothers would call him the "token." "Sometimes, I let it go," he said. "Sometimes, I said, 'That's not a cool thing to say.'" James felt like his presence made a difference. A white member from a small town in Oklahoma confided in him about his own father, who had referred to someone as "a colored guy at the store." "It felt dirty to him," James said, suggesting a shift in his brother's consciousness. Once, members considered throwing a party with the theme "forty ounces of frat." They and their dates would dress up as rappers and their entourages. They would dance to hip-hop and drink malt liquor—hence, the title. In other words, it would be a classic "ghetto party," the kind that so often ends with a fraternity lambasted online and in news articles. James saw the problem right away. Gently, he suggested it could come across as racist. "Let's not do that," one of the organizers said. Imagine if someone had said those simple words when the racist song made its way from the leadership school to the University of Oklahoma.

JAMES'S ACCOUNT REMINDED me of the words of Ben Johnson, another African American SAE member. At the 2015 convention, Johnson addressed members about the racial history of SAE. A 1987 graduate of the University of California at Irvine, he was president of SAE's alumni association. He also chaired a national diversity committee, and he urged the gathering to reckon with its racial history, not ignore it. "SAE was founded in 1856 at the University of Alabama," he said. "It was a bad place, a bad time. SAE must respect its history, understand its history, but not be a part of it."

Other institutions of higher education are starting to account for their roles. More than a dozen universities, including Harvard and Brown, have taken steps to acknowledge their ties to slavery. Colleges are erecting memorials, renaming buildings, and sponsoring research. Georgetown University, a Jesuit institution, said it would offer admissions preferences to the descendants of 272 slaves it sold in 1838 to shore up its finances.

After the Oklahoma incident, rather than reassess its past, SAE removed references to its Southern roots from its website. I decided to delve into SAE's archives to understand what had happened generations ago, at the dawn of the era of integration. I found an extraordinary account of an SAE convention in 1951. It had long been a carefully guarded secret, and it helped explain the roots of the fraternity's racial hostility and why it is something of a miracle SAE ended up with any black members at all.

6

DISCRIMINATING GENTLEMEN

"Who Speaks with Frankness
but Always with Sincerity and Sympathy"

On a September night in 1951, the Sigma Alpha Epsilon convention in Chicago radiated exclusivity. At the Edgewater Beach Hotel, a famed resort on Lake Michigan that attracted celebrities such as Frank Sinatra, Judy Garland, and Nat King Cole, SAE members and their guests danced. They swayed to the Latin rhythms of bandleader Xavier Cugat and the voice of the singer Abbe Lane, known for her sultry Spanish ballads. The men of SAE may have enjoyed their cosmopolitan, multiethnic entertainment, but they had no interest in opening up their fraternity to that kind of diversity. They agreed with US senator Richard B. Russell Jr., one of the most powerful men in Washington, who was about to become their honorary president. Russell, a politician from Georgia, was a defender of segregation.

Behind the convention's closed doors, fraternity members were struggling to preserve their exclusionary membership rules. Fraternity leaders debated a section of SAE's governing laws dating to the early 1900s:

> Any male member of the Aryan race, of good moral character and intellectual ability, who is a student at the domicile of the Chapter Collegiate, is eligible to membership in the Fraternity, except that (1) No person, either of whose parents is a full-blooded Jew, is eligible, and (2) No person who is or has been a member of another college social fraternity is eligible.

The "Aryan race" requirement, not to mention the exclusion of the children of "full-blooded" Jews, sounded as if it had come straight out of Hitler's Germany. After the liberation of Nazi death camps, such attitudes were becoming less acceptable. The US government was beginning to fight discrimination, and public universities started pressuring fraternities to drop racist membership rules. The University of Connecticut threatened to shut down its thriving SAE chapter. The University of Rhode Island and the University of Massachusetts were expected to be next, as would colleges throughout the North.

On the last full day of the convention, more than 170 men gathered in a hotel ballroom. More than once, Emmett B. Moore, SAE's president, asked the brothers to ensure no outsiders were present. Unlike all the other business of the convention, no transcript of this "executive session" would be published, not even, as was the custom, in the *Phi Alpha*, itself a secret publication of the fraternity. One member suggested barring the stenographer. Showing a lawyer's regard for preserving the record, Alfred Nippert, an Ohio judge, disagreed. Nippert, who grew up in Germany during the nineteenth-century Franco-Prussian

War, also had a keen sense of history. During World War I, he had acted as an emissary between the German leader Kaiser Wilhelm and President Woodrow Wilson. Now, Nippert took the floor to press his point, saying that they owed an accounting of their actions to the next generations. "We ought to know why and how we did it, when our sons and grandsons come to be members of SAE," he told the crowd, his faint German accent giving him a sense of worldly authority. Nippert had authority for another reason. The lead financier of the fraternity's headquarters, he was married to the heir of the Proctor & Gamble soap fortune. Nippert prevailed. Others remained worried that word of their deliberations would leak out. "For God's sake, be careful, because this may be reproduced some day in every paper in the United States," one member warned.

To save the Northern chapters, a panel of prominent members had already determined before the convention that SAE had no choice but to change the language of its laws. The group included a former president of the Federal Reserve Bank of Boston, William W. Paddock, who gained notoriety in 1934 when the Boston papers said his institution processed part of the ransom money for the kidnapped Lindbergh baby. Other members inhabited the upper reaches of law, sports, and medicine: Samuel G. DeSimone, a state judge in New Jersey; Walter "Doc" Meanwell, a legendary former basketball coach at the University of Wisconsin at Madison; and M. Brittain Moore Jr., who became director of venereal disease research at what would become the US Centers for Disease Control and Prevention, where he published research on the Tuskegee syphilis experiment, infamous for failing to treat hundreds of black men who had the disease.

The SAE leaders had concocted a recommendation that seemed straightforward: instead of insisting on an Aryan brotherhood, the fraternity's law would allow as members all men "of sound moral character, of creditable intellectual attainments, and socially acceptable throughout the fraternity." The SAE elders weren't actually opening up the fraternity to blacks and Jews—far from it. They promised the convention crowd that the new language amounted to a public-relations move, a shift from explicit to unspoken discrimination. "We are all united on one thing, I am very sure, and that is that we cannot have certain people in the fraternity," proclaimed Albert M. Austin, a past SAE national president. "We just can't do it. We won't do it, and, if that happens, if any of you walk out, boys, I'll be number one."

Austin lived in New York City, where he was a distinguished patent lawyer whose firm worked on a pivotal case involving Henry Ford's intellectual rights to the automobile. But he told the audience he was "a Southerner by instinct." He had grown up in Franklin, Tennessee, vacationed in the mountains of North Carolina, and spoke the language of SAE's conservatives: "No power on Earth can keep us from selecting our friends. In Soviet Russia, they can't make a man select his friends." Sounding like a Southern demagogue, he gave a stem-winder: "Get rid of these words, but stick to our standards, stick to our standards, boys, until death do us part." The crowd gave Austin a standing ovation.

Austin's speech failed to convince traditionalists, who continued to fight in favor of the racist and anti-Semitic language. In their view, words mattered, and a change could open the door to black and Jewish members. Joseph Walt, a member of the University of Tennessee chapter, said his alumni were "unalterably opposed" to striking the discriminatory clause. Speaking of the admission of blacks and Jews, he said that his alumni "must be absolutely guaranteed that no such thing can or ever will take place." G. Holmes Braddock, a member from the University of Miami, predicted the controversy would blow over as it had two years earlier at his alma mater when Jewish students briefly protested their exclusion. "We had a member of our faculty who was a Jew, and we had a fight on our hands," he said. Braddock urged the fraternity to resist outside pressure: "I don't want to see SAE deteriorate, and neither do I want to see us back down when the fight is just beginning." Nevertheless, 122 members, more than the two-thirds majority required to pass the altered language, supported striking the discriminatory language. The word "Aryan" was out. Under the letter of the law, a member need only be "socially acceptable throughout the fraternity," though it would still be understood what that really meant: no blacks or Jews.

But that gentlemen's agreement failed to satisfy some members, who proposed merely shifting the discriminatory language from SAE's publicly disclosed laws into the words of its secret ritual. They considered the ritual sacred because it had been passed down from Noble Leslie DeVotie, their founder. Pledges wearing robes and holding candles chanted its words in dark rooms. On the last day of the convention, Walt, who headed the ritual committee, suggested the private words of the ritual specify that only "white Christian Gentiles" could join SAE. The federal government might not abide discrimination in its public laws, but why couldn't the offending language be included in the ritual? One speaker suggested the discriminatory phrase be written in Greek, so legislators wouldn't understand it. Meanwell, the Wisconsin basketball coach loved the idea. "We would certainly put something in the ritual that we could stand on and know that we would have no persons of other color or of another race except pure white-blooded Americans, or red-blooded Americans," he said. John Graves of the George Washington University chapter added, "We have to take something back to our brothers that is ironclad, something with teeth in it. We have to be able to say, 'Brothers, here is what we did; we have all the safeguards in the world to keep the non-Aryan, the Negro and the Jew out of our fraternity.'"

Armistead I. Selden Jr., an Alabama state legislator who had been a World War II US Navy lieutenant, put forth a compromise. He focused on the words in the public law that had already been approved: members must be "socially acceptable throughout the fraternity." Selden offered what he thought was a clever solution. What if the convention secretly defined the meaning of "socially acceptable"? What if members proclaimed it to mean, in fact, "white Christian Gentile"? To the Reverend Charles E. McAllister, dean of St. John the Evangelist in Spokane, Washington, the group was playing with words. McAllister was a member of the Washington State College of Regents and the convention's keynote speaker. However, instead of arguing the fine points of his position, he used his time to tell a racist joke about "an old Negro Mammy . . . way down South" who called her child Morphy, short for Morphine. When asked why she had named her child after a narcotic, she replied that she had looked up the word in the dictionary: "Well, Mister, it said there that morphine was the product of the wild poppy and if ever a child had a wild poppy, this is the child." The joke may have had little relevance to the matter at hand, but the audience laughed all the same.

As their 3:00 p.m. checkout time approached, the men were forced to make a decision. They turned to one of their luminaries, Eminent Supreme Recorder John O. Moseley, the fraternity's executive director, who spoke up for the first time. No one had more standing than Moseley, except perhaps the late Levere. Moseley, courtly and bespectacled, was a Rhodes scholar and classics professor who became president of the University of Nevada. Perhaps most important, Moseley first introduced the True Gentleman creed as a cornerstone of SAE education. (In 1899, John Walter Wayland, a historian at what is now

James Madison University in Virginia, wrote its words to win a contest at the *Baltimore Sun* for the best definition of a "true gentleman.")

Moseley, born in Mississippi, was very much a Southerner of the old school. At the 1945 SAE convention, Moseley gave a keynote speech filled with racial overtones. He told Uncle Remus stories in a stereotypical black accent. He called Levere, the temperance activist and SAE historian, "a Northern boy who adored the South and loved to tell of the chivalry of our Southern SAEs in that War between the States." He made casual use of racial epithets, saying apropos of nothing: "Like the nigger said, 'He should have zigged when he zagged.'"

At the 1951 convention, Moseley backed Selden's approach. Moseley assured the crowd that SAE would keep its door shut to the wrong people. "I was born and raised in the state of Mississippi and if anybody brings someone contrary to my social standards into this fraternity, Albert Austin said he would be the first to leave, and I'll be the second," Moseley said. He called for a voice vote on Selden's compromise: that they would agree that day that "socially acceptable," in fact, meant "white Christian Gentile." In other words, SAE could tell college administrators it had changed its rules and ended discrimination, even though it hadn't. It was an appealing strategy, although perhaps difficult to square with the creed of the True Gentleman, "who speaks with frankness but always with sincerity and sympathy." The motion carried.

The True Gentlemen had voted in favor of a lie.

To create an American elite, the fraternity movement had long practiced discrimination, while its members praised it and its official literature codified it. Fraternity men liked the other definition of *discriminating*: a cultured person with refined taste, a *discriminating* gentleman. "Who made it a bad word, anyhow?"

David A. Embury, chairman of the National Interfraternity Conference asked at a 1947 meeting. "I love the discriminating tongue, the discriminating eye, the discriminating ear, and above all the discriminating mind and the discriminating soul." Or, as Coach Meanwell told members at SAE's Chicago convention four years later, "You are chosen because of your traits, because of the manly traits you possess. Let's face it. We do discriminate."

The SAE men defending prejudice were some of the most respected leaders in the history of the fraternity and are still held up as models for members. Moseley founded SAE's leadership school in 1935. The University of Oklahoma students had learned the racist chant from other members attending the John O. Moseley Leadership School. Moseley had deep ties to Oklahoma. He had joined SAE when he was a graduate student at the University of Oklahoma; undergraduates later named the chapter after him. Walt, the Tennessee undergraduate pushing to add discriminatory language to the secret ritual, became a fraternity historian. For half a century, from 1959 through 2008, Walt edited the *Phoenix*, the manual given to all new members that outlined SAE's values and history. He died in 2013, but his words still appear in the foreword of the edition handed out to undergraduates: "The basic principles that drive Sigma Alpha Epsilon are the same today as they were more than 155 years ago."

Other members wielded influence in American society. Selden, who first suggested the compromise that created the unwritten rule that only "white Christian Gentiles could be members," later became an Alabama congressman, an assistant secretary of defense, and an ambassador in the Nixon administration. Braddock, the alumnus from Miami opposed to Jewish membership, served on the Miami-Dade School Board from 1962 to 2000. There, in an instance of historical irony, he led the effort to desegregate Miami's public schools. One school is named in his honor. "The world was different then," Braddock, who was now ninety-one years old, told me. "I was born and raised a Southerner. As all Southerners did in those days, I grew up in segregation. I didn't know any better."

SAE's Southern roots influenced its racial attitudes. When Noble Leslie DeVotie and his seven friends christened the fraternity by candlelight at the University of Alabama in March 1856, they shared prevailing Southern views. DeVotie's own family had roots in both North and South. His father, James H. DeVotie, was born in upstate New York and was a descendant of French Protestants who arrived in the New World before the Revolutionary War. But the elder DeVotie, a severe, rugged-looking man with an unruly white beard, had become a diehard Alabamian. As a teenager, he was born again as a Southern Baptist, a denomination that advocated for slavery. James DeVotie became a preacher, then married into a prominent Montgomery, Alabama, family. Not surprisingly, his son, SAE's founder, held similar views. Over the next three years, the younger DeVotie and his minions founded SAE chapters on other campuses. Staunch believers in slavery and the second-class status of black people, they chose not to venture above the Mason-Dixon line, instead opening chapters at ten Southern schools, including the University of North Carolina and the University of Virginia.

For the Southerners of SAE, a black person's smallest missteps could provoke violence. In 1857, a student at the University of Nashville's Western Military Institute beat a black waiter whom he believed had offended him. The college demanded the student apologize to the waiter or be expelled. "To the young white men of the South, the demand was one they deemed unacceptable," wrote William Levere, the SAE historian. Henry Halbert, an SAE member from Mississippi, petitioned the administration in favor of the white student, who had been expelled. The school demanded an apology from

Halbert, too. He refused and was also kicked out. Halbert then transferred to Union University, a Southern Baptist institution whose president had no quarrel with Halbert's behavior. There, he helped found an SAE chapter, the second in Tennessee.

Of the 369 men then initiated into SAE, nearly all fought for the Confederacy. One founder, DeVotie's closest friend, John Barratt Rudulph, lost his arm to General Sherman's forces in the Battle of New Hope Church in Georgia. Of the seven founders who were alive when the war began, six enlisted. Three of the enlisted men died, including DeVotie, who fell off the dock in Mobile, Alabama, at age twenty-three, hit his head, and was swept to sea. In all, seventy SAE members died in battle. Only one chapter survived, at what is now George Washington University. SAE later expanded into the North, starting with an outpost in Gettysburg, Pennsylvania, the site of the South's bloody Civil War defeat. The northern expansion sparked furious debate within the fraternity. Finally, one of its most successful leaders won the Southerners over by couching it as a quasi-military campaign to conquer "the best colleges and universities of the great North, East and West."

In the early years of the movement, fraternities had no need for explicitly discriminatory policies because only a relative handful of Jewish and black students attended college, and it would have been unimaginable to consider admitting them. Even Catholics weren't welcome. In response, these outsiders began to form their own organizations. In 1895, three Yale students founded nonsectarian Pi Lambda Phi, which became a haven for Jews. In 1899, students at Brown created the first Catholic fraternity. The first black fraternity, Alpha Phi Alpha, followed in 1906 at Cornell, where Asian Americans established Rho Psi ten years later. The Latino fraternity, Phi Iota Alpha, founded in 1931, can trace its roots to 1898 and the formation of the Union Hispano Americana at Rensselaer Polytechnic Institute in Troy,

New York. Members of these groups look with pride on their traditions, and many make an affirmative choice to belong. Yet they are creations of discrimination, of historically white Greek organizations seeking to preserve one of their core values: separation by race, religion, and ethnicity.

In 1900, Levere revealed what might happen when a student tried to cross these strict boundaries. He wrote a novel set at his alma mater, Northwestern University. In the book, a penniless "Persian boy" tries to join a fraternity and no one will choose him. "That dago has been rushing the frats so hard it's a pity he cannot be accommodated and given a first-class initiation," one fraternity man says in the novel. The brothers make up a fake fraternity called Alpha Sigma Sigma, whose initials stand for "ass." On a dark, rainy night, they pick the outsider up in a carriage, blindfold him, and take him off campus for a mock initiation. There, he is beaten, forced to drink a mixture of milk and vinegar, stripped to his underwear, poked with sharp sticks, plastered with flypaper, and baptized with molasses. Finally, members deposit him in front of the Northwestern president's house, where he would be picked up by the police. Levere presented the episode as all in good fun.

In the nineteenth century, SAE's attitudes reflected many of the prevailing prejudices of the times. But certainly by the early twentieth century, Greek organizations displayed less tolerance than other elite groups. Ivy League schools, eager to attract the brightest students, began accepting immigrants, especially Jews, and, with the exception of Princeton, a small number of blacks. To be sure, these new members faced discrimination on campus and sparked a backlash. According to the sociologist Jerome Karabel, Harvard, Yale, and Princeton changed their admissions requirements to limit the number of students considered "socially undesirable," namely, Jews from Eastern Europe. Rather than base decisions on academic performance, where Jews excelled, admissions officers turned to the subjective criteria of "character," "manliness," and "leadership." These were the same characteristics prized by the historically white fraternities. The Ivy League, like Greek-letter groups, deemed that Jews lacked these qualities. In this context, elite college admissions officers sounded much like the fraternity leaders at SAE's fateful 1951 convention. Robert Nelson Corwin, chairman of Yale's board of admissions, called Jews "an alien and unwashed element" that "graduates into the world as naked of all the attributes of refinement and honor as when he was born into it." Under the more subjective admissions standards, rich white Anglo-Saxon Protestant men received preference, and Jewish enrollment was suppressed by quotas.

Still, bigoted Ivy League admissions officers accepted some Jews and blacks. Not so, fraternities. Consider the contrast between SAE and Princeton, often considered the most "Southern" member of the Ivy League. Woodrow Wilson, who was president of Princeton from 1902 to 1910, held racial views that were similar to the leaders of SAE. Wilson, a member of the University of Virginia's Phi Kappa Psi chapter, grew up in the South and worked to keep blacks out of Princeton. As president of the United States, he oversaw the segregation of the federal workforce. Yet even Princeton admitted its first African American student in 1945, decades after other Ivy League schools and six years before the Chicago SAE convention reaffirmed the fraternity's commitment to discrimination.

Before World War II, fraternities made no effort to conceal their admissions policies. In a 1936 Ohio State University catalog, dozens of Greek chapters were listed with descriptions and membership requirements, their racial and ethnic divisions multiplying to the point of absurdity. Like SAE, Delta Tau Delta and Phi Delta Theta were restricted to "the Aryan race." Lambda Chi Alpha accepted "non-Semitic" students. Phi Delta

Chi was open to "Protestant pharmacy and chemistry students" and Alpha Zeta to "Gentile agricultural students." Alpha Rho Chi was looking for "white male students registered in the departments of architecture, architectural engineering or in professional courses in landscape architecture, interior decoration or sculpture."

After World War II, politicians, colleges, and the public began questioning such restrictions. The 1947 movie *Gentleman's Agreement* attacked the kind of anti-Semitism on display at the SAE convention. It won three Academy Awards, including best picture. That year, President Harry Truman, a former Missouri farmer who had been known to use racial epithets, began a campaign for civil rights. He formed a committee to fight discrimination and appointed a commission to study the state of higher education as 1 million veterans flooded campuses. This older, more diverse group no longer reflected a country-club vision of college life. The Truman commission called for a doubling of college enrollment to 4.6 million, by 1960. It decried racial and religious discrimination, particularly quotas restricting blacks and Jews. The commission viewed those policies as reminiscent of the Nazis and "one of the plainest inconsistencies with our national ideal." Truman, by executive order, desegregated the military and prohibited discrimination in federal employment.

Truman's actions alarmed fraternities. In 1946, L. G. Balfour, a Sigma Chi member from Kentucky who ran a business selling fraternity pins and rings, distributed a bulletin about the threat of integration. He called it an assault on democracy. In his view, it resulted from the jealousy of "the unadjusted and the frustrated." The statement quoted an unnamed judge and fraternity supporter who questioned "the theory that all races and religions should associate and intermarry" and "the old outmoded Russian theory of Communism that all must be reduced to the social level of the lowest." Fraternities at the universities of Alabama, Mississippi, and North Carolina incorporated racially tinged themes into their symbols and parties, according to the historian Anthony James. Confederate flags flew over chapter houses at the Kappa Alpha Order, Kappa Sigma, SAE, and Phi Delta Theta fraternities. Parties with minstrel shows and blackface proliferated. SAE at the University of Georgia chapter started holding a Magnolia Ball, where the "clock was turned back 100 years" to the days of "stately Southern gentlemen with long plantation coats and top hats." From 1945 to 1963, the fraternity section of the University of Alabama yearbook had thirteen Confederate-themed photographs, James found. Entries featured captions such as "The South Shall Rise Again" or "The Klan in their afternoon formals." In 1947, members of SAE at the University of Oklahoma performed in blackface at a Christmas party. When I was at the University of Oklahoma, I found a 1949–1950 SAE scrapbook that featured a photo from an "International Ball" showing "Walter K and his Southern girl." Both wore blackface. Walter looked like a hobo, wearing a top hat and vest with no shirt. His date had bones in her short hair and a nostril ring.

Outside the South, colleges pressured fraternities to integrate, pitting Greek alumni against more open-minded students. In 1946, Amherst College in Massachusetts decided that no fraternity could operate on campus if it restricted membership based on race, religion, or ethnicity, as the historian Nicholas Syrett recounts. Two years later, the school's Phi Kappa Psi chapter pledged a black freshman. Its national headquarters revoked the chapter's charter. Phi Sigma Kappa took the same step when its Boston University chapter pledged an African American. The University of Connecticut, in 1949, and the State University of New York system, in 1953, both told fraternities they had to eliminate discriminatory practices. Many fraternities, like SAE, dropped discriminatory language while continuing to keep blacks and Jews out of their chapters.

During the civil-rights era, conflicts intensified between colleges and fraternities, as well as between students and alumni. In 1962, Williams College announced a ban on fraternities, saying they were interfering with its academic and social mission. After the passage of the federal Civil Rights Act of 1964, fraternities faced pressure to desegregate or shut down. When national fraternities refused, some chapters broke away to form separate local organizations that could offer membership bids to any student. Sigma Chi's Stanford University chapter won praise from the college when it sent two members on the dangerous "Freedom Summer" civil rights rides to Mississippi in 1964. The next year, Sigma Chi's national headquarters suspended the organization when it pledged a black student. Still, some members of SAE played high-profile roles in defense of civil rights. Ivan Allen Jr., mayor of Atlanta for much of the 1960s, worked with Martin Luther King Jr. to fight segregation and testified in favor of President John F. Kennedy's civil-rights legislation. Edward Breathitt Jr., the governor of Kentucky, then led the state to pass antidiscrimination laws considered stronger than those in Washington.

As higher education began to embrace diversity, Harvard, Yale, and Princeton dropped Jewish quotas and instituted affirmative-action programs to enroll blacks and other minorities. Fraternities headed in the other direction; rather than adopt the spirit of the civil-rights movement, they fought against it. Often, they relied on a particularly effective way to preserve the white brotherhood: the requirement of a unanimous, secret vote approving new members. Under the time-honored blackball system, brothers would pass around a box into which they would deposit balls that were typically the size of marbles. A white ball represented approval of a pledge and a black ball, rejection. A single, prejudiced member could "blackball" a Jewish or black pledge, no questions asked.

In 1966, Daniel Sheehan, a white student who was social chairman at SAE's Harvard chapter, nominated as a member Tommy Davis, who was African American. "He was the first black man ever to receive a nomination for membership in SAE in the entire history of that old, traditional Southern fraternity," Sheehan, who became a civil-rights lawyer, wrote in a 2013 book. Davis was blackballed. "I stood up and announced that I was going to blackball every single other nominee until whoever had thrown the black balls against Tommy Davis fessed up and gave us their reasons." Sheehan blackballed the next ten nominees, until one member, from Cleveland, said he had heard Davis dated white women: "If he were to show up at one of our SAE social gatherings with a white date, why, I just don't know what I would do."

"He's on the dean's list. And he is one of the nicest guys I've ever met at Harvard," Sheehan recalled saying in reply. "And, besides, I understand that he presses twice his weight in the varsity weight room. So exactly what *would* you do if he came to one of our social functions with a white date?"

Sheehan said the room was silent, and he suggested the member could just leave the party if Davis showed up with a white date. The blackballing continued, until Sheehan said he wouldn't approve any new brothers as long as he was a voting member of SAE. Davis won a bid. But when Sheehan explained how it had happened, Davis declined. "I knew he wanted to join our fraternity, but he wouldn't under those circumstances," Sheehan said.

SIGMA ALPHA EPSILON held its June 1969 convention in San Francisco, the capital of the counterculture. Yet the music the members danced to at the Palace Hotel, known for hosting presidents and debutantes in its luxurious Beaux Arts decor, wasn't Janis Joplin or Jimi Hendrix. Suggesting little had changed since the 1950s, members and their guests enjoyed the twelve-piece band of Ray Hackett, the music director for the 1960 Republican national convention. Once again, the business of the meeting was discrimination and how to preserve it. At least a dozen colleges had indicated they couldn't allow chapters on their campuses whose national organizations required unanimous approval of every pledge because they understood how the black-balling system excluded African American members.

Steve Walker, a consultant to the national SAE office, had toured seventy-two chapters, from Florida State University (FSU) to the University of Maine. He had concluded that fraternities would be expelled from campus if they continued to require unanimous approval of pledges. SAE had faced a similar threat in 1951 because of the "Aryan" clause in its national laws. At the convention, conservative alumni wanted to stick with the tradition of the blackball. They argued that they had a constitutional right to choose members however they liked, federal law notwithstanding. Richard Generelly, a Washington lawyer, called abandoning the blackball a "suicidal experiment" and an "inexcusable surrender of the freedom of association guaranteed our fraternity under the First Amendment." An internal SAE survey showed that undergraduates were split. About half favored preserving the blackball. Forty percent said a black brother would hurt their chapter, and more than half said they wouldn't welcome a black student who was already an SAE member transferring from another campus.

Walker wanted to save SAE chapters in the North and West. Echoing his forerunners at the 1951 convention, he drew on his impeccable Southern credentials to convince the skeptical crowd. As an alumnus of the University of Alabama, he belonged to the "mother," or first, chapter. Walker had established his conservative bona fides when he fought against Students for a Democratic Society, activists who opposed the Vietnam War, supported racial justice, and viewed fraternities as part of an unfair American social system. "I am certainly no left-wing radical," Walker told members of the convention.

To win over fellow Southerners, Walker summoned the same argument that prevailed in 1951. He suggested a way to eliminate the language about the blackball without changing the practice itself. It would all hinge on the words *at least*. The national laws would require *at least* a majority vote, but chapters would have the authority to set a stricter standard, including a unanimous vote. The law would specify that "the election of pledges shall be the sole prerogative of the individual chapters." Again, it was public relations and semantics. When a college president asked if SAE required a unanimous vote, the national office could say, truthfully, that it mandated merely a majority. The rest was up to students. Walker offered powerful evidence that the status quo would remain. He invoked the 1951 decision to eliminate the discriminatory clause, which he said had no effect on the fraternity's membership practices. "There were many, many people throughout the fraternity . . . who threw (their) arms up in despair and said, 'If we pass this law there is going to be a great influx of black members,'" Walker said. "I submit to you that simply hasn't happened."

The motion passed, and the next year an SAE field report showed that the lawyerly language had done its job. In April 1970, Thomas M. Rigdon, president of SAE's University of Missouri chapter, described a fraternity in ascendance. He chronicled a string of victories: a successful rush; improving grades; a van for blood donations; a Christmas party for a school for the deaf; victories in football, golf, and swimming; eight men on the varsity basketball team; writers for the school newspaper; students in the campus branch of the US Army's Reserve

Officers' Training Corps; and class officers. One piece of news would have especially interested alumni at the San Francisco convention. A black student had tried to join the chapter. Rigdon offered a window into the deliberations:

> Thoughtful conflict arose over the bidding of a Negro during this rush week with the 100 percent rule being severely criticized by some. The Negro was not bid, and the 100 percent rule withstood. Emotions were stirred by both issues. During the heat of debate, I was touched by the deepest feeling felt in fraternity life as I observed young men debating complex issues in a tolerant, thoughtful manner. Everyone in the chapter gained from this experience.

The "100 percent rule"—namely, the blackball—had worked just as the convention had hoped it would. Still, Rigdon felt sure the times were changing: "I predict that within two or three years the 100 percent rule will fall, and, in the future, if a qualified man enters rush, no matter what his color, he will be pledged."

Rigdon's prediction proved optimistic, though even the unspoken prohibition on black and Jewish members gradually disappeared, in most chapters, over the next few decades. SAE doesn't have records detailing the first members to break those barriers. Whereas Jews would rise to occupy even the highest levels of SAE national leadership, blacks faced tougher barriers, as well as conflicted emotions when they did gain acceptance.

W. Ahmad Salih, an African American who graduated from MIT in 1972, joined SAE, though only briefly. In a collection of oral histories of black MIT students, Salih said he knew of another black student, a senior, who also belonged to the fraternity. Salih grew up in Chicago, the child of poor, uneducated parents who had emigrated from the South. He chose the chapter because its members were known as serious students and athletes. But soon after he read the *Autobiography of Malcolm X* and a book on lynching, he changed his mind. "That book got me so upset at white people in general that I started losing weight," he said. "I couldn't eat and I couldn't live in the fraternity anymore." The robes and hoods in SAE's initiation reminded him of the Ku Klux Klan. Even though he was already a brother, he decided to quit. "I mean we didn't have a burning cross, but the image was painful," said Salih, who became an emergency-room physician in California.

America's racial history haunted these SAE members, white and black. Their recollections illustrated the tug-of-war between progress and resistance in the fraternity movement. To understand this dynamic more fully, I decided to travel to the University of Alabama, where SAE's story began.

7

OLD ROW

"Who Does Not Make the Poor Man Conscious of His Poverty . . . or Any Man of His Inferiority"

Sigma Alpha Epsilon's mansion at the University of Alabama looks more like a Southern plantation house than a frat. Two gilded lions, their heads resting languidly on giant paws, flank an entrance framed by towering white Corinthian columns. SAE's oldest chapter holds a privileged place among the Neoclassical buildings that form the grandest fraternity row in America. In the taxonomy of Greek life in Alabama, SAE is "Old Row." These organizations, which have the longest histories on campus, dominate the social food chain. Some "New Row" chapters may have bigger and more modern houses, but they don't have the prestige, the deepest ties to tradition and power. Like other Old Row fraternities, SAE selects many of its members from the state's most prominent and blue-blooded families, whose sons have presided over the South since the nineteenth century.

I came here to meet one of those sons, Benjamin Carter Goodwyn, the twenty-one-year-old president of the Alabama SAE chapter. The Goodwyns can trace their lineage to John Tyler, a Virginian and states'-rights advocate who became the tenth US president in 1841. On a warm October afternoon in 2015, Carter Goodwyn waited for me on the front steps in shorts and sandals and a backpack by his side. With his mop of red hair and light stubble on his chin, he hardly looked like the leader, or "Eminent Archon," of one of the most powerful organizations on campus. But Goodwyn had every reason to feel at home. Both his great-grandfather and grandfather served as chapter presidents. His father, the chapter's house manager, met his mother, an Alpha Gamma sorority girl, on Old Row. Her father and grandfather also belonged to SAE. Goodwyn has three SAE uncles, too. In the fraternity world, Carter Goodwyn qualifies as aristocracy—he is the ultimate fraternity "legacy," or child of an alumnus, with a diamond-shaped Eminent Archon badge carved with the initials of his ancestors. As he settled into an oversized leather couch in the chapter-house living room, he told me, "I'm big on family tradition."

Goodwyn showed me a weathered fraternity album and pointed to the generations of relatives who paved the path before him. Here was George Thomas Goodwyn, Carter's grandfather, who teamed up with a pledge brother in 1947 to found one of the Southeast's largest engineering and architecture firms. Both civil engineers, they built hotels, hospitals, schools, dormitories, and sports centers from Selma to Charleston to Oklahoma City. He flipped the page, and there was Carter's father, George Thomas Jr. He also went into business with a pledge brother. Together, they formed the Goodwyn Building Company, which develops residential subdivisions of affordable homes with names such as Cotton Lakes. Goodwyn, who is earning a joint engineering-MBA degree, stood ready to take his place among those builders. In every way, Goodwyn's family, friends, and business relationships are so tightly intertwined with SAE's first chapter that they form a kind of rope extended from one generation to the next.

These family connections open doors on Old Row. Like football coaches scouting for prospects, fraternities start recruiting in high school. Chapters have feeder schools, and alumni lobby for their children long before less privileged freshmen figure out the best route to the dining hall. The most likely candidates come from affluent enclaves in Birmingham, Mobile, and Montgomery.

SAE has long favored Goodwyn's private school, Montgomery Academy, founded in 1959 by white families fleeing public schools after the US Supreme Court mandated desegregation in its landmark *Brown v. Board of Education* decision. Seven percent of the students at the onetime "segregation academy" were now black, 15 percent members of minority groups, but its hometown still revels in its traditional ways. Each spring at the Montgomery Country Club, the Southern Debutante Cotillion introduces sorority sisters wearing white ball gowns and long white gloves. Goodwyn escorted his girlfriend, an Alabama Tri-Delt, or member of the Delta Delta Delta sorority.

Of course, not all SAE members are legacies, or even from Alabama. Still, it helps to have a connection. Goodwyn introduced me to Holden Naff, a twenty-year-old junior who was expected to succeed him as president. Naff graduated from Birmingham's Mountain Brook High, a public school that is also a feeder into Old Row. Naff, who planned to go to medical school, wasn't an SAE legacy. His father belonged to Delta Kappa Epsilon at Tulane University, and his grandfather was also a DKE at Alabama. But his father's boss, a prominent Birmingham money manager, was a member of SAE at Alabama. It also helped that Naff played competitive golf in high school. "Where I'm from, where you go is centered on the fraternities," Naff told me. "A lot of golfers come to this house from Birmingham."

With the right calling card, membership confers social entrée, especially to mixers that are called "swaps" at Alabama. Swaps offer up hundreds of sorority women, selected in no small part because of their attractiveness to fraternity men. (A former Alpha Omicron Pi sister told me her sorority rated prospects' looks from one, which meant too unattractive to join, to four, "drop-dead gorgeous" and a shoo-in.) SAE holds its swaps at an annex called the Band Room. At 10:00 p.m. on a Thursday night that fall, the men had transformed the cavernous space into a nightclub pounding with pop music. Young women in short dresses and stilettos arrived in SUVs so packed that some of them tumbled out of tailgates before heading to the party. SAE's signature event is the "Stockholders Ball," one of the hottest tickets on campus. The extravaganza costs $20,000, and brothers must pay a "special assessment" of $250 apiece. During a week each spring, hundreds of people attend parties Thursday through Saturday, when the event culminates in a black-tie gala flowing with champagne and featuring an ice sculpture shaped like an SAE lion.

Old Row offers the amenities of a private men's club, yet its dues and room-and-board fees can be competitive with the $13,000 estimated cost of living on campus with a meal plan. It helps that the university subsidizes fraternities. SAE's house sits on public land, and the fraternity has a $1-a-year, 150-year lease. The chapter employs a staff of seven, including cooks and housekeepers, all supervised by Cindy Patton, the "house mom." She is an ardent booster of Alabama Crimson Tide football: she wore crimson earrings that are replicas of its elephant mascot, crimson nail polish, and a crimson belt and ballet flats. A cook known as "Miss Angie" prepares such Southern favorites as macaroni and cheese, collard greens, corn bread, fried chicken, and catfish. For "guy" time, the men retired to a poolroom featuring a big-screen television that might not look out of place in a multiplex.

Beyond all the perks, the top fraternities wield power. The Old Row Greek organizations formed a secretive voting bloc, Theta Nu Epsilon, a kind of uber-fraternity known universally as the "Machine." This cabal traced its birth to 1870, when Theta Nu Epsilon broke away from Yale's Skull and Bones secret society. It spread nationwide before it reportedly died out except in Alabama, where it has dominated student government for generations, and SAE is a charter member. When I asked Goodwyn the name of the fraternity's Machine representative, he laughed and looked away. "I don't know," he said, then added, "The Machine doesn't exist." Goodwyn's response was not surprising. It is said that members are fined for acknowledging the Machine's existence.

Those with the Machine's backing nearly always win the student-government presidency. In the last six years alone, two members of SAE, Hamilton Bloom and R. B. Walker, won the presidency. Like Goodwyn, both were graduates of Montgomery Academy. Bloom, son of one of Alabama's top lobbyists, was known on campus for his seersucker suits, bow ties, and impressive collection of fashionable socks. He now works in Washington for Richard Shelby, the powerful Republican senator from Alabama. Shelby is said to have been a Machine president as a Delta Chi at Alabama in the 1950s. Walker, a former lobbyist for Alabama Power Company, became director of government relations for the University of Alabama system. Goodwyn, who was a student-government senator, drew inspiration from their success. "I've gotten the kind of leadership experience that I can't get anywhere else," he told me. "SAE is a good stepping-stone if you want to go into politics."

Secrecy heightens SAE's appeal and power. When I visited, members had sequestered themselves in their chapter room to learn about fraternity rituals. As a nonmember, of course, I couldn't attend that meeting, but later I took a tour of one of SAE's most sacred spaces. DeVotie Memorial Hall is named after founder Noble Leslie DeVotie and was decorated in SAE colors of purple and gold. Gold chandeliers hung from the high ceiling and deep purple drapes framed the floor-to-ceiling windows, while purple candles in gold sconces gave the room an air of luxury. One wall displayed a fraying brown manuscript, the original chapter minutes from 1856. Nearby, gold-framed portraits of DeVotie and seven other severe-looking founders seemed to look down disapprovingly at the ease and informality of a younger generation. One founder, the bearded John Barratt Rudulph, wore a double-breasted Confederate uniform. Outside this shrine, the rest of the house gave you the eerie feeling of being watched. In room after room on the main floor, the photos of hundreds of young men in coats and ties hung on the walls. In the 1930s, the brothers wore their hair slicked back like matinee idols. In the 1970s, a few sported long hair and striped blazers with wide lapels and ties. In more recent years, short, neat hair and jackets with cleaner lines evoked a timeless preppie style.

The unspoken truth of this world was clear. This was a white fraternity. One hundred and fifty years after the end of the Civil War, sixty-four years after SAE dropped the discrimination clause from its laws, seven years after the election of the first African American president of the United States, the founding chapter of Sigma Alpha Epsilon had never had a black member.

On that late afternoon, one African American man made his way through the halls. In SAE's lexicon, he was known as the "butler," but he was really a custodian. He mopped the hardwood floors, then buffed them until they gleamed so brightly he could see his own reflection.

SAE's FOUNDING CHAPTER reflects the social barriers that keep minority and low-income students out of historically white fraternities. Their recruiting practices, opaque and favoring insiders and legacies, all but guarantee a candidate pool dominated by white students. Even if a black student were welcomed into an old-line fraternity house as a candidate, he would have trouble seeing himself inside walls covered with portraits of white students and Confederate soldiers. The flare-ups of overtly racist episodes, such as the Oklahoma video, have further discouraged minorities from joining. For lower-income students, both white and minority, the cost can be prohibitive; an environment of assumed affluence—of $250 "special assessments" for a party—has repelled students from modest backgrounds. An Alabama political science professor described this system, with its unspoken rules and assumptions, as textbook "institutional racism," the kind that may not always be intentional but can be just as hard to overcome.

These barriers reveal themselves most clearly in the South. At the time I visited Alabama, I was told its SAE house was among several Southern chapters without black members. Like Oklahoma, the region includes some of the largest SAE chapters in the country, and their recruitment focused on legacies. Clark Brown, an SAE member who graduated from the University of Arkansas in 2007, told me nearly all his fraternity brothers were legacies who had secured spots when they were in high school. Others had to stand out in some way. Brown wasn't a legacy, but he was a member of the varsity tennis team and a Chancellor scholar, an honor for entering freshmen. At the same time, African American and other minority fraternities pushed hard—and early—for members. "By the time rush comes along, they've already picked the smartest, most accomplished, most athletic guys," said Brown, now general counsel for SAE at its headquarters. "There aren't many left who you'd want to join your fraternity. The stars would have to align perfectly for an African American to join the Arkansas chapter."

After the Oklahoma video became public, SAE hired Ashlee Canty, its first director of diversity and inclusion, who planned to visit campuses such as the University of Mississippi to encourage them to welcome minority students. Canty is African American and, amid the controversy about SAE, at first resisted taking the job. Her friends questioned her judgment. "I didn't know if this was a public relations move or a legitimate position that will have some clout in the fraternity," she told me. She came to view the fraternity as committed and sincere. She also had an abiding belief in the virtue of Greek life. As an undergraduate at North Carolina State University, she joined the historically African American Zeta Phi Beta sorority, as had her mother before her, and worked as a graduate assistant in the Department of Fraternity and Sorority Life. Growing up in Winston-Salem, North Carolina, she never considered joining a historically white fraternity because her mother's sorority experience inspired her.

Canty considered the racial divisions of Greek life a matter of self-selection. "At the core of it, SAE is a historically white fraternity," she said. "They are always going to be majority white. People want to join with people they connect with—and the first thing they connect with is 'people who look like me.'" Canty said fraternity chapters reflect a college's culture as much as the national organization's. SAE leaders said they won't institute the kind of admissions policies that universities rely on to increase diversity, namely, racial preferences. Fraternity leaders criticize that approach as amounting to "quotas." Although controversial, such "affirmative action" plans have repeatedly been upheld by the US Supreme Court as serving a compelling national interest. I asked her if she would track each chapter's racial composition to encourage less diverse houses to reach out to minorities. "I don't want it to get to the point of counting brown faces," she replied.

When black students choose African American fraternities, they often lose out on the amenities and career networks taken for granted at historically white organizations. This inequality extends well beyond the South. For a study published in 2012, the sociologists Rashawn Ray and Jason Rosow spent nine months observing and interviewing fifty-two members of historically white and black fraternities at Indiana University. Even in the Midwest, they found unfairness reminiscent of the Jim Crow era. White students held private parties in their palatial chapters. Black fraternities had no houses, and African American men were excluded from parties at historically white fraternities because they were open only to members or recruits. Class played an explicit role, too. Men in white fraternities placed socioeconomic barriers to admission. One of the top chapters asked for parents' income on its membership application. Members cultivated an aura of privilege, bragging of their chapters' wealth and influence. As one member said, "There are kids in our house worth $400 million."

In 2015, the Indiana University Faculty Senate, which had been troubled by such divisions, received a rare glimpse of Greek demography. The professors asked the Student Affairs Division to poll its chapters. Through a public-records request, I obtained a summary. On a campus where 20 percent of US students were members of minority groups, several big chapters reported a minority membership of less than 5 percent. Others, including SAE, were more diverse. One-sixth of SAE's roughly 110 members were minorities. The university didn't collect data about subgroups of minorities. Andrew Cowie, SAE's Indiana University president, told me the chapter had three black members. Cowie said his house took pride in its diversity and marched with an African American fraternity after the Oklahoma video surfaced. Steve Veldkamp, the university's director of student life and learning, said the survey's results surprised him because all fraternities of any significant size had minority membership. "There was more than tokenism," Veldkamp said. "This isn't 1950. We're headed in the right direction."

Veldkamp, like many administrators who oversee Greek life, is a true believer in fraternities and sororities. From his office at the Indiana University Student Union, he also directs the Center for Fraternity and Sorority Research, a nonprofit funded in part by Greek organizations. Veldkamp, tall and lean with a neatly trimmed beard flecked with gray, comes from a white, working-class background. He grew up in Flint, Michigan, and his father worked construction and drove trucks. As a first-generation college student at Grand Valley State University, he joined the Sigma Phi Epsilon fraternity, which he credits with teaching him leadership and social skills. "It was the ideal fraternity experience," he told me. Still, others on campus hardly see fraternities as a haven for the working class. In contributing to the school's strategic plan, a group of thirty-three Indiana students, faculty, and alumni issued a 2016 report that found, for all its philanthropy and leadership, Greek life contributed to an "elitist social hierarchy" that is "replicated in recruitment and social opportunities."

Campus geography reinforces the inferior circumstances of non-white students in Greek life. Indiana University's main fraternity row sits on a ridge above the campus—a visual reminder of its privileged position. In the 1950s, the university gave fraternities and sororities twenty acres of prime real estate, land that then president Herman B. Wells, a member of Sigma Nu, called "admirably suited to give large houses a dignified setting." The university also backed loans for financing new houses and for expansions and renovations that feature imposing stone entrances, Tudor-style gables, manicured hedges, and porches with swings.

A few blocks away on a fall afternoon, an Indiana University junior named Frank Bonner, the son of a middle-school math teacher, worked the front desk at a dorm to earn money to help pay for college. Bonner was president of Iota Phi Theta, an African American fraternity that has no chapter house. Like many black students who join African American fraternities, he was drawn to their legacy of providing a haven for students shunned by white Greek-letter organizations. Rather than Confederate soldiers, their alumni have included W. E. B. DuBois, Thurgood Marshall, and Martin Luther King Jr., who all belonged to Alpha Phi Alpha. "You have a history of black organizations advancing equality and social justice," Bonner told me. Once, as a freshman, Bonner tried to go with friends to what he called the "mansion house" of a historically white fraternity. "We didn't know anyone, so we couldn't get in," he said. He hadn't been to a "mansion house" party since. Bonner, who was also president of the organization representing black fraternities and sororities, said his members aren't pushing for houses of their own. It would be hard to pay for them; his fraternity charged an initiation fee of $700 and $125 in annual dues. Bonner said he would rather push for economic and academic help that would benefit all minority students, not just those in Greek organizations. "In the grand scheme of things, trying to cause an uproar to have a mansion house doesn't make sense," he said. "There are other battles."

Greek organizations at Indiana and other big public universities may not have a formal fraternity "Machine" that dominates elections, but they still tend to exert a powerful influence on campus politics. At the University of Texas in 2013, fraternity and sorority members made up 15 percent of students but 45 percent of those elected to the Student Government Assembly. Suchi Sundaram, a columnist for the *Daily Texan*, the student newspaper, criticized the result of this imbalance: a succession of white fraternity men as presidents. "The Greeks have ultimately created a dynasty out of a democracy," she wrote.

After college, these student-government positions burnish résumés and form networks propelling students into successful careers in politics and business. Lauren Rivera, an associate professor at Northwestern University's Kellogg School of Management, determined that bankers prefer fraternity heads to candidates with better grades. "People like people who are like themselves," Rivera, who interviewed 120 professionals involved in hiring graduates for banking, law, and consulting jobs, told *Bloomberg News*. A 2001 study of seniors at Dartmouth found that those who networked with fraternity and sorority members and alumni were more likely to get higher-paying jobs, especially in investment banking or Wall Street sales or trading. In 2013, Dartmouth's Alpha Delta fraternity received an e-mail from an alumnus working at a unit of Wells Fargo and Company, the largest US mortgage lender. Its San Francisco office had hired Alpha Deltas for four straight years. If they mailed résumés to a fraternity brother, the e-mail said, it would go to the top of the pile. That year, Conor Hails, the twenty-year-old head of the University of Pennsylvania's Sigma Chi chapter, recalled exchanging a secret handshake with an executive at a recruiting reception for banking giant Barclays PLC. "We exchanged a grip, and he said, 'Every Sigma Chi gets a business card.'" Hails recalled in the same *Bloomberg* article, "We're trying to create Sigma Chi on Wall Street, a little fraternity on Wall Street."

AT THE UNIVERSITY of Alabama, the administration explicitly embraces two conflicting goals: promoting diversity and Greek life. To attract out-of-state students, including top scholars, the college has been distancing itself from its racial past. In 1963, a few blocks from the university's fraternity row, Governor George Wallace made the "stand in the schoolhouse door," his infamous failed effort to keep black students out of the college. When I visited, African Americans made up 12 percent of undergraduates, less than half the percentage in the state, though similar to the US average. In 2016, President Stuart Bell called "an accepting and inclusive community that attracts and supports a diverse faculty, staff and student body" one of four pillars of a new strategic plan. At the same time, Alabama takes pride in holding "the coveted honor of being the largest fraternity and sorority community in the country." More than 11,000 students, or 36 percent of undergraduates, belong to Greek organizations. The school endorses—and financially backs—a system that benefits rich, white students and largely excludes blacks. Over the last decade, in a kind of Greek arms race, fraternities and sororities have spent more than $200 million to build or expand thirty mansions, each one larger and grander than the last. The university has leased its own public land for as little as $1 a year. To finance the houses, the college sells bonds, which let Greek organizations borrow more cheaply because the public is assuming the financial risk of default. Chapter members and alumni, who pay off the debt, then own the mansions, which have cost as much as $13 million for a single building.

This public support of a racially divided Greek system has long infuriated campus critics, including the editors of the *Crimson White*, the student paper. In the 1990s, Pat Hermann, a white English professor, accused the school of subsidizing segregation. "I am very, very tired of apologists for apartheid," he said. In 2011, amid renewed calls for integration, then president Robert E. Witt drew a rebuke from the *Crimson White* for words that seemed a defense of segregation: "It is appropriate that all our sororities and fraternities—traditionally African American, traditionally white and multicultural—determine their membership," said Witt, who became chancellor of the University of Alabama system.

In 2013, public outcry finally sparked change. That year, undergraduate sorority members wanted to offer bids to two accomplished African American students, including the step-granddaughter of a University of Alabama trustee. Their alumni advisers blocked their admission. In previous years, black women tended to be eliminated in the early rounds of deliberations. That year, they progressed further, sparking intense debate, according to Yardena Wolf, then a member of the historically white Alpha Omicron Pi. "Girls were saying there would be so much media coverage, and boys won't swap with us anymore," Wolf told me. "I thought, 'What the hell? This is 2013.'" Students from outside Alabama no longer took racial attitudes for granted. Wolf was Jewish and, though she was born in Tuscaloosa, grew up in Oregon. Pressure mounted. The *Crimson White* ran a story about the black women's rejection. Wolf and other white sorority women marched in protest. Their efforts provoked a national media firestorm. Breaking with the past, Judy Bonner, the university's first female president, insisted that the sororities integrate. By fall 2015, most of the historically white sororities included from one to three black members. It was hardly representative of the campus, considering some chapters had more than four hundred members, but it was progress.

Out of the media spotlight, however, fraternities remained stubbornly segregated. Kathleen Cramer, who retired in 2012 as senior associate vice president for student affairs after thirty-six years at the university, said sororities changed because undergraduate women pushed for diversity. "The same thing would have to come from the fraternities," she told me. "It's definitely been slower to happen." In the fall of 2015, twenty-five of thirty-one historically white fraternities—including all the Old Row chapters—had no black members, according to internal university documents I obtained. Along with SAE, they included some of the largest chapters on campus, such as Delta Kappa Epsilon, Sigma Nu, Kappa Alpha, and Phi Gamma Delta, each of which had more than 120 members. "Even in the age of Obama, it may be easier for a black man to sit in the White House than in a University of Alabama fraternity house," wrote Lawrence Ross in a 2015 book on race at American college campuses. In 2016, without fanfare, Phi Gamma Delta, an Old Row stalwart, became one of six additional fraternities initiating black members, doubling the number from the year before, a faculty senate report found. In an e-mail, Monica Greppin Watts, a university spokeswoman, pointed out that the school now requires non-discrimination clauses in student-group constitutions, as well as diversity training. She noted that, in 2016, three African-American women became presidents of traditionally white sororities.

Despite these changes, newcomers often viewed Alabama's social life as straight out of the 1950s. "I was horrified when I came here," said Amanda Bennett, an African American senior who grew up in Atlanta. "It's completely segregated." Longtime observers saw progress, though halting and slow. Norman Baldwin, a University of Alabama political science professor, blamed institutional roadblocks more than overt racism. Baldwin, who is white, had been fighting Greek segregation for fifteen years. In his classes, he surveyed racial attitudes and documented increasing tolerance. For example, in 2012, three-fourths of students said they would marry a person of another race, up from one-half in 1999. Baldwin, who co-chaired a faculty committee on diversity, said any reform must include a requirement that the Machine emerge from the shadows. In his view, the officers should be made public, so it can be held accountable for practices that limit opportunities for minorities. "We now have what I call institutional barriers," Baldwin said. "We have institutional racism."

Most of all, in Baldwin's view, fraternities must change their recruiting. As a first step, he recommended shifting to the approach long favored by Alabama's traditionally white sororities. It was known as formal recruitment and was conducted as follows. In August, sororities all held a week of scheduled events before making their bids. This increases the chance that a newcomer would consider joining. It also made it obvious when all the black women received no bids, or offers of membership. By contrast, the historically white fraternities used "informal" recruitment. By and large, they selected members and extended bids in the spring and summer before classes even began. This practice disadvantaged outsiders, especially black students. In addition, white and minority fraternities held separate recruitment drives, which encouraged racial sorting. Baldwin proposed instituting a unified recruitment program. In that way, black students would be more likely to consider historically white Greek groups, and vice versa. The university has adopted many recommendations from Baldwin and other members of its faculty senate: the school outlawed "social boycotts" of campus organizations that accept black students; ordered the tracking of the racial and ethnic composition of fraternities and sororities; required new house construction to include plans to promote diversity; and ordered Greek organizations to "neutralize the effects of legacy preference" on minority recruits.

I WITNESSED THE conflict between the school's racial history and its desire for progress when I visited the University of Alabama's Ferguson Student Center. After a recent $45 million renovation, it had all the amenities of a twenty-first-century hub of campus life: a food court with Wendy's and Subway, a theater, and a space for "sustainable service and volunteerism." The gleaming campus hub acknowledges, in a small way, the school's racial history. Visitors encounter a portrait of a bespectacled Birmingham school teacher named Autherine Lucy. In the 1950s, Lucy fought a three-year court battle to become the first African American to enroll at the University of Alabama. Because of mob violence, she lasted only three days as a graduate student. The school expelled her "for her own safety." Only in 1988 did the university's board overturn her expulsion, and she finally received her master's degree four years later. Lucy's story represents the sluggishness of change at Alabama.

Most students here know about Lucy, but few could tell you much about the center's namesake, Hill Ferguson. At the dawn of the twentieth century, he was a Big Man on Campus, a fraternity brother at Sigma Nu, a Phi Beta Kappa, and quarterback of the football team. Ferguson was a Birmingham insurance executive who served for forty years on the Board of Trustees before stepping down in 1959. He has been described as "Alabama's most loyal alumnus." He was also a die-hard segregationist. As a trustee, he fought against Lucy's enrollment, going so far as to hire a private investigator to dig up dirt on her and another black student. In the words of the Southern historian E. Culpepper Clark, Ferguson "never gave up his quest to 'keep 'Bama White.'" The university makes no mention of a head-spinning irony: Lucy's portrait hung in a student center that honored a fraternity man who fought to keep her off the campus.

On the Ferguson Center's second floor, I met Elliot Spillers, president of the Student Government Association. He left his office and headed for lunch at the food court. In his plaid shirt and khakis, Spillers had the easygoing charm of a natural politician. He also inherited a sense of discipline and government service from his family. He was a US Air Force brat who had lived in Turkey and Germany and all over the United

States before settling in Alabama. Both his parents were officers: his father, a lieutenant colonel and congressional liaison to the Pentagon; his mother, a nurse who had advanced to major. When we spoke, his younger brother, a high school junior, was considering playing football at the US Naval Academy. Spillers envisioned his next step as a Fulbright scholarship abroad, law school, and work in the State Department. He would seem a natural choice as student body president, but he wasn't, because he was black. In 2015, Spillers became the first African American student-government president in almost forty years. "What drew me was the opportunity to make a difference," Spillers told me. "I wanted a challenge."

That challenge required Spillers to confront the most powerful force in Alabama student life, the Greek establishment's Machine. Not coincidentally, his achievement represented twin firsts. He was the first African American to become president in four decades, as well as the first candidate to win without Machine backing since the mid-1980s. Even his triumph highlighted the barriers posed by Greek life.

In 1976, when a black student named Cleo Thomas matched his achievement and won the presidency, men in white sheets burned crosses. Spillers was aware of this history and figured his candidacy would be a struggle. He didn't belong to a fraternity but knew he had to court the Greek community. He had support from Alpha Tau Omega, a New Row fraternity with four black members in the fall of 2015. The fraternity hung an Elliot Spillers banner across the front of its house. One night, it was mysteriously removed, an act of vandalism many on campus attributed to the Machine, which has long been known for electioneering and dirty tricks. Even though the Machine opposed him, Spillers had plenty of friends in Greek life. He was part of a historic power couple. His girlfriend, Halle Lindsay, was one of the African American women who integrated Alpha Gamma

Delta, an Old Row sorority. He attended fraternity and sorority parties and referred to members as "my Greek friends."

I pointed out that the Student Government Association and the Office of Fraternity and Sorority Life face each other across a hall, as if they were two branches of a bicameral government. "The location is no accident," Spillers said. "Alabama isn't subtle. Student government is Greek life, and Greek life is student government."

Spillers gave plenty of credit to the sorority women who stood up to alumni who wanted to continue excluding African Americans. He also praised then president Bonner, who risked the wrath of donors by forcing integration. "She was so brave," Spillers said. "I respect her completely." Spillers said the current administration needed to focus more on Old Row fraternities. "It's one of those conversations everyone wants to have but no one wants to have," Spillers said. That afternoon, Spillers was headed to a conference where he was pushing for what he hoped would be a signature achievement of his tenure: a full-time administrator to promote diversity. Spillers would like to see houses for minority fraternities. More broadly, he said, the university should promote social life for independent students. "Where is our money to have a party?" he asked. It will require a wholesale rethinking of campus life. "I'm afraid when I leave, it's going to go back to the way it was," he said. "I'm looking for a more sustainable solution."

Five months after our conversation, the crosscurrents of change and resistance swept the campus. Lillian Roth, a sophomore political science major, won the presidency as Spiller's successor. The founder of her own jewelry business and a former intern for Martha Roby, a Republican Alabama congresswoman, she joined only a handful of other female Student Government Association presidents in the University of Alabama's history. In other ways, she still symbolized the old order.

She was white and a sorority sister at Chi Omega, part of the Machine, which had swept back into power. Like the two former student-government presidents from SAE, she was a graduate of Montgomery Academy. Roth was also a debutante and the daughter of an Alabama Chi Omega. Her father, Toby, had been president of the Theta Chi fraternity at Alabama and later worked as the chief of staff for Bob Riley, the Republican Alabama governor. After her victory, Roth declined to answer a student newspaper reporter's question about the Machine.

FAR FROM PUBLIC view, Old Row fraternities had been taking the first steps toward integration. The year before my visit, Jackson Britton, president of Kappa Alpha Order's chapter, privately pushed to admit a black member. He had been discussing integration with Yardena Wolf, one of the students who had fought to open up sororities. The two belonged to a prestigious campus institute that focused on ethical leadership. Although Britton was politically conservative and Wolf was liberal, they had become friends. Britton's father, who was in Kappa Alpha Order, was a first-generation college student and a descendant of Southern sharecroppers. Britton sympathized with those who found themselves living on the margins. He asked KA members if they would consider circumventing the pledge process entirely and extending a bid to a black student. "No one was opposed," Britton told me. "Members were enthusiastic about the idea." Britton then suggested an African American junior who was friends with almost everyone in his pledge class. The student, whose name he declined to share, had top grades and a record of community service. "Everyone agreed we needed to give him a bid," Britton said. In a decision that was never made public, KA made the offer. Five minutes later, the junior called back. He declined. He told Britton he couldn't afford the cost of more than $7,000 a year in dues.

Wolf, who ended up quitting her sorority, said she was disappointed in her friend. "It was frustrating," she said. "I thought he would do more than he did."

To Britton, the episode illustrated why the entire recruitment system had to change. He described the informal fraternity rush as "governed by a set of unspoken rules" that assured a white membership. The chapter receives about two hundred recommendation letters from alumni, typically legacies, for a pledge class of forty. The fraternity throws three informal rush parties on campus for graduating high school seniors and two more in the summer. Those who live nearby, legacies, and wealthier students are far more likely to attend. The result is predictable. KA skews heavily in-state, drawing many of its members from the small towns that have always been its lifeblood. "If you were to ask people who KA attracts, they would say, small-town Alabama guys, the good old boys," he said. Later, as speaker of the student Senate, Britton co-authored a resolution supporting a "formal" rush open to all students.

Britton said KA had also been toning down its Southern pride. Established in 1865 at what is now Washington and Lee University in Lexington, Virginia, the Kappa Alpha Order calls Confederate general Robert E. Lee its "spiritual founder." KA is known for its signature "Old South" parties where men dress in Confederate uniforms and women in hoop skirts. In 2009, Kappa Alpha had apologized after it paused its "Old South" parade in front of a historically black sorority. A year later, the national organization said members should no longer wear Confederate uniforms because they were "trappings and symbols" that could be "misinterpreted or considered objectionable to the general public." In Alabama, members started wearing gray clothing and caps, so it wasn't clear how much had really changed. Britton said the fraternity then eliminated gray clothing, as well as the "Old South" name for its end-of-the-year party. I asked Britton how many black students would want to join KA as long as it continues to honor Robert E. Lee. Britton replied that KA's reverence for Lee could be divorced from his support for slavery. KA members say they try to live by Lee's definition of a True Gentleman, which is much like SAE's. "The manner in which an individual enjoys certain advantages over others is a test of a true gentlemen," Lee wrote in papers found after his death in 1870. "The Southern values we embrace are really Lee's definition of a true gentleman," Britton said.

At the SAE house, I asked Goodwyn, the chapter president and fourth-generation SAE, why his house had no black members. He considered it a matter of self-selection. Goodwyn said one African American friend picked Alpha Phi Alpha, the historically black organization to which Martin Luther King belonged. "No one is keeping anyone out," Goodwyn said. "People are going to go where they want to go." Still, in his view, the social scene was starting to open up. After my visit, SAE had scheduled a joint philanthropy event to fight pediatric cancer. For the first time, rather than having separate events, this one included white, black, and other minority Greek-letter organizations.

Goodwyn and Benton Hughes, SAE's rush chairman, said they had courted a black student named Justin Woolfolk in 2014. Like Goodwyn and Hughes, Woolfolk attended Montgomery Academy, where he was a tailback on the football team. "He would have been the first black SAE," Goodwyn told me. Later, Woolfolk told me he understood the historic nature of joining the chapter. At Montgomery Academy, one of his teachers, an Alabama graduate, pulled him into his office and told him, "You know what a big deal it is." Woolfolk said he felt welcome when he spent time in the SAE house during his rush visit in high school. "I wasn't treated like a token black person," he said. "They embraced me like I was anyone else." Woolfolk ended up going to Birmingham Southern College instead because he could continue to play football. Without changing recruitment practices, Goodwyn's approach—looking at only a handful of black students from fraternity feeder schools—guarantees any progress will be slow. Still, Goodwyn predicted that one day the chapter will accept a black member. 'It will definitely happen," he said. "It's not a matter of if. It's a matter of who and when."

PART THREE

REBIRTH

8

THE PHOENIX

"Whose Conduct Proceeds from . . .
an Acute Sense of Propriety"

On a cloudless spring afternoon in Newport Beach, California, Bradley Cohen was on his home turf. As T. Boone Pickens, the famed oil tycoon, flew in on his Gulfstream jet, and other guests made their way to the Marriott Hotel and Spa with its stunning views of the Pacific Ocean, Cohen, Sigma Alpha Epsilon's national president, prepared for what he knew would be a contentious 159th annual convention. Cohen was under fire. He had been barnstorming the country to defend an unpopular decision: eliminating a fraternity's most cherished tradition—pledging. Cohen believed the months-long initiation period for new members had become embroiled in horrific abuse. Now, traditionalists had gathered against Cohen. In a move unprecedented in the modern era, they were running a candidate to oppose his vice president and designated successor.

His legacy, not to mention the lives of future undergraduates, hung in the balance.

The SAE men, some in seersucker suits and bow ties, sat outside in the hotel's rose garden, where Cohen had been married twenty-four years before. Inside, on a stage, Cohen interviewed Pickens. In his trademark Oklahoma twang, the eighty-seven-year-old investor recounted his own hazing at Texas A&M and Oklahoma State. The beating with a paddle left his behind red for a week. He derided political correctness and said he was "lucky" his college basketball team had had no black players because it gave him the chance to compete. Pickens spoke of his conservative politics, his worship of Ronald Reagan, and his disdain for Barack Obama.

The mostly white crowd—albeit with more than a few Latino and black members—applauded.

It wasn't exactly the message Cohen hoped to send at the convention, and it certainly wouldn't have played well on most college campuses. But Pickens's star turn represented an important vote of confidence in Cohen's leadership. Pickens had questioned SAE's decision to ban pledging but eventually came to publicly endorse it. Cohen needed all the help he could get in challenging this tradition.

SAE's national president seemed ideally suited to the task: the fifty-two-year-old Cohen was both a fraternity insider and outsider. The son of a champion athlete, he was square-jawed, six foot one, and muscular. A self-made Southern California real-estate entrepreneur, he and his wife, Kim, a former stage actress, had three children, the eldest in high school. Like Pickens, Cohen was a Republican who revered Ronald Reagan. Cohen also reveled in the fraternity's more nostalgic traditions: he once suggested that flowers and sorority serenades could be antidotes to misogyny and sexual assault. "We have to get back to the old ways," he told the men during a seminar on the annual leadership cruise.

Yet Cohen's very presence as the head of this convention in June 2015 was remarkable. He was SAE's first Jewish president. In a fraternity that had long prized its ties to families tracing their roots to the antebellum South, he was also an immigrant, a naturalized American citizen who spoke with an accent. It was the lilting, musical cadence of his native South Africa, where he grew up under the policy of racial separation known as apartheid. When Cohen was a teenager, his family had fled to America because of fears of violence as the regime collapsed. Because of his background, Cohen understood the need to respond to critics who called for more diversity in fraternity chapters after the racist Oklahoma video became public. Still, when asked how he felt being part of a racist organization, he had a stock answer that demonstrated tone-deafness to matters of race: this white native of apartheid South Africa described himself as SAE's first "African American president." Although Cohen supported the hiring of SAE's first full-time diversity director, he, nonetheless, remained true to his conservative bona fides. He opposed any kind of affirmative action. "This organization was not going to enter into an era of quotas," he said.

But Cohen understood—and rejected—SAE's racist and anti-Semitic history. He once brandished a 111-year-old volume of the fraternity's laws so he could tell hundreds of shocked undergraduates about the "Aryan" requirement and the prohibition of members with a parent who was "a full-blooded Jew." He considered himself a case study in the evolution of the fraternity. Now he was offering a vision of an organization that no longer forced young men to drink until they passed out. To illustrate this renewal of purpose, he liked to wear a necktie emblazoned with SAE's cherished symbol.

"We're like the phoenix," he would say. "We're rising from the ashes. It's a new beginning."

Brad Cohen's title, "Eminent Supreme Archon," made him sound like a king ruling by divine right. But, in fact, he headed a volunteer board with little power to rein in the fraternity's alarming behavior. Until the adults in headquarters confronted that reality—and changed it—they were doomed to oversee a never-ending parade of insurance claims, court judgments, injuries, rape allegations, and deaths. To a large degree, fraternities' legal strategy depended on the national fraternity keeping its distance so the organizations could avoid liability. But that strategic distance is not a recent phenomenon. The political structure of most fraternities resembled the United States before the Constitution, when the federal government had little authority. At SAE, each chapter functioned, by and large, autonomously. The national organization could confer a charter—and suspend it. It could offer guidance, but its national staff of thirty-nine was hardly in a position to police 15,000 undergraduates. Most important, any significant decision—any change to fraternity law—was subject to a vote at a national convention, held once every two years. A two-thirds majority had to approve a change. Because only 1 percent of alumni were active volunteers, undergraduates were overrepresented at the convention. Quite simply, the kids were in charge.

The power of adolescents within the organization had doomed SAE's two recent attempts to curb drinking. In 2011 and 2013, SAE's board proposed banning alcohol in chapter houses. Over a decade, that approach had reduced injuries, deaths, and sexual assaults at rival Phi Delta Theta, which required dry houses starting in 2000. Its claims plunged 90 percent, and its per-man liability insurance fee decreased by half, to $80 a year. SAE brothers paid as much as $340.

"If your founders were in this room today considering all the facts and information, what would they do? Would they allow your culture to be defined by alcohol in *Animal House*?" Christopher Lapple, Phi Delta Theta's national president had asked the SAE convention in 2013.

Perhaps they wouldn't. But Chris Smith, president of SAE's Florida State University chapter, would. "FSU is known for being a party school," Smith said. "Kids go there for the social atmosphere, you know. They go there for the football. I mean, the academics is mediocre, I mean, I'll be honest."

Smith said SAE couldn't enforce the policy: "Going dry is just going to force a lot of these chapters to just blatantly lie to the nationals. That's not really going to solve anything." He said eliminating alcohol had eroded Phi Delta Theta's social capital at Florida State.

"The chapter's culture has completely changed," he said. "I mean it's not very often you can literally tell, like, the different pledge classes just by the way they look. I'm not trying to be superficial here, but that's the case. One of the most prestigious chapters at my school has now become a laughingstock."

A brother from a decidedly non-party school agreed: Dylan Moses, president of the chapter at Johns Hopkins University.

"It seems as though their time away from the chapter collegiate and into the bureaucracy that is the SAE national has left them with a deficit of what it means to be an undergraduate brother of SAE and what college life entails," Moses said.

With the bombast of a young man impressed with his own education, not to mention the sound of his own words, Moses called the older men cowards.

"While I'm all in favor of keeping the honor of our fraternity sacred and our virtue safe, I feel that it is a mistake to quiver in the fear that has been shown by this council," Moses said. "Drinking in our houses doesn't seem to be the issue. Rather the issue seems to be drunk brothers doing dumb things, which unfortunately is a commonality amongst most fraternity men, sorority women, and society in general."

Moses treated the virtue and honor of the True Gentleman as an afterthought. He defended the inalienable right to be drunk and stupid.

THAT YEAR, 2013, when Cohen became SAE's president, he began to realize that he would have to challenge the right of adolescents and young adults to wield this kind of power over the fraternity. Otherwise, he feared, it was headed for extinction. To Cohen, this was a frightening and unacceptable prospect. He counted his SAE initiation as among the most moving ceremonies of his life, along with his wedding and the naming of his children. Cohen credited the fraternity for his life's trajectory. He was sixteen and a high school junior when his family immigrated to Phoenix, Arizona. Cohen's father, Desmond Vernon Cohen, a doctor then in his fifties, faced the challenge of establishing an obstetrics and gynecology practice in a new country. He left behind deep ties to his former nation, having twice represented South Africa in the Olympics on the swimming and water polo teams. Wanting to stay close to his family, Cohen enrolled at the University of Arizona at Tucson. As a foreign student—and like many at big public universities—he felt lost. "I hated my freshman year," he told me. "I was lonely. I was in a dormitory. I didn't know where or what anything was."

As a sophomore, when SAE alumni started recruiting to re-establish a chapter, Cohen jumped at the chance to belong to a fraternity. From the beginning, Cohen understood the duality of Greek life. The chapter had been shut down in the late 1970s for hazing. Members had branded pledges' buttocks with "Phi Alpha," the SAE salutation and motto. Once the chapter reopened, Cohen had also been hazed, if gently. He had been required to do menial tasks and was the subject of practical jokes such as being made to sit for an entirely fictional national exam. "It was just silly old pranks from way back when," he said. "But, by today's standards, they wouldn't fly."

In the fledgling chapter, Cohen rose quickly, serving two terms as president. He enjoyed theme parties, including one where he dressed as a Zulu warrior in a scanty leopard-print outfit. (Today, of course, the affair would be considered offensive on a college campus.) "My parents had no idea what fraternity was all about, and literally watched me grow from a shy and timid boy to a confident young man because of SAE," said Cohen, who graduated with a bachelor's degree in psychology and business administration in 1985. By the end of his undergraduate career, Cohen had helped build one of the fraternity's largest chapters, with 140 members. Cohen's hustle impressed SAE's national leadership, which offered him the position of director of expansion at the Illinois headquarters. In two years, Cohen helped establish more than twenty new chapters, including one at Yale. In 1988, Cohen moved to Southern California and made his name in the real-estate escrow business. In 2009, after the housing market collapsed in the financial crisis, he opened his own company, Granite Escrow Services, which grew to have annual revenue of more than $10 million, with almost one hundred employees and seven offices.

Cohen kept up the Greek tradition of philanthropy. He focused on a personal cause. He and his eldest son, Devon, have Type 1 diabetes. Both were diagnosed at age eleven. Cohen served on the executive board of the University of California at Irvine diabetes research center. In 2012, Devon held a fundraiser for his bar mitzvah that raised almost $30,000 for diabetes research. He also donated two hundred teddy bears with medical identification bracelets to Children's Hospital of Orange County. As he started high school, Devon shared his father's love for SAE. He liked to wear a purple-and-gold bow tie and knew the fraternity's handshake. But the Cohen family knew that, for a diabetic, heavy drinking could be fatal. "As a mother, I would have been scared to put him in an environment like that," Kim Cohen told me. It was a stunning admission. The wife of SAE's president wasn't sure her son would be safe in the fraternity. Neither was the president.

Outside pressure mounted. In December 2013, my colleague David Glovin and I published a 5,000-word *Bloomberg News* article that detailed nine drinking, hazing, and drug-related fatalities at SAE, which we called "the deadliest fraternity." That same month, a drunk SAE member at Washington and Lee University drove off the road after a party and slammed into a tree, killing a passenger, a twenty-one-year-old female student. The next month, a drunk freshman at Alma College in Michigan left an SAE party wearing a polo shirt and no coat. Two days later, he was found dead of hypothermia. Lloyd's of London became increasingly concerned about the risk of insuring SAE and threatened to drop coverage. In February, Cohen learned that JPMorgan Chase & Co., which handled the SAE foundation's investment account, was reconsidering its relationship. JPMorgan worried its association with SAE could tarnish its reputation. "If JPMorgan is going to turn us down, who's next?" Cohen asked himself. "What if universities start saying SAE's not welcome?"

Cohen and the four other members of SAE's volunteer board, the Supreme Council, worried that the loss of insurance could end the fraternity. As they had twice failed to ban drinking in chapter houses, they decided to fight hazing instead. But how? The fraternity had long ago banned it, to no avail. They decided then to outlaw pledging. The pledge period was the time freshmen were most vulnerable to abuse and most likely to die of alcohol poisoning. The decision was revolutionary, as much for its approach as for its substance. The members of the Supreme Council decided to take action without putting it to a convention vote. They had learned from experience with the proposed alcohol ban; they might never get the two-thirds majority required for passage. What's more, they decided they couldn't wait until the next convention. Cohen invoked an emergency exception. Out of his own pocket, he paid $800 an hour for an attorney to review SAE's laws in order to defend the decision.

Even then, the men knew the council could be voted out of office at the next convention. The volunteer members could live with that consequence. But Cohen was especially worried about Blaine "Boomer" Ayers, the only leader approving the decision who worked full time for SAE. The $150,000-a-year executive director had four young daughters. Ayers, the Kentucky native known for his bow ties and sessions on etiquette, was a teetotaler who cautioned undergraduates about making the fraternity the center of their lives. In his view, it should be faith, family, and country. Ayers, who had been hired in 2011, backed the decision without reservation. "How many more new members have to die before everyone is willing to change the way we operate?" he asked.

So the council sketched out a plan. Under the new initiation system, SAE chapters would extend recruits a "bid," or invitation to join, and students who accepted would become full members within ninety-six hours. Cohen kept the plan under wraps. He feared that hazers would accelerate their abuse of pledges before the program was eliminated. On March 7, coinciding with the celebration of the anniversary of the fraternity's founding, Cohen announced the pledging ban—the same day JPMorgan finally terminated its relationship with SAE.

"As an organization, we have been plagued with too much bad behavior, which has resulted in loss of lives, negative press and large lawsuits," he said in a video address.

The move made national headlines, drawing praise from many quarters that had once condemned SAE. E-mails and phone messages poured in from college administrators, fraternity members, and families whose sons had suffered from hazing. The most meaningful reaction came from the Starkey parents, whose son had died of alcohol poisoning during an SAE initiation ritual at California Polytechnic State University. "I will tell you my proudest moment was seeing the relief of the Starkey family—that their son hadn't died in vain," Cohen said.

But the pledge ban immediately stirred a backlash. "It doesn't feel right," Christian Couch, a twenty-one-year-old junior from California State University at Long Beach, told me. "You just sign up and you're automatically in. It's the easy way out."

On a Facebook page called "SAE Cause for Change," posts warned that brotherly bonds would fade or pledging would go underground. They questioned whether the SAE board had the authority to ban pledging.

Some angry students complained that the new recruits would become "insta-bros."

"Doing away with the pledge program is like giving all the kids on a youth soccer team trophies at the end of the season for doing 'a good job,'" one critic wrote. "People need to face adversity in order to feel accomplished."

By June 2015, the next convention, Cohen had a revolt on his hands.

AT THE OPENING session, four hundred members filed into the Marriott resort's ballroom, finding their places behind rows of long tables organized by region. Flanked by two flags—the American and SAE's purple and gold—Cohen delivered an impassioned defense of his board's action.

"We were faced with being labeled, correctly so, the deadliest fraternity in America, whether we liked it or not," Cohen said. "We had killed more undergraduate members through forced alcohol hazing than any other fraternity or sorority out there, and it was time to make a change. This wasn't five guys sitting in a dark room and some conspiracy theory to override and screw over the convention. This was a survival mode to save and protect SAE. We would not have survived."

Cohen painted a grim picture: "I am not an alarmist. I am a realist. And I am here to tell you, brothers, if we hadn't acted as quickly and as swiftly as we did, and we would've had another incident, God help us all. Our insurance might've been canceled. It guaranteed would've gone up to the point we couldn't afford it. Universities would've said we're done with SAE. And can you imagine Oklahoma hitting two months ago, and SAE still having all these hazing incidents?"

As Cohen wound down his speech, he told the members they still hadn't tackled the most significant problem: "Every one of our deaths, every one of our closings of a chapter we had problems with has in some way or shape or form involved alcohol." He warned of the lawsuits over the deaths at Arizona State and Cornell, as well as the sexual assaults at Johns Hopkins.

"How does a chapter allow anybody into their house, not only a minor—I mean, an underage drinker, but a minor—who then got brutally raped in the bathroom?"

In closing the speech, he suggested the worst could be over. "This last eighteen months has probably been one of the most challenging times in our fraternity's history since the Civil War, bar none. Despite what we've read, despite all the negative publicity, despite the embarrassment, despite the upheaval, we have come through it shining. We have made this fraternity better than it was, and I am proud more than ever to be an SAE."

Ayers made just as impassioned a plea. "We were getting questions: 'Why are you not doing more, and why didn't you do more to protect my son?' And, as a parent and your executive director, that haunted me." The fraternity would vote on a measure that would give the Supreme Council the authority to act between conventions. Their decision would then later be subject to a convention vote—but requiring a simple, not a two-thirds, majority. The change would empower the council as never before.

The opposition complained that Cohen and his board were violating democratic traditions. Their presidential candidate was Darin Patton, a Florida lawyer and financial planner, as well as a former University of Central Florida student-body president and homecoming king.

"The Supreme Council ruled by decree when they changed fraternity laws without the consent of the fraternity convention," said Marco Pena, a Central Florida classmate, hospital executive, and unsuccessful Republican candidate for the statehouse. "One person or even five should not make the decisions for the fraternity. That's why we have these laws."

One of the dissenters was Michael Scarborough, the former national president. Scarborough had been furious when Cohen shut down his chapter at Salisbury University for hazing. Before, he had been one of Cohen's fans. In 2009, Scarborough had nominated Cohen for a board position and praised him effusively. "Brother Cohen is the true Renaissance man, the true gentleman and a true leader," he had said. "This fraternity certainly would be poorer without him." Now, he was supporting a candidate for a board position who opposed Cohen's approach. Scarborough later told me he was skeptical of the ban, believing it would push hazing underground. Mostly, he objected to how Cohen took action. "It was an edict," he said. "This was something that was shoved down a lot of people's throats. Candidly, it wasn't graciously delivered."

Austin Alcala, an undergraduate from Ball State University, said many in his chapter opposed ending pledgeship. Even more, he worried that its authority would lead to something else: an alcohol ban.

"Basically, this gives the Supreme Council the ability to remove—I know that alcohol-free housing has been talked about without our permission—giving them the ability to basically initiate alcohol-free housing without the convention's approval,"

Alcala said. "I honestly believe the convention should be the ones deciding this for us as a community, not five people."

Despite several days of complaints and opposition, Steven Churchill, Cohen's vice president, won, as did the measure giving the board the authority to change laws between conventions. Cohen's legacy survived.

During his tenure, Cohen and his council had shut down nineteen chapters. Even as SAE opened new chapters, membership dropped from a peak of almost 15,000 to 12,000 by 2017. But several facts were undeniable. Its per-member cost for liability insurance dropped 15 percent. Most significant, the fraternity hadn't had another death related to hazing or drinking.

Cohen had offered a path forward. The question hung over the convention: Would undergraduates continue to take it?

ON THE FINAL night of the convention, the men gathered again in the ballroom, around tables with purple tablecloths and gold napkins and centerpieces the size of chandeliers. SAE had brought in a tailor to measure members for tuxedos, and many of the college students wore black tie. Past "Eminent Supreme Archons" filed in, wearing fraternity pins and service medals on their lapels as they escorted their wives on their arms. Earlier, on a ninety-foot yacht that SAE had hired for an evening cruise, Kim Cohen had told me she was now ready for her son to join SAE in college. The ban on pledging reassured her. "He can go, 100 percent," she said. "He'll do it the right way, with the right guys." Later, on bended knee, Cohen and hundreds of men serenaded her. In a turquoise dress, with glitter on her eyelids, she looked again like the actress making her curtain call. She clutched a bouquet of sunflowers while the sea of men sang to her: "Violet, violet. You're the fairest flower to me. Violet, violet. Emblem of fraternity."

Cohen, who reveled in a sentimental gesture, never passed up the chance to make a speech. Some members made under-over bets based on the length of his addresses. A safe wager would be fifty minutes. For this, his swan song, Cohen invited his three children onto the stage. Cohen's thirteen-year-old daughter, Syd, wore a purple dress with a gold bow in her blonde hair. Devon, fifteen and now nearly as tall as his father, wore a suit with a purple-and-gold tie.

"Syd, you'll always be my little SAE sweetheart," he told his daughter.

Then, he turned to Devon and his brother, Zach, Syd's twin.

"You two boys, may you all be SAEs, brothers of mine, someday."

Cohen loved the rhetorical set piece, and brothers would also bet on which one would appear once he stepped before a microphone. One was an early twentieth-century verse by the poet Ella Wheeler Wilcox. He didn't disappoint. Cohen's accent and the timeworn language evoked a British boarding school:

> One ship sails East,
> And another West,
> By the self-same winds that blow,
> 'Tis the set of the sails,
> And not the gales,
> That tells the way we go.

IT WAS A poem about agency, a belief in the ability to shift course in an often hostile world. On this night, the betting men won the jackpot. Cohen offered both of his favorite speeches. As it became clear where he was headed, Cohen heard cheers in the audience, perhaps even the rustling of a few bills changing hands:

People say fraternity men are nothing more than a bunch of guys who lie, drink, steal and swear. I say, yes we are. We lie down every single night, grateful for this incredible experience we call SAE. We drink from the fountain of youth when we initiate young members into the bloodline of this fraternity. We steal a little time to give back to those less fortunate than ourselves. We swear that we'll leave this fraternity better than we've found it.

Cohen wanted to confront the reality of the fraternity man, not deny it. He seized on the double meaning of powerful verbs— lie, drink, steal, and swear. They promised a road to redemption. As someone who reveled in language, Cohen believed the meaning of these words could be reversed, as if a kind of linguistic alchemy could reclaim the soul of the fraternity.

9

THE LIONS

"Whose Deed Follows His Word"

The lions had always bothered Chris Hallam. Standing on either side of the entrance to the chapter house, they looked forlorn and neglected, their paint chipped, discolored, and faded, as if they were animals left behind in the cages of a traveling carnival. The sad cats lacked the right scale. Maybe half the size of the real thing, they were far too small for the white columns in front of the once-grand home. The statues sent a message about the state of the chapter—an accurate one, Hallam understood quite quickly.

The young men of Ohio State University's Sigma Alpha Epsilon chapter had turned to him for help. They needed a new volunteer adviser. They elected Hallam, though "elected" might have been too strong a word. After a few beers, they sent him an e-mail. Hallam, in his late twenties, had never even belonged to a fraternity. When he was an undergraduate at Allegheny College in Pennsylvania, Theta Chi had blackballed him. Now, working as an Ohio State residence hall director, he had grown to like some of SAE's members. With his master's in higher education and student affairs, Hallam also appreciated a challenge, a way to use his newfound knowledge about adolescent development and social dynamics. Energetic, trim, and youthful, even if his hair hadn't survived his post-collegiate life, Hallam had always wondered about the potential of fraternities to mold young men. Here was his chance to make a difference.

The lions were the least of his problems. The membership rolls had atrophied to several dozen, hardly enough to fill the dilapidated house. The boiler kept breaking, lead paint needed removal, and thousands of dollars appeared to be missing from the chapter treasury. Its few members were so disorganized that they had thrown a philanthropy event, a sorority powder-puff football game, that had actually managed to lose $50. They screamed at each other in chapter meetings. Some arrived drunk. The house even had a "slush fund" for alcohol. A pledge had nearly passed out after being told to drink a bottle of vodka. The "pledge educator" used to teach new members how to break beer bottles on their own heads. Although the lions were the chapter's official mascot, another animal might have better embodied the state of the fraternity: its pet rabbit, which left droppings all over the house.

Yet SAE at Ohio State had a proud history. On the day of its installation in 1892, three other Ohio chapters came to mark the celebration in Columbus, Ohio, in a suite of rooms at the luxurious Chittenden Hotel, which then served as the residence of Governor William McKinley. To mark the occasion, SAE made McKinley an honorary member. Later, McKinley wore his SAE badge at his inauguration as the twenty-fifth US president in 1897 and, to this day, the only one to have belonged to the fraternity.

Ohio State remains fertile territory for fraternities. One of the largest public universities in America, with a football stadium bigger than those housing NFL teams, Ohio State has 60,000 students, and its size can make the bonds of Greek life seem especially attractive. But the twenty-first century had been unkind to SAE. In 2001, Ohio State administrators shut the chapter after 108 years on campus. The members had become best known for throwing beer bottles and frozen water balloons at pedestrians, cars, and other houses. One of the chapter's own advisers had called its behavior "inexcusable."

Now, to turn the chapter around, Hallam befriended the young men while setting boundaries. He met each member for a meal and joined the chapter's Sunday dinners at a Japanese steak house. He visited before parties and sat with members as they watched professional wrestling on TV. He encouraged the men to require ties and jackets at chapter meetings, which he attended himself.

"You can choose to break the rules," he would tell them. "But, if you are caught, no one gets to complain, and you admit it. My job comes first. I would never lie to the university or hide anything."

Hallam urged the men to dream big. He said they should compete for national SAE honors and, one day, the John O. Moseley Zeal Award, which honors the chapter in the United States that best reflects the values of a True Gentleman.

The response from his charges was less than enthusiastic: "Do not be an idiot," a member named Kevin Bowen told him. "You're looking for greatness. We're just not there."

Hallam also insisted the chapter would get new lions. Bowen was skeptical. "Are you kidding me?" he said. "We're never getting new lions."

The adviser viewed the young men, like the house, as fixer-uppers. Hallam had to ask the university to make an exception for one prospective member with poor grades. "I didn't know where I was going in life," the member would recall later. "Hallam saw something in me and put his neck on the line." To fulfill Hallam's vision, the chapter changed the way it recruited new members. Officers ignored legacy preference and began judging prospects on their merits. The chapter welcomed more first-generation college students and members of minority groups. In 2009, the brothers initiated Hallam himself as a member of the fraternity. "It's a privilege to be an SAE," Hallam told me. "I waited thirteen years for that badge."

Hallam was proudest of how the chapter's members shifted their attitudes. The brothers looked out for each other. Over the years, three members had been hospitalized for depression; one had tried to kill himself by drinking Drano. The members rallied around the men and visited them in the hospital, which eased the transition back onto the campus and through graduation. "I'm here for you," individual members would tell the returning brothers. After the racist Oklahoma video surfaced in 2015, the chapter hosted a campus-wide diversity presentation and helped minority fraternities raise money for their philanthropy events.

Hallam, who is openly gay, worked from the beginning to make the chapter more welcoming to brothers who didn't fit the traditional vision of fraternity masculinity. When he started out as an adviser, Hallam heard a member lash out at a chapter meeting by calling another member "a pansy faggot."

"You know I'm gay, right?" he said, pulling the member aside.

A couple of years later, he witnessed the same student admonish a housemate who said "faggot": "We don't use that word here." In 2012, Donovan Golich, a freshman member, stood up in front of thirty-nine pledges and let them know he was gay. "It was really a nonissue with them," said Golich, who said he would bring his boyfriend to chapter events. "You come as you are. We are going to accept you that way."

The Ohio State chapter's greatest test came in February 2015, when Mike Moore, the president, began hearing reports of a member's aggressive treatment of women. The culminating incident occurred during spring break in Panama City Beach, Florida, when the member brought a woman to his hotel room, then allegedly performed a sex act on her after she told him to stop. "He eventually stopped and apologized profusely, but she still felt incredibly uncomfortable and was not OK with what happened," a member told Moore in a text. Moore, who had not been on the trip, interviewed members and the woman, who was also an Ohio State University student. She confirmed what had happened. "That was pretty much it for me," Moore told me. "I didn't feel comfortable with this anymore."

Moore called Hallam, who had since taken a position as associate director of housing at the University of Cincinnati but was still overseeing SAE volunteer advisers. SAE expelled the fraternity member accused of the sexual assault. Moore shared his report with the university and also testified before a disciplinary proceeding. It was difficult for him to turn on a brother, but he felt he needed to protect the fraternity. "I knew this was not the chapter I joined," Moore said.

Soon after, the chapter applied for the Zeal Award. Its application noted that members won many university-wide Greek awards such as Man of the Year, Outstanding Chapter President, and Volunteer of the Year. The chapter raised $14,000 for Children's Miracle Network, SAE's favored charity, which provides for pediatric care, and that was a 50 percent increase from the previous year. Over four years, chapter membership had tripled, to 115.

In August 2015, on the national fraternity's annual leadership cruise, members filed across a stage. At long last, they had won the Zeal Award. Hallam had so inspired the chapter that its members fulfilled their dream, which many had considered unattainable. Several weeks later, this achievement would become even more pivotal in Hallam's life in a way no one could have anticipated. One day at work, he collapsed and had to be rushed to the hospital. There, at thirty-six years old, he was diagnosed with terminal brain cancer. The doctor gave him a year to live. After he told his parents, he called Moore. Over the course of their time at the fraternity, they had become like family—like brothers.

On a Monday evening several months later, Hallam asked to make a guest appearance via Skype at the Ohio State chapter house. Moore put a laptop on a high table so that Hallam could see the signs of his handiwork. Through the computer screen, he addressed seventy-five men in ties and jackets. Hallam knew the formality was the result of a $5 fine the fraternity had instituted for showing up to chapter meetings in jeans, sweatshirts, and flip-flops. Hallam looked pale but otherwise spoke clearly and with purpose.

"Before I pass, I'm going to get the chapter some new lions," he said. "It's the one goal I have left to achieve."

The men shouted and cheered: "Phi Alpha!"

Hallam wanted the lions to be special. They would be tall, fierce, and hewn from marble. They would rival the sentinels standing before the grandest old chapters of the South. They wouldn't come cheap, but Hallam had a plan.

He had life insurance. He wasn't married and didn't have children. It would be his final gift to the fraternity he loved.

FRATERNITY LOYALTY RUNS deep. Many SAE brothers told me a version of a story that ended with, "The fraternity changed my life," or even "The fraternity saved my life." One student had suffered a devastating rejection from a first love; another lost his sense of mission after an injury kept him sidelined from varsity sports. A third worried he couldn't cut it academically.

Each time, they said their brothers helped them survive and even thrive. Sometimes, this loyalty can be writ large. In 2012, Bob Dax, the longtime alumni adviser of the Carnegie Mellon University SAE chapter, was diagnosed with ALS, the degenerative illness often called Lou Gehrig's disease. In his honor, his brothers dedicated their goofy, annual fund-raiser to Dax. It was called the Donut Dash. Members run a mile, eat half a dozen donuts, then run another mile. In 2016, the event raised a record $175,000. Other efforts remain private. At California State University at Northridge, Alexi Sciutto found out his mother had been diagnosed with late-stage breast cancer. His SAE brothers helped him raise money to fight the disease; then, on his mother's deathbed, they made her an honorary member. "I'll do whatever needs to be done to keep SAE alive," Sciutto told me. "And I'll do it until I die."

These bonds can't be dismissed lightly in a world where scattered families and social media make genuine human connection increasingly precious. But can they be saved from the pathologies of Greek life? Fraternities have all kinds of power: financial, political, and historical. Do they also have the power to change? Despite their love of dubious traditions, fraternities have, in fact, evolved during their two-century history in higher education. Often, it has been from necessity. Outside pressure forced reform. Fraternity men have reimagined their values to welcome other religions and races. They have even led campaigns to abolish their own organization when they became convinced it served the greater good.

Consider the evolution of the first fraternity, the Phi Beta Kappa Society, founded in 1776. In 1831, it abandoned secrecy, a core feature of the brotherhood. Setting itself apart from the newer social fraternities, Phi Beta Kappa would focus on scholarship. Whereas early fraternities worked in opposition to faculties, professors became key members of Phi

Beta Kappa. The organization, perhaps because of its focus on academic merit, dispensed with discrimination long before social fraternities did. In the 1870s, chapters at the University of Vermont and Wesleyan inducted the first women. Yale and the University of Vermont elected African Americans. Today, the organization has 286 chapters and half a million members. Since its founding, its inductees have gone on to have illustrious careers, among them seventeen presidents, thirty-nine Supreme Court justices, and more than 130 Nobel laureates. Many social fraternities have sought to improve their standing by incorporating students' grade-point average and other achievements into their selection criteria. They have also publicized their members' GPAs.

Other fraternities focused on community service. A latecomer to the movement, Alpha Phi Omega, was created in 1925 at Lafayette College in Pennsylvania. Its founder was a returning World War I sailor named Frank Reed Horton who wanted to found a service organization open to men of all religions. At the time, Horton was also a member of SAE, with its Aryan-only policy. President Bill Clinton joined Alpha Phi Omega as an undergraduate at Georgetown University in the 1960s. In 1976, inspired by the women's liberation movement, the organization voted to become co-ed. "Why discriminate because of sex?" Joseph Scanlon, the fraternity's executive director wrote in 1970. "Forty-five years ago, Alpha Phi Omega dared to differ with the times. It set out to prove an organization committed to service, opposed to membership discrimination because of race, creed, color, economic status or national origin, could exist on college campuses." As a "service fraternity," the organization had no houses, and members of single-sex social fraternities could become members. It offered many of the same features as traditional fraternities: pledgeship and other rituals, friendship and parties. Today, the group has

375 chapters and 400,000 members. Alpha Phi Omega proved that a fraternity could reject discrimination while flourishing on a modern campus.

Some members of traditional fraternities found they had to separate from their national organizations if they wanted to embrace more egalitarian principles. At Dartmouth, for example, Phi Tau broke away from Phi Sigma Kappa over racial segregation in the 1950s and, in 1972, admitted women. Similarly, at Brown, members of Zeta Psi withdrew from that organization to form Xeta Delta Xi in the 1980s so they could include female members. Unlike the more recent efforts to promote co-ed fraternities at Trinity, Harvard, and Wesleyan, change came from within chapters. Members, interpreting fraternal values for themselves, rebelled against older restrictions.

At Williams College, a fraternity man named John Edward Sawyer led one of the earliest and highest-profile campaigns against the excesses of Greek life. As an undergraduate, Sawyer had been president of Zeta Psi, as had his brother and father. As an insider, he understood the negative influence of Williams's fraternities, which had become bastions of debauchery and intolerance. After World War II and through much of the 1960s, the Williams trustees worked to eliminate fraternities. They gradually reduced their power while offering attractive alternatives for living and dining. In the 1950s, for example, Williams, then all male, banned freshman rushing. It also built a new dining hall for first-year students. In the 1960s, Sawyer became president of Williams and created an alternative to fraternities. The school established its own residences for students and converted fraternity houses into dorms. By 1968, only 10 percent of upper-class students belonged to fraternities. The school then ordered the end of all fraternity activity by 1970. Sawyer's timing was excellent. Fraternities had become less popular during the anti-establishment 1960s, and national organizations' opposition to racial integration undermined their support, especially on Northern campuses. Abolishing fraternities "would be a lot more difficult to pull off today," his successor as president, John W. Chandler, told me. "We thought the line behind us would be long. It really wasn't." Williams stuck with the policy even amid the more recent Greek revival. To this day, Williams prohibits fraternity membership and promises to suspend or expel students who join.

Williams paid no price for confronting its fraternities and, in fact, prospered because of it. In his history of Williams and fraternities, Chandler argued that the death of fraternities made it easier for the college to start admitting women in 1970. Williams may have bucked wealthy fraternity alumni, but its academic standing improved as it drew students with top grades and standardized test scores. In fact, Williams became the richest US liberal arts college, with a $2.3 billion endowment. Chandler called Sawyer "the most transformative leader in Williams' history" and the abolition of fraternities "the key to his accomplishments and his crowning achievement."

The success of Williams College put pressure on its New England peers, sometimes referred to as the "Little Ivies." In the 1980s and 1990s, other colleges—Amherst in Massachusetts, Colby and Bowdoin in Maine, and Middlebury in Vermont—banned their fraternities. Williams and its rivals demonstrate that colleges can eliminate Greek organizations, even when they are a powerful part of a school's tradition. All these schools say they benefited academically and socially from eliminating fraternities. Of course, they have continued to struggle with drinking and sexual assault; but, unlike colleges with Greek life, they don't find themselves on lists of top party schools or those with the most alcohol-related arrests. In 1996, a year before Bowdoin began eliminating fraternities, 29 percent of graduating seniors were "satisfied" or "very satisfied" with the "sense of community on campus." Ten years later, that figure had risen to almost 70 percent. These schools needed alumni support for prioritizing academics over social life and the wherewithal to invest heavily in housing and dining.

Private colleges have more freedom to promote bans. Small, wealthy liberal arts colleges can more easily afford new residence halls. Private institutions also face fewer legal constraints. As Greg Lukianoff, a lawyer and campus free-speech advocate, has explained, the First Amendment and its freedom of assembly provision don't directly bind private universities, though many have their own policies that protect expression; as government agencies, public universities are fully subject to constitutional limits.

Yet short of banning fraternities, public colleges can still institute tougher regulation. In the 1990s, one president, Robert Carothers, decided to attack the culture of drinking at the University of Rhode Island. The *Princeton Review* had named the college the country's number one party school for three consecutive years. The university, whose initials are URI, had earned a nickname: "You are high." At homecoming, students would regularly be hospitalized for alcohol poisoning, and students had been known to bring kegs to commencement. Henry Wechsler, then director of the Harvard School of Public Health, found that an astonishing 70 percent of students there were binge drinking. Carothers was horrified, and he understood the challenge.

As Williams had done decades before, Carothers sought to improve his university's academic standing and its image by attacking the fraternity culture. Like Sawyer, he was a fraternity member. In the 1960s, he had been president of Delta Sigma Phi at Pennsylvania's Edinboro University. Still, at the University of Rhode Island, Carothers led the charge to ban alcohol at any social function on campus sponsored by the school—and that included fraternities. Students who violated policies three times were suspended for two semesters—a three-strikes policy. Seven fraternities that resisted were kicked off campus; the university bought their houses and either razed them or used them for dorms or administrative offices. The change all but eliminated the kind of tragic alcohol-related deaths that had been a regular occurrence. A 2009 study found a decrease in the number of drinking-related police reports, as students became more aware of the consequences of flouting the law. When he took on fraternities, Carothers heard warnings about a backlash from alumni. But he said older graduates understood the seriousness of the problem, and he found himself getting congratulatory notes, with $1,000 donations. The college attracted students with higher grades and test scores and had more success shepherding them through graduation. After the crackdown, "People would say, 'I hate to see my fraternity come to this,'" Carothers told me. "But they would also say, 'You have to do what you have to do.'"

More recently, Philip Hanlon, Dartmouth's president, took on his school's famed fraternity culture. Half of Dartmouth students belong to Greek organizations, among the largest proportion of any US college. Previous presidents had tried and failed to rein in fraternities. In 2015, the school banned hard liquor. Hanlon also urged professors to curb grade inflation, and to stop canceling classes the morning after party nights. As at Williams, Dartmouth created a new residential system, which would assign first-year students to "houses" based around a cluster of dormitories. Again, it apparently took a fraternity man to make some inroads. Hanlon, a 1977 Dartmouth alumnus, had belonged to Alpha Delta, whose Dartmouth chapter had inspired the movie *Animal House*. When Hanlon announced the measures to curb the party culture in 2015, he wouldn't rule out banning fraternities: "If in the next

three to five years, the Greek system does not engage in meaningful, lasting reform, and we are unsuccessful in sharply curb-
ing harmful behaviors, we will need to revisit its continuation
on our campus."

Dartmouth and the University of Rhode Island turned to what
Wechsler has called a "comprehensive community intervention."
Rather than focus on discipline and individual compliance, the
schools employed the same kinds of tools that succeeded in
public-health campaigns against drunk driving and smoking.
This approach combines a variety of measures aimed at reduc-
ing the behavior that society wants to discourage: heightened
enforcement, higher penalties and financial costs, and consistent, clear public messaging. The goal wasn't prohibition, but a
reduction in drinking. Wechsler recommended enlisting local
authorities to make sure bars and stores insist on proof-of-age;
pushing to raise state and local taxes on liquor; and passing or-
dinances forbidding the serving of cheap shots and huge bowls
of alcohol. Wechsler also praised colleges that have offered in-
expensive, attractive alcohol-free housing. These methods have
more impact than the alcohol-education programs offered on
most campuses. "You can't just tell students how dangerous it
is," Wechsler told me. "You have to change the environment."

Any discussion of college drinking inevitably leads to what
sounds like a logical approach: lower the drinking age to eighteen. Proponents argue that this approach will bring alcohol
into the open, eliminating the secrecy and associated luster,
thus leading to more moderate and responsible drinking. Its ad-
herents hold up Europe as a model.

In 2008, a group of more than one hundred college presidents,
led by John McCardell, the former leader of Middlebury College, suggested just that. But public-health authorities have come
to an overwhelming consensus supporting the higher drinking
age. Since the increase in the 1980s, alcohol consumption has

declined among high school students and adults aged eighteen to twenty, with most of the drop occurring in the 1990s. Countering the college presidents in 2008, public-health experts noted that the number of sixteen-to-twenty-year-old drunken drivers killed annually had fallen by half. The National Highway Traffic Safety Administration has estimated the law saved more than 26,000 lives since the 1970s. Still, college students drink more than their peers who aren't enrolled. Wechsler blamed lax enforcement and an environment awash in cheap alcohol. It's worth repeating that studies show that white men in general—and fraternity members in particular—drink more heavily than anyone else on campus.

Judson Horras, who became president of the North-American Interfraternity Conference in 2016, has embraced the public-health approach. Horras was a longtime executive at Beta Theta Pi, which has shut down many chapters since the 1990s, then reopened them as alcohol free. Horras proposed working with fraternity councils and building a campus consensus on stricter alcohol rules. It would be a gradual approach, tailored to the current state of behavior. At an out-of-control campus, he would advocate starting with a ban on hard liquor; such a ban would lower the risk of alcohol poisoning. Then, the conference might push for restricting the number of parties with alcohol. The next step would be "damp" fraternity houses. Members could have no alcohol in common spaces—in other words, no social events with alcohol. Members who were twenty-one and older could have alcohol in their own rooms. The final step could be dry houses. Any event with alcohol would have to be held at a restaurant with professional bartenders. Or, as Bob Biggs, the chief executive of Phi Delta Theta, likes to say: the fraternities would finally get out of the bar business.

Horras has also pledged to help fraternities replace an aggressive vision of masculinity with another ideal, a man who acts with "humble confidence." In his experience, new chapters tend to be idealistic, open to adult guidance and members who show leadership on campus. As they grow more successful, they often shift away from those qualities and seek members who are "cool." They start lying to their advisers and prizing a brand of outlaw culture that is celebrated on social media and websites such as Total Frat Move, ostensibly a satire that often functions as a how-to guide for young men's darkest impulses. Horras said he viewed increasing diversity as both a moral and a business imperative. Catering primarily to white males will relegate organizations to irrelevance. "Diversity is the next big wave of growth for our organizations," Horras told me. "We are going to embrace it. We are embracing it."

HALLAM'S LIONS WERE stuck in customs. They had been crafted out of marble in the mountains of Southeast Asia. A Vietnamese SAE member had found craftsmen who would carve a pair for about $4,000. It was a bargain, and it meant the brothers could raise thousands more for landscaping at their new home. Hallam could even keep his life-insurance money to help his parents with end-of-life expenses. With all the delays, the men worried that Hallam might not live to see his lions. Finally, on a Friday in April 2016, a flatbed truck pulled up in front of the chapter house. A Bobcat crane hoisted the two giant wooden crates and carried them up the hilly lawn. The lions each stood five-foot-eight-inches tall and weighed 5,000 pounds, as much as a midsize SUV. They were gold, their manes flecked with red. Each had a giant paw resting on an SAE badge, as if protecting the fraternity's legacy. A plaque dedicated them to Hallam. "The epitome of a True Gentleman," it read.

The next day, Saturday, was rainy and overcast. Men from across the country descended upon the Ohio State chapter. Hallam arrived late, his wingtips sinking into the mud around the new lions. He wore a pink Oxford shirt and an SAE pin on the lapel of his black blazer. He had dark circles around his blue eyes and a red rash on his throat from chemotherapy. On this afternoon, though, he had plenty of energy. He had taken a break from his medication, so he wouldn't feel so tired for the day's events. "They're a lot bigger than I thought," Hallam said as members gathered around the lions. "It means so much that I can be here to see this."

Inside, the chapter overflowed with fraternity brothers. They spilled out of the basement meeting hall and up into the stairs to the first floor. In his tribute, Kevin Bowen, the undergraduate who had recruited Hallam, remembered the sorry chapter his adviser had adopted.

"People were paying dues only because they forgot they were members," Bowen said sarcastically. "It speaks volumes to the lives you've impacted and the changes you've made here that this many people are here on a Saturday when Ohio State students could be drinking. The improvements you've made to this house will live on far beyond the time you've spent here. I couldn't be happier that you're a brother of mine."

Mike Moore, the chapter president who had investigated the sexual-assault allegation, told the crowd how Hallam changed his life. He never would have dreamed he could be speaking without notes in front of this crowd of two hundred. He struggled to check his emotions.

"You see him living his values every day," Moore said. "I was lucky to be as close to Chris Hallam as I was. He was truly dedicated to improving every single person in this room. He had his own career, his own life. He didn't have to dedicate this much time to us, to making sure all of us developed and grew into the men we are today. That's admirable. You don't find a lot of people like that. Over this past year, I've started to consider him a friend. I know he feels the same way. I can't tell you how much it means to me. Phi Alpha, brother."

Moore stepped down and gave Hallam a hug.

Hallam sat in the front row with his mother, Debbie, a retired medical secretary, and his brother, Scott, and a cousin, Rebecca, and her fiancé. His father, Paul, a retired special-education teacher and administrator, stood several rows behind, videotaping the proceedings.

Hallam usually favored notecards but he hadn't prepared for this address—one of the most meaningful of his life. He spoke from the heart, his voice strong, breaking at times with raw emotion.

"Thank you for bringing SAE into my life," he said. "When people talk about the negative side of fraternities, it hurts. They don't understand us. We grow men. We educate men. We develop men. Yes, they make mistakes. But there's a culture of growth and development and advancement. We can be better men."

Hallam said he would never have imagined the bonds he had to the members of the chapter.

"I've asked three members to be pallbearers at my funeral," he said. "That's what this has meant to me."

Hallam spoke of the power of symbol.

"Thank you for knowing what the lions meant to me. That is the culmination of my dedication to this chapter. Know there are always people before you. That is the legacy you are leaving. It is a brotherhood that does not end. The choices you make build on the choices made before you. The fraternity will continue after me. The lions will live on after me."

Before the dedication ended, before the men scattered across the campus, they stood with arms around each other. They recited the words of their creed.

"The True Gentleman is the man whose conduct proceeds from good will and an acute sense of propriety. . . ."

Its words were etched on the walls of the chapter room. But the brothers didn't need to read them. They knew them by heart. They shouted them until the walls vibrated with the sounds of their voices.

CONCLUSION

Like America's founders, the men who started the first college fraternities sparked a revolution. They helped breathe life into stodgy institutions obsessed with theology and Greek and Latin. Fraternities offered students a path to careers in courtrooms, boardrooms, and the corridors of political power. Young men found a place to make friends for life, develop social skills, and forge character. The brothers' energy invigorated college life. But today, fraternities, once so forward-looking, seem hobbled by their own past. With their history of segregation, racial hostility, and misogyny, these distinctive organizations embody many of the unresolved conflicts still plaguing the United States.

WHEN I EMBARKED on my journey into the heart of fraternities, I suspected I would find a culture in its twilight. Women were ascendant on college campuses. The country had twice chosen a black president who, unlike most of his recent predecessors, had not belonged to a fraternity. Voters appeared ready to select the first female president. But the 2016 election of President Donald Trump reflected a backlash against the multicultural America that had been embraced on college campuses, in the military, and at many corporations. His followers' disdain for "political correctness" echoed the language inside racially isolated chapter houses—places that sociologists have described as "nurseries for the sense of white victimization." Like the conservative revival of the Reagan years, the age of Trump could mark the beginning of another fraternity boom based on retrenchment rather than reform.

But many fraternity members want to chart a different future. The Chris Hallams of this world see young men of all backgrounds desperately seeking community, guidance, and purpose. These male students often feel lost and alone. In an age of family fragmentation, of identity forged on social media, undergraduates are looking for authentic connections. They need role models and friends. They need to learn how to thrive in a diverse world, alongside workers of all backgrounds.

Some critics continue to find fraternities irredeemable and look to abolish them. It is a simple and elegant solution that has succeeded at a handful of private campuses with the commitment and wealth to offer genuine social alternatives. I'm not so sure it can work as broadly as many believe. Public universities—governed by the First Amendment—would no doubt be barred from restricting the right to freedom of association. Even more, fraternities are durable organizations for a reason and are likely to survive. It makes sense to ask: Could they change?

Public pressure can help. Consider the impact of Doug Fierberg, the lawyer who made his career by suing fraternities. The threat of financial extinction motivated Sigma Alpha Epsilon to eliminate pledging, a move that has halted the once-inevitable hazing-related deaths. The savviest leaders, such as Brad Cohen, can seize the spotlight to reform their own organizations. Even this change required constant vigilance. In July 2017, SAE was scheduled to consider a proposal to end its pledging ban, which had been in effect for more than three years. But the proposal was withdrawn at its biennial convention in Boston. The fraternity's governing board, the Supreme Council, had offered compelling evidence of the ban's success that reached beyond the most important goal of saving lives. SAE now averaged two insurance claims a year, down from thirteen when it still had pledging.

That SAE would consider reinstating an initiation period was especially surprising in light of a recent high-profile hazing death at another fraternity. In May 2017, a grand jury indicted eighteen Pennsylvania State University fraternity brothers after a nineteen-year-old pledge died from traumatic brain injuries sustained in a liquor-soaked Beta Theta Pi initiation. The death and its aftermath showed why fraternities must fight to preserve promising reforms if they want to survive. Penn State's president demanded changes on fraternity row. Otherwise, he warned of chapter closings and, potentially, "the end of Greek life."

Short of shutting down fraternities, colleges have another less dramatic tool at their disposal: information. In exchange for conferring recognition, they have the power to collect and publish data about alcohol-related hospitalizations, especially at fraternity houses and other sites of underage drinking. This information has the potential to point toward effective solutions, from banning hard liquor to requiring dry fraternity houses. Colleges also have a mechanism to increase the cost of drinking, assessing a per-student fee for fraternity houses and other organizations that host parties with alcohol. This money could be used either to step up enforcement or to fund other student activities without drinking. Colleges could advise fraternity parents to buy liability insurance policies if their sons host parties with alcohol. Economists and public-health scholars agree that raising the cost of a behavior can reduce its prevalence. Fraternities form the heart of the drinking problem on campus; these measures have the potential to reduce their members' alcohol consumption, bringing it more in line with the average student's drinking.

These approaches rely on making tangible the costs of behavior and providing consumers with accurate, up-to-date information. Imagine if colleges demanded that fraternities disclose their disciplinary histories, each chapter detailing specific infractions in a prominent, easy-to-read online format. Public colleges must already provide these data if confronted with public-records requests, as they did for me when I researched this book. But such disclosures are haphazard, infrequent, and out of date. Universities could also document the sites of all reported sexual assaults. This would provide an incentive to hold safe parties and warn women about the most dangerous spaces on campus.

This kind of openness could help heal fraternities' complicated racial histories. Why not require individual chapters to publish a racial breakdown of their memberships? Universities, which often offer financial assistance to fraternities, have the leverage to do so. Some legal scholars have suggested that the federal government could threaten the tax exemptions of fraternities that discriminate—as it did successfully with Southern "segregation academies."

In the current political environment, fraternities must make a choice. They can fight alcohol abuse and hazing, and fully welcome women and minorities as equals, even members—or they can double down on the familiar attitudes of a bygone era. If they want change, fraternity members themselves, with prodding from college administrators, must step up. The new leadership of the North-American Interfraternity Conference has committed to working with colleges.

Change won't come easily. At the 2017 convention, SAE's national leadership sought to amend its laws to declare that no chapter could discriminate against "a potential new member due to his race, his color, his religion, his sexual orientation, his national origin, his age or his physical ability." On its website, SAE had already declared its support for diversity and inclusion. Still, at the convention, men queued up during a plenary session to speak against the antidiscrimination clause. Although opponents said they welcomed potential members of all backgrounds, they worried that the amendment would expose the fraternity to litigation for discrimination. Some even questioned the need for an explicit commitment. "Is this an issue?" asked Ronald Doleac, a Mississippi judge and SAE national president in the 1990s. "Is this really a problem we're having in our fraternity?"

With the men evenly split, the motion failed. The next morning, members reintroduced the antidiscrimination clause. At the microphone, Ga-Lhiel Dillard introduced himself as a "small town Catholic boy from Birmingham, Alabama." Now a junior at California State University, Fresno, he said he was the first African American SAE chapter president. "All of us are going to have experiences with brothers who may be homosexual, Muslim, African American, Hispanic, etc.," he said. "We are going to love those brothers either way. But now we make history."

Steven Churchill, the national president and Brad Cohen's successor, gave the final push. Like Cohen, Churchill embodied change. Cohen was the first Jewish SAE president; Churchill, the former Republican state legislator from Iowa, was the first who was openly gay. He appealed to undergraduates' ambition, saying the aspiring Fortune 500 CEOs in the room will need to promote diversity to attract talent. "It seems to me, honestly, that this should be a no-brainer," he said. "This is what being a True Gentleman is. This is who we are." Members took another voice vote. The motion passed, and supporters broke into applause.

This rejection of the past is only a first step. Individual fraternities could experiment with new approaches, bringing the kind of fresh energy that animated the movement at the beginning. Some could decide to raise their academic standards and become scholarship organizations like Phi Beta Kappa. Others could admit female students as members, righting one of the original wrongs of the movement—the treatment of women as second-class students. Fraternities are already considering the admission of transgender students, as the brothers of Ohio State told me during my visit. Why not women? Why couldn't black and white fraternities form partnerships? Fraternities should also consider abandoning their history of advantaging the advantaged. They could abolish legacy preference and instead offer social and academic support to first-generation college students. Or following the model of Alpha Phi Omega, they could decide to get out of the housing business and focus entirely on philanthropy to become true service organizations.

None of these changes will happen by relying entirely on the collective wisdom of adolescents. Fraternities need adult supervision. Most members enjoy their four years and move on. If they care about the organizations, they need to make membership a lifelong commitment. Wealthy fraternity alumni need to donate money that could be designated for scholarships, as well as for staff to oversee chapters—including live-in advisers. Fraternity members may ask: Why are they being singled out? Are they responsible for all the ills of the modern college experience? Of course not. But the evidence shows that they account for more than their share. Just as important, their creeds explicitly hold them to a higher standard.

In this book, I have chronicled the ways in which fraternities have failed to live up to their words. Many members have chanted noble pledges out of obligation. They have even forced teenagers to memorize them under penalty of paddle or worse. But I have also met leaders who believe that the brotherhood must stand for more than Fireball shots. They can imagine a reinvention of the fraternity, a disentangling of the best strands of the past from the worst. Displaying a characteristic kind of American optimism, they ask themselves: What if a man's deed really did follow his word, and brothers, in fact, lived as True Gentlemen?

ACKNOWLEDGMENTS

I AM GRATEFUL to the generations of Sigma Alpha Epsilon members who welcomed me into their world. From the beginning, Brad Cohen, then the national president, embraced the idea of a book, inviting me both to SAE's convention and leadership school. Cohen showed uncommon openness and belief in the essential strength of the organization and encouraged others to share their views with me. I am also indebted to Cohen's successor, Steven Churchill, and the fraternity's hardworking headquarters staff, especially Blaine Ayers, Brandon Weghorst, Clark Brown, and Ashlee Canty. Undergraduate chapter members Mike Moore, Carter Goodwyn, Jack Counts III, and Andrew Cowie were especially helpful in explaining the cultures of their particular outposts and introducing me to other members. Alumni Jack Counts Jr., Ian Gove, Michael Scarborough, and, of course, Chris Hallam gave me a sense of their passionate commitment to fraternity life. I appreciate their assistance and good humor during the years I worked on *True Gentlemen*.

The victims of fraternity behavior rarely have a voice. Doug Fierberg, who devoted much of his legal career to representing those hurt at Greek houses, helped me understand these tragedies and what can be done to prevent them. To protect other

255

students, Justin Stuart broke the code of silence around hazing and came forward to expose its horrors. The attorneys Trey Parker and Matthew Fraling offered their experience in navigating the complexities of a sexual-assault trial. Gabriela Lopez, most of all, showed uncommon bravery, both on the stand and in agreeing to talk with me. Despite my initial uneasiness, she insisted on using her name as her contribution toward helping other assault survivors.

This book would never have happened without my colleagues at *Bloomberg News*. David Glovin, a dogged investigative reporter and former prosecutor, came up with the idea of looking at fraternity deaths and exploring the little-understood world of insurance and liability. David had already written several first-rate stories when he invited me in as his partner for the articles that would increasingly focus on SAE. David was unable to join me in writing the book because of a well-deserved promotion as editor, but he offered tremendous support from conception to research to his careful reading of the draft. Dan Golden and Jonathan Kaufman, my longtime mentors and friends, provided their characteristically brilliant insights as editors on the original series and, afterward, in helping me with the manuscript. Matt Winkler, the founding editor of *Bloomberg News*, and his top deputy, Laurie Hays, championed the series and all investigative reporting on education. *Bloomberg* editor in chief John Micklethwait and his deputies, Reto Gregori and Laura Zelenko, generously supported my book leave. My current editors, David Gillen and David Papadopoulos, were unfailingly patient and flexible as I finished the manuscript.

Ben Adams, my editor at PublicAffairs, shared my vision of a book about fraternities and then took a risk on a first-time author. Ben offered great wisdom in how to structure a nonfiction narrative and followed up with wise and careful revisions. Clive Priddle, publisher of PublicAffairs, and Peter Osnos, its founder, showed great enthusiasm for the subject. The rest of the team at PublicAffairs—Melissa Veronesi, Melissa Raymond, Katherine Haigler, Michele Wynn, Jaime Leifer, Lindsay Fradkoff, Josie Urwin, and others—expertly guided *True Gentlemen* from manuscript to bookstores.

I wouldn't have found PublicAffairs without my tireless agent, Lynn Johnston, who introduced me to Ben and then educated me in the ways of New York publishing. She contributed vital suggestions in the early stages of the manuscript and championed the book's promotion.

Early readers of the book offered great insight. Along with my colleagues at *Bloomberg*, I owe much, in this and all other endeavors, to my brother Paul Hechinger, a veteran journalist who offered moral support and editing suggestions. My good friend Jeff Frieden somehow managed to read chapters almost overnight and offer sharp critiques while teaching college government courses and traveling the world.

My parents, Fred and Grace Hechinger, set an example for me to follow. As education journalists, they understood the central role of schools and colleges in America. My father, in particular, a Jewish refugee from Nazi Germany, helped me understand how colleges must be held to their promise of welcoming newcomers to the United States. My daughter, Rachel Hechinger, offered the invaluable perspective of a young woman in college. For as long as I can remember, she has asked me when I was going to write a book. She inspired me with her fierce determination and her sense of social justice.

I am indebted, most of all, to my wife, Ricki Morell. I am blessed to share my life with a brilliant journalist and editor. She spent countless hours on the manuscript, pushing me to rewrite and refusing to let me send it before it met her high standards. She has taught me much of what I know about writing—not to mention life, love, and the proper use of the semicolon.

NOTES

I spent more than two years reporting and writing *True Gentlemen*. I visited college campuses in ten states and interviewed scores of students and fraternity alumni. I reviewed thousands of pages of documents from public-records requests and court files and visited university and Sigma Alpha Epsilon archives for historical materials. I attended SAE gatherings, including the fraternity's biennial conventions and annual leadership school. Some of the reporting has its roots in a series of *Bloomberg News* articles about fraternity deaths that I wrote with my colleague David Glovin and which appeared from March 2013 through March 2014. I did much of my additional reporting for this book during the 2015–2016 school year. Although firsthand reporting informs most of the book, I benefited enormously from the excellent work of historians, sociologists, and journalists who have written articles and books about fraternities. I'm also indebted to the work of campus reporters who have long been the first line of inquiry into student organizations.

Introduction

I attended Sigma Alpha Epsilon's John O. Mosely Leadership School, convened aboard the Royal Caribbean ship *Majesty of the Seas*, from August 2 to August 7, 2015.

6   **$3 billion in real estate:** See Sean P. Callan, "The Chapter House Rules: How Corporate Structure Can Handcuff

a House Corporation," *Fraternal Law* 122 (Cincinnati: ManleyBurke, November 2012), p. 3, at http://fraternallaw .com/wp-content/uploads/2012/11/Fraternal-Law-Newsletter -November-2012.pdf.

6   **eight hundred US campuses:** For these and most of the other statistics about membership and members, past and present, I relied on the North-American Interfraternity Conference.

6   **About 40 percent of US presidents:** The North-American Interfraternity Conference counts Bill Clinton, who is an honorary member of Phi Beta Sigma, a historically black fraternity. Clinton also belonged to a service fraternity, Alpha Phi Omega at Georgetown University. See http://nicindy.org /about/notable-fraternity-alumni/political-leaders.

7   **2014 survey:** "Fraternities and Sororities: Understanding Life Outcomes," Gallup-Purdue Index, February 4–March 7, 2014, at http://products.gallup.com/170687/fraternities -sororities-understanding-life-outcomes.aspx.

7   **60 percent of all donations:** Response to public-records request, April 2016.

7   **just above toxic-waste dumps:** "FIPG Risk Management Manual," January 2013, p. 2, at http://fea-inc.org/Websites /fea/files/Content/5454667/FIPG_MANUAL.pdf.

8   **One in six men:** This is my estimate. The North-American Interfraternity Conference counts 380,000 members. About 2.4 million men attend four-year universities (both public and nonprofit) full-time, according to US Education Department data. No one can be entirely sure about changes in fraternity market share over time because fraternity statistics haven't always been tabulated reliably. One book placed the high-water mark in the 1920s, at almost 12 percent of undergraduates: Clyde Sanfred Johnson, *Fraternities in Our Colleges* (New York: National Interfraternity Conference, 1972), p. 89. Heather Matthews Kirk, a spokesperson for the Interfraternity Conference, told me the group has kept consistent data for the last ten years. Her survey of editions of *Baird's Manual of American College Fraternities*, the bible of the movement, places the modern record at 401,460 in 1990, up from 195,712 in 1981.

9   **36 percent of students:** University of Alabama website: http://ofsl.sa.ua.edu.

9   **336,000 brothers:** Figures on initiates and information about members, as well as discipline of chapters, are from Sigma Alpha Epsilon's website, at www.sae.net.

9   **claims the distinction:** Brandon E. Weghorst, ed., *The Phoenix: The Manual of Sigma Alpha Epsilon* (Evanston, IL: Sigma Alpha Epsilon, 2012), p. 152.

10   **ten people died:** Examining news reports, court records, and interviewing officials, my colleague David Glovin put together a database of more than sixty fraternity deaths from 2005 through 2013. See David Glovin and John Hechinger, "Fatalities in Michigan Spotlight Deadliest Fraternities," *Bloomberg News*, January 31, 2014, at www.bloomberg.com/news/articles/2014-01-31/fatalities-in-michigan-virginia-spotlight-deadliest-fraternity.

Chapter 1: Drinking Games

To reconstruct George Desdunes's final night and morning, I relied on the voluminous record of the investigation into his death. These sources include the 580-page transcript of the trial of three students accused and later acquitted of hazing Desdunes: *New York v. Sigma Alpha Epsilon Fraternity, Max Haskin, Ben Mann, and Edward Williams* at the Tomkins County Courthouse in Ithaca, New York, May 21–23, 2012. I also relied on documents related to the Desdunes family's civil case against the fraternity: *Marie Lourdes Andre v. Sigma Alpha Epsilon et al.*, New York Superior Court, Kings County, filed September 7, 2011. The case file includes records related to the police and prosecutors' investigation, including witness statements, text messages, and forensic records. Unless noted, quotations are from trial testimony, depositions, or statements to authorities.

15   **twice the legal limit:** I used the Cleveland Clinic's online blood-alcohol content calculator. See www.clevelandclinic.org/health/interactive/alcohol.asp. If Desdunes, who weighed 170 pounds, drank nine ounces of 80-proof (40 percent alcohol) liquor in half an hour, his blood alcohol would have been .15 percent.

16   **Built in 1915:** Information about the house, its history, and
      its members is from the chapter's website, at www.sae-cornell
      .org/public6.asp.

20   **In December 1776:** For history of Phi Beta Kappa and the
      Kappa Alpha Society and the early social fraternities, see
      William Raimond Baird, *Baird's Manual of American Col-
      lege Fraternities*, vol. 9 (Menasha, WI: G. Banta, 1920), pp.
      4–7.

21   **the "collegiate revolution":** Roger L. Geiger, *The History
      of American Higher Education: Learning and Culture from the
      Founding to World War II* (Princeton: Princeton University
      Press, 2014), p. 365.

22   **"well-known drinking bout":** Nicholas L. Syrett, *The Com-
      pany He Keeps: A History of White College Fraternities*
      (Chapel Hill: University of North Carolina Press, 2009),
      p. 156.

22   **"fiery flavor of sin":** John Addison Porter, *Sketches of Yale Life*
      (Washington, DC: Arlington Publishing Company, 1886),
      p. 225.

22   **At Ohio's Miami University:** Walter Benjamin Palmer, *The
      History of Phi Delta Theta Fraternity* (Menasha, WI: G. Banta,
      1906), p. 231.

22   **SAE's birth in 1856:** For the early history, I relied on a 1,500-
      page, three-volume history of SAE by one of its most im-
      portant leaders: William C. Levere, *The History of the Sigma
      Alpha Epsilon Fraternity*, vol. 1 (Chicago: R. R. Donnelley
      and Sons, 1911), p. 25.

22   **Pale and with brooding gray eyes:** See William C. Levere,
      "The Life of Noble Leslie DeVotie," serialized in the SAE
      Record from 1906 to 1910, in the Levere Memorial Temple
      library, Evanston, Illinois. See also Nancilee D. V. Gasiel,
      "Rediscovering DeVotie," SAE *Record*, undated.

22   **mediocre students and troublemakers:** Landon Cabell Gar-
      land letters, University Libraries Division of Special Collec-
      tions, University of Alabama, boxes 636–638. DeVotie grades
      exceed 96, while others were in the 70s.

22   **"tended only toward evil":** Ibid.

22   **a stormy day with choppy seas:** William C. Levere, "Death
      of DeVotie," SAE *Record* 30 (1) (May 1910).

23   **seventy-seven cases of beer:** Alex Hickey, "IUPD Raids SAE Party; President Arrested," *Indiana Daily Student*, February 5, 2002.

24   **apocryphal story:** Members tell many versions of the Paddy Murphy story. See Cole Garrett, "Legend of Paddy Murphy," May 2015, USC Digital Folklore Archives, at http://folklore.usc.edu/?p=29677.

24   **One of the movement's fiercest advocates:** For the life of William Levere, I relied on Joseph W. Walt, *The Era of Levere: A History of the Sigma Alpha Epsilon Fraternity, 1910–1930* (Evanston, IL: Sigma Alpha Epsilon Fraternity, 1972).

24   **David Starr Jordan, another teetotaler:** Syrett, *The Company He Keeps*, p. 177. Syrett also provided me with archival documents from his research at Stanford University.

25   **equivalent of $6 million today:** *The Phoenix: The Manual of Sigma Alpha Epsilon*, 2012, p. 182. The building cost $400,000 when it was dedicated in 1930.

26   **"underage drinking clubs":** Simon J. Bronner, *Campus Traditions: Folklore from the Old-Time College to the Modern Mega-University* (Jackson: University Press of Mississippi, 2012), p. 246.

26   **"Kegs, party balls, beer trucks":** "FIPG Risk Management Manual," p. 2.

27   **College Alcohol Study:** Henry Wechsler and Toben F. Nelson, "What We Have Learned from the Harvard School of Public Health College Alcohol Study," *Journal of Studies on Alcohol and Drugs* 69 (2008): 481–490. See also Henry Wechsler and Bernice Wuethrich, *Dying to Drink: Confronting Binge Drinking on College Campuses* (New York: Rodale, 2002).

29   **minors drinking themselves unconscious:** University of California at San Diego, disclosed in public-records request.

29   **more than 130 chapters:** Sigma Alpha Epsilon website, 2010–2016, "Chapter Health and Safety History," at www.sae.net/2013/pages/resources/2013-parents-chapter-risk-management-history.

29   **falls from windows and porches:** Caitlin Flanagan, "The Dark Power of Fraternities," *Atlantic*, March 2014, at www.theatlantic.com/magazine/archive/2014/03/the-dark-power-of-fraternities/357580.

30　**surpassed all others:** John Hechinger and David Glovin, "Deadliest Frats Icy 'Torture' of Pledges Evokes Tarantino Films," *Bloomberg News*, December 30, 2013, at www.bloomberg.com/news/articles/2013-12-30/deadliest-frat-s-icy-torture-of-pledges-evokes-tarantino-films.

30　**became easier to sue:** For discussion of liability and fraternities, see Kerri Mumford, "Who Is Responsible for Fraternity Related Injuries on American College Campuses?" *Journal of Contemporary Health Law and Policy* 17 (2001).

31　**sixth-worst risk:** "FIPG Risk Management Manual," p. 2.

31　**national fraternities came up with a strategy:** See David Glovin, "Frats Worse Than Animal House Fail to Pay for Casualties," *Bloomberg News*, March 28, 2013, at www.bloomberg.com/news/articles/2013-03-28/frats-worse-than-animal-house-fail-to-pay-for-casualties. See also Flanagan, "Dark Power of Fraternities."

32　**Lee John Mynhardt, a senior at Elon University:** Glovin, "Frats Worse Than Animal House."

32　**"risk-management" policies:** Ibid. See also Flanagan, "Dark Power of Fraternities."

38　**Marie Lourdes Andre, Desdunes's mother:** For the heartrending account of a mother's discovery of her son's death, I relied on Michael Winerip, "When a Hazing Goes Very Wrong," *New York Times*, April 12, 2012.

40　**The court sealed the proceeding:** Ibid.

42　**confidential settlement:** April 23, 2017, e-mail from Clark Brown, SAE general counsel.

43　*Cornell Alumni Magazine*: "Fraternity Man," *Cornell Alumni Magazine* (November–December 2010), at http://cornellalumnimagazine.com/index.php?option=com_content&task=view&id=894&Itemid=9.

44　**Barnum, the president of the chapter, and his parents sued:** *Eric Barnum, Mark Barnum, Sally Barnum v. Lloyd's, London et al.*, New York State Supreme Court (2015), 153485/2015.

Chapter 2: Broken Pledges

In December 2013, I interviewed Justin Stuart for more than five hours, first on the campus of the University of Maryland and then several more times by phone. To document his account, David Glovin and I tried to speak with every fraternity member who could have been a witness. None of the pledges who joined would comment. A pledge who chose not to join, Max Kellner, confirmed much of his account of what happened during the first night in the basement. Stuart provided us with copies of text messages from members that confirmed his account. His father offered e-mails that detailed correspondence with the college administration. Through a public-records request to Salisbury University, we obtained scores of pages of records detailing Stuart's report to the school and to the campus police. The disciplinary board backed his account. Some of the reporting for this chapter originally appeared in *Bloomberg News*: John Hechinger and David Glovin, "Deadliest Frat's Icy 'Torture' of Pledges Evokes Tarantino Films," December 30, 2013, at www.bloomberg.com/news/articles/2013-12-30 /deadliest-frat-s-icy-torture-of-pledges-evokes-tarantino-films.

51   **"fagging"**: Hank Nuwer, *Wrongs of Passage: Fraternities, Sororities, Hazing, and Binge Drinking* (Bloomington: Indiana University Press, 2001), pp. 100, 123, 238.

52   **fraternities favored "tubbing"**: Nicholas L. Syrett, *The Company He Keeps: A History of White College Fraternities* (Chapel Hill: University of North Carolina Press, 2009), pp. 151–153.

53   **"The practical joke is war . . ."**: G. Stanley Hall and Arthur Allin, "The Psychology of Tickling, Laughing, and the Comic," *American Journal of Psychology* 9 (Worcester, MA: Clark University, 1897–1898), p. 23. See also Michael Kimmel, *Guyland: The Perilous World Where Boys Become Men* (New York: HarperCollins, 2008), which contains an excellent chapter on fraternity hazing and its use to enforce a certain vision of masculinity.

53   **"horseplay" or "rough house"**: Syrett, *The Company He Keeps*, p. 152.

53   **an entire issue of the *Record***: I examined decades of issues of the SAE *Record*, SAE's magazine, and the *Phoenix*, its pledge manual, at the library of Levere Memorial Temple, SAE's headquarters, in Evanston, Illinois.

56   **University of Maine survey:** Elizabeth J. Allan and Mary Madden, *Hazing in View, College Students at Risk: Initial*

Findings from the National Study of Student Hazing (Collingdale, PA: Diane Publishing, 2009).

57   **"developed 'pledge ass'":** Charles M. Blow, *Fire Shut Up in My Bones* (Boston and New York: Houghton Mifflin Harcourt, 2014), p. 176.

57   **blindfolded and forced to wear a backpack:** Rick Rojas and Benjamin Mueller, "Defiant Baruch Fraternity Pledge Fought Back in Fatal Hazing," *New York Times*, September 15, 2015.

58   **shocked them with a cattle prod:** Stephen Keller, "Former Fraternity Leaders Sentenced," *Daily Texan*, April 29, 2008.

58   **"Brown Bag Night":** John Hechinger and David Glovin, "Cal Poly Brings Back Freshman Pledging After Lobbying," *Bloomberg News*, October 15, 2013, at www.bloomberg.com /news/articles/2013-10-15/cal-poly-brings-back-freshman -pledging-after-lobbying.

59   **a litany of hazing:** Josephine Wolff and Matt Westmoreland, "In the Hot Seat: Hazing at Princeton," *Daily Princetonian*, April 25, 2010.

59   **kiddie pool full of vomit:** Andrew Lohse, *Confessions of an Ivy League Frat Boy* (New York: Thomas Dunne Books, 2014), p. 69.

70   **consistency of "black leather":** Carrie Wells, "Hazing at Maryland Colleges Includes Humiliation, Coercion, Hospital Trips," *Baltimore Sun*, November 22, 2014.

Chapter 3: Sexual Assault Expected

I attended Ethan Turner's criminal trial on Friday, February 12, 2016, and from Tuesday through Thursday, February 16–18, as well as his sentencing on Thursday, April 7. The account of the SAE party and its aftermath relies primarily on court testimony. I also examined records related to the trial and criminal investigation, including statements by Ivan Booth and Evan Krumheuer. Through his lawyer, Turner declined comment. I was not able to secure an interview with Chaz Haggins. I interviewed his mother, who provided details about her son and told me she believed her son was innocent. I met Gabriela at the courthouse and later interviewed her by phone in February 2017. I offered to use a pseudonym, but she said she preferred to use her real name. After

Turner's sentencing, I spoke with Gabriela's parents, who provided more details about her life both before and after the party.

77   **most likely to be sexually assaulted in her first months:** "Factors That Increase Sexual Assault Risk," *National Institute of Justice*, October 2008, at www.nij.gov/topics/crime /rape-sexual-violence/campus/pages/increased-risk.aspx.

78   **sexual assault represented 15 percent of liability losses:** Mick McGill, vice president, client advocacy, Willis Group, August 12, 2011, presentation, claims 1998 to present.

78   **one and one-half times more likely:** Christopher P. Krebs et al., "The Campus Sexual Assault Study," *National Institute of Justice,* October 2007, p. xv.

78   **three times the risk of rape:** Meichun Mohler-Kuo et al., "Correlates of Rape While Intoxicated in a National Sample of College Women," *Journal of Studies of Alcohol* 65 (January 2004): 41.

78   **indisputable link between alcohol and . . . sexual assault:** Krebs and Lindquist, "Campus Sexual Assault Study," p. ix.

79   **one in five women:** Christopher P. Krebs et al., "Campus Climate Survey Validation Study Final Technical Report" (Washington: Bureau of Justice Statistics Research and Development Series, January 2016), p. 73.

79   **Stanford student named Brock Allen Turner:** Liam Stack, "Light Sentence for Brock Turner in Stanford Rape Case Draws Outrage," *New York Times*, June 6, 2016.

79   **"No means yes":** Sam Greenberg, "DKE chants on Old Campus Spark Controversy," *Yale Daily News,* October 14, 2010.

79   **"luring your rape bait":** Janel Davis, "Georgia Tech Disbands Fraternity Responsible for 'Rapebait' E-mail," *Atlanta Journal-Constitution*, April 4, 2014.

79   **members cheered on pledges:** Tess Bloch-Horowitz, "On Living in Fear of Telling the Truth: My Experience with SAE, Retaliation and Title IX," *Stanford Daily*, May 20, 2015.

80   **"Freshman daughter drop off":** Elisha Fieldstadt, "Old Dominion University's Sigma Nu Frat Suspended During Probe into Sexually Suggestive Signs," *NBC News*, August 25, 2015, at www.nbcnews.com/news/us-news/old-dominion -universitys-sigma-nu-frat-suspended-during-probe-sexually -n415056?cid=par-time-article_20150824.

80 **"when I rape you"**: "NC State, Pi Kappa Phi Decry 'Unacceptable and Offensive' Book," *WRAL.com*, March 20, 2015, at www.wral.com/nc-state-fraternity-placed-on-interim -suspension-after-embarrassing-scary-book-found/14528066.

80 **a member of SAE was expelled**: Nicholas Syrett, *The Company He Keeps: A History of White College Fraternities* (Chapel Hill: University of North Carolina Press, 2009), p. 177.

81 **"considerable merriment in the fraternity"**: William C. Levere, *The History of the Sigma Alpha Epsilon Fraternity* (Chicago: R. R. Donnelley and Sons, 1911), vol. 2, p. 88.

81 **double standard . . . "easy lays" . . . eight naked fraternity men**: Syrett, *The Company He Keeps*, pp. 264, 280–281.

82 **a woman on leave**: Andy Merton, "Hanging on (by a Jockstrap) to Tradition at Dartmouth," *Esquire*, June 19, 1979.

82 **fifty such campus attacks**: Julie K. Ehrhart and Bernice R. Sandler, "Campus Gang Rape: Party Games" (Washington, DC: Association of American Colleges, Project on the Status and Education of Women, November 1985), p. 2.

82 **eight members of the Alpha Tau Omega chapter**: Peggy Reeves Sanday, *Fraternity Gang Rape: Sex, Brotherhood, and Privilege on Campus* (New York: New York University Press, 1990), pp. 38–89. Sanday, following the conventions of social-science research, doesn't name the fraternity or college, but its identity is clear from contemporary news accounts. See Tamar Lewin, "In Short: Nonfiction," *New York Times*, April 28, 1999.

82 **In a variety of surveys**: Joetta L. Carr and Karen M. Van Deusen, "Risk Factors for Male Sexual Aggression on College Campuses," *Journal of Family Violence* 19 (2004): 279.

82 **two studies . . . fraternity members are three times more likely**: John D. Foubert, Johnathan T. Newberry, and Jerry Tatum, "Behavior Difference Seven Months Later: Effects of a Rape Prevention Program," *NAPSA Journal* 44 (2007): 739; and Catherine Loh et al., "A Prospective Analysis of Sexual Assault Perpetration," *Journal of Interpersonal Violence* 20 (2005): 1339.

82 **"rape-supportive attitudes"**: See R. Sean Bannon, Matthew W. Brosi, and John D. Foubert, "Sorority Women's and

Fraternity Men's Rape Myth Acceptance and Bystander Intervention Attitudes," *Journal of Student Affairs Research and Practice* 50 (2013): 72–87.

82 **"A 2016 university task force":** Harvard University Task Force on the Prevention of Sexual Assault, Final Report, March 7, 2016, at http://sexualassaulttaskforce.harvard.edu /files/taskforce/files/final_report_of_the_task_force_on_the _prevention_of_sexual_assault_16_03_07.pdf.

83 **"predictable outcome":** Elizabeth A. Armstrong, Laura T. Hamilton, and Brian Sweeney, "Sexual Assault on Campus: A Multilevel Integrative Approach to Party Rape," *Social Problems* 53 (November 2006): 483–484. For an eye-opening inside look at the college scene, see Elizabeth A. Armstrong and Laura T. Hamilton, *Paying for the Party: How College Maintains Inequality* (Cambridge: Harvard University Press, 2013). Following social science conventions, the book and study do not name Indiana University, but it has since become public.

84 **23 percent of sexual-assault reports:** "Community Attitudes and Experiences with Sexual Assault—Survey Report" (Bloomington: Division of Student Affairs, Indiana University, October 2015), p. 5, at http://stopsexualviolence.iu.edu /doc/climate-survey/climate-survey-full-report.pdf.

84 **a member of Delta Tau Delta:** Samantha Schmidt, "Accused in Two Rapes, Former Student at Indiana University Avoids Prison with Plea Deal," *New York Times*, June 27, 2016.

84 **Sociologists at Lehigh:** Ayres A. Boswell and Joan Z. Spade, "Fraternities and Collegiate Rape Culture: Why Are Some Fraternities More Dangerous Places for Women?" *Gender and Society* 10 (April 1996): 136–138.

85 **"the 'rapey' one":** Rebecca Leitman Veidlinger, "Does Your Chapter Tolerate Sexual Assault? The Answer Is More Complicated Than You Think," *FRMT Risk Management Newsletter (Willis of Nebraska)* 35 (Spring 2015): 3, at www .frmtltd.org/wfData/files/FRMT_Spring_2015.pdf.

86 **at fifteen of 230 SAE chapters:** This is a conservative number. I excluded some cases where it was difficult to determine the facts of the report.

86 **"was charged with rape and assault":** Massachusetts District Court, criminal docket number 1662-cr-002604, April 19, 2016.

86 **"I am directing you and members of your chapter":** University of Iowa, result of public-records request.

87 **SAE member was handcuffed and arrested:** Ibid.

87 **five separate reports:** San Diego State University and California State University, Long Beach, results of public-records requests.

87 **longest trail of sexual-assault reports:** University of New Mexico, result of public-records requests.

87 **lawsuit filed by an eighteen-year-old freshman:** *Jane Doe v. Sigma Alpha Epsilon et al.*, U.S. District Court, New Mexico, June 22, 1999, CV 99–0693.

88 **the initials A. O.:** *A. O. v. Phi Alpha Inc. d/b/a Sigma Alpha Epsilon-New Mexico Chapter et al.*, New Mexico District Court, County of Bernalillo, January 29, 2014, CV-2014–00836.

88 **"This is where my memory stops":** Public-records request, University of New Mexico.

91 **in the SAE chapter house at Emory University:** SAE and Emory statements. In February 2017, Emory said, "the victim decided not to pursue criminal prosecutions." Citing privacy rules, the school declined to release information about possible disciplinary proceedings. Clark Brown, SAE's general counsel, said the chapter wasn't found responsible for the alleged attack but underwent sexual-assault training.

92 **according to her parents:** Parents of an LMU Student, "First-Person Feature: Parents of a Rape Survivor Tell Their Story," *Los Angeles Loyolan*, April 15, 2015. Brown, the SAE lawyer, said the chapter, which was a provisional "colony" was shut down soon after for alcohol violations.

94 **"during his interview with detectives":** Transcribed DVD statement of Ivan Alexander Booth, November 2, 2014.

96 **"It is beyond just alcohol":** "University Formalizes SAE Chapter Suspension," *Johns Hopkins News-Letter*, March 5, 2015.

96 **In a March 2015 editorial:** "SAE Suspension Wrong, Requires Reversal," *Johns Hopkins News-Letter*, March 5, 2015.

97   **$2 million insurance policy:** University Policies and Procedures, Insurance, Johns Hopkins University, at http://studentaffairs.jhu.edu/fsl/policies.

Chapter 4: The SAE Law

I based my account of SAE's disciplinary hearing on November 13, 2012, on the results of a public-records request to the University of North Carolina at Wilmington. It yielded the 175-page transcript of the proceedings, as well as the voluminous records of e-mails, letters, and documents related to the incidents, the investigation, and its aftermath. I also traveled to Wilmington from April 26 through April 28, 2016, to meet with Ian Gove and other fraternity members and alumni.

108   **could pull off a purple seersucker suit:** Molly Farker, "Sen. Goolsby Takes Last Lap with Eye on House—His Own," *StarNewsOnline.com*, May 15, 2014, at www.starnewsonline.com/article/NC/20140515/news/605041629/WM.

108   **"This is a kangaroo court":** Interview with Ian Gove.

111   **college professors are more likely to be liberal:** See Neil Gross, *Why Are Professors Liberal and Why Do Conservatives Care?* (Cambridge: Harvard University Press, 2013), and Mitchell Langbert, Anthony J. Quain, and Daniel B. Klein, "Faculty Voter Registration in Economics, History, Journalism, Law, and Psychology," *Econ Journal Watch* 13 (3) (September 2016): 422–451.

111   **defining characteristic of the American right's:** Arlie Russell Hochschild, *Strangers in Their Own Land: Anger and Mourning on the American Right* (New York: New Press, 2016), p. 235.

114   **judicial officer later sued SAE:** *David Fiacco v. Sigma Alpha Epsilon*, U.S. District Court, Maine, September 15, 2005, 1:05-cv-00145-GZS. I relied mostly on records related to this case.

115   **"I knew those men":** Pete Smithhisler, speech to Lambda Chi Alpha, published September 2014, at www.youtube.com/watch?v=PKclW4MoHX0. Smithhisler declined to speak with me.

115   **make up about 40 percent of fraternity-related deaths:** John Hechinger and David Glovin, "CalPoly Brings Back Freshman

Pledging After Lobbying," *Bloomberg News*, October 15, 2013 at www.bloomberg.com/news/articles/2013-10-15 /cal-poly-brings-back-freshman-pledging-after-lobbying.

116   **report, prepared by fraternity executives:** Ibid.

116   **Trinity College, a well-regarded:** David Glovin, "Wall Street Pipeline Trinity Sees President Resign," *Bloomberg News*, May 7, 2013, at www.bloomberg.com/news/articles/2013-05 -06/wall-street-pipeline-trinity-sees-president-quit-amid -frat-fight.

117   **Wesleyan Student Assembly had conducted a survey:** "Survey Data Regarding Greek Life and Sexual Assault," Wesleyan Student Assembly, April 26, 2014, at http://wsa .wesleyan.edu/2014/04/26/survey-data-regarding-greek -life-sexual-assault.

117   **saw a broader need to remake Greek life:** "On the Record with President Michael Roth: Sexual Assault, Frats, Need Blind," *Wesleying*, December 1, 2014.

118   **"I think it's a really tragic loss":** "Future of Wesleyan's DKE Frat in Hands of Judge," CBS News, April 29, 2015, at www .cbsnews.com/news/wesleyan-university-lawsuit-delta-kappa -epsilon-fraternity-accuses-school-of-discrimination.

118   **re-examine the policy:** Graham W. Bishai, Claire E. Parker, and Leah S. Yared, "Social Organizations Sanctions Could Be 'Revised or Replaced,'" *Harvard Crimson*, January 26, 2017, at www.thecrimson.com/article/2017/1/26/sanctions-may-change -khurana-says/.

118   **committee advocated:** Hannah Natanson and Derek G. Xiao, "Faculty Committee Recommends Social Groups Be 'Phased Out,'" *Harvard Crimson*, July 13, 2017, at www .thecrimson.com/article/2017/7/13/new-sanctions/.

118   **"I sincerely hope":** C. Ramsey Fahs, "In Most Extensive Comments in Centuries, Porcellian Club Criticizes Final Club Scrutiny," *Harvard Crimson*, April 13, 2016.

119   **this $500-a-plate cocktail reception:** I attended the early portion of the evening, along with Steven Churchill, president of SAE.

120   **39 percent of senators:** North-American Interfraternity Conference.

120   **its share of kingmakers:** Bruce D. Hornbuckle, "Brother Bill Brock: A Profile of the SAE and Republican Party Chairman," SAE *Record* 99 (May 1979), pp. 2–14.

121   **more than $1.3 million in campaign contributions:** Center for Responsive Politics, OpenSecrets.org, at www.opensecrets .org/orgs/summary.php?id=D000021992.

122   **FratPAC bore down on US representative Frederica Wilson:** David Glovin, "Mother of Golf Prodigy in Hazing Death Defied by FratPAC," *Bloomberg News*, July 24, 2013, at www.bloomberg.com/news/articles/2013-07-24/mother-of -golf-prodigy-in-hazing-death-defied-by-fratpac. In a February 2017 e-mail, O'Neill said of Wilson, "We have spent a lot of time talking with her and her staff about the most effective ways to combat hazing and to penalize those who haze students. Many other groups did so as well, and it was clear that crafting a federal anti-hazing law presents a number of challenges." His firm is now called Arnold & Porter Kaye Scholer LLP.

123   **The coalition spent $250,000 lobbying:** OpenSecrets.org, at www.bloomberg.com/news/articles/2013-07-24/mother-of -golf-prodigy-in-hazing-death-defied-by-fratpac.

123   **"We believe our sisters":** Tyler Kingkade, "Alpha Phi Becomes First Sorority to Say It Doesn't Support Safe Campus Act," *Huffington Post*, November 12, 2015, at www .huffingtonpost.com/entry/alpha-phi-safe-campus-act_us _56441c26e4b045bf3dedce0d.

127   **an episode from 2008:** Parks Griffin provided records related to the football game.

127   **"Whoever's able to hire":** Allie Grasgreen, "Students Lawyer Up," *Inside Higher Ed*, August 26, 2013, at www.inside highered.com/news/2013/08/26/north-carolina-becomes-first -state-guarantee-students-option-lawyer-disciplinary.

128   **student right-to-counsel bills have been introduced in seven states:** February 2017 e-mail from Joe Cohn, legislative and policy director, Foundation for Individual Rights in Education.

129   **"The real problem for the fraternity":** "Fraternity Suspension Hounds UNCW Chancellor," 2014, *WECT*, at www.wect .com/story/25478372/fraternity-suspension-hounds-uncw -chancellor.

130   **"a victim of North Carolina good old boy politics":** Kristen
       King, "Miller New Chancellor at the University of Wisconsin-
       Green Bay," The Daily Clips, *StarNews Online*, June 3, 2014.

Chapter 5: Sing, Brothers, Sing

I visited the University of Oklahoma campus in Norman from November 4 through November 10, 2015. I pieced together the history of the song through interviews with several members: Garrett
Parkhurst, Drew Rader, Sam Albert, and Jack Counts III. These
University of Oklahoma students also offered details of the singing on the bus, as did their dates, Corina Hernandez and Lindsay
Strunk. I met with Jack Counts Jr., who walked me through the
chapter's rich archival material and introduced me to other alumni
who shared details about SAE at Oklahoma. The university's Western History Collections provided valuable archives related to the
chapter's history—including photographs of its blackface party—
and of the early history of fraternities on campus.

138   **equivalent of $4 million today:** The 1965 cost, $550,000,
       and other details of construction come from Jack Counts Jr.'s
       chapter archives.

138   **largest networks of Ford auto dealerships:** Fred Jones Fam-
       ily Foundation, at http://fredjonesfamilyfoundation.com
       /history.html.

138   **"Singing Fraternity":** For lyrics, see SAE's Facebook page,
       at www.facebook.com/notes/sigma-alpha-epsilon-fraternity
       /the-many-songs-of-sigma-alpha-epsilon-fraternity
       /88343331136, or to hear the songs, mthetgi.sae.net/TheTrue
       GentlemanInitiativeLibrary/81/Module?module=Songs.

140   **The song had traveled:** University of Oklahoma "Inves-
       tigation and Findings," released under a public-records re-
       quest, reported earlier by Tyler Kingkade, "SAE Fraternity
       Members Learned Racist Song at National Leadership
       Event, University Finds," *Huffington Post*, March 27, 2015,
       at www.huffingtonpost.com/2015/03/27/sae-fraternity
       -racist-song_n_6956790.html. See also SAE's statement on
       the investigation, at www.sae.net/home/pages/news/news
       -media-statements-oklahoma-investigation-findings.

141   **had been a top golfer . . . Jesuit prep school:** Faith Karimi and Justin Lear, "Who Are the Two Fraternity Students Expelled at the University of Oklahoma," *CNN.com*, March 12, 2015, www.cnn.com/2015/03/12/us/oklahoma-who-are-expelled -students. I couldn't reach Parker Rice for comment. Through a family spokesman, Pettit declined my request for an interview.

142   **"To those who have misused their free speech":** David Boren, University of Oklahoma statement.

143   **At Princeton University, three-fourths:** "Report of the Working Group on Campus Social and Residential Life," *Princeton University Reports* (May 2011) at www.princeton .edu/reports/2011/campuslife/obs-rec/fraternities-sororities.

144   **found rigid segregation:** Matthew W. Hughey, "A Paradox of Participation: Nonwhites in White Sororities and Fraternities," *Social Problems* 57 (November 2010): 653–679.

144   **"American apartheid":** John D. Sutter, "Are Frats a Form of American Apartheid," CNN.com, March 10, 2015, at www .cnn.com/2015/03/10/opinions/sutter-oklahoma-fraternity -racist.

144   **"racially isolating environments":** Julie J. Park, "Clubs and the Campus Racial Climate: Student Organizations and Interracial Friendship in College," *Journal of College Student Development* 55 (October 2014): 641–660.

144   **"ethnic clubs for White students" . . . "White victimization":** Jim Sidanius et al., "Ethnic Enclaves and the Dynamics of Social Identity on the College Campus: The Good, the Bad and the Ugly," *Journal of Personality and Social Psychology* 87 (July 2004): 107.

145   **more likely to report verbal and physical assaults:** Nella Van Dyke and Griff Tester, "Dangerous Climates: Factors Associated with Various Racist Hate Crimes on College Campuses," *Journal of Contemporary Criminal Justice* 30 (July 2014): 290–309.

145   **many previous episodes:** See Tyler Kingkade, "SAE's Racist Chant Was Not an Isolated Incident," *Huffington Post*, March 10, 2015, at www.huffingtonpost.com/2015/03 /10/sae-racism_n_6831424.html; Jake New, "Deadliest and Most Racist?" *Inside Higher Ed*, March 10, 2015, at

www.insidehighered.com/news/2015/03/10/several-sigma
-alpha-epsilon-chapters-accused-racism-recent-years; and
Tasneem Nashrulla, "A History of Racism at Sigma Alpha
Epsilon," *BuzzFeed News*, June 29, 2015, at www.buzzfeed
.com/tasneemnashrulla/a-history-of-racism-at-sigma-alpha
-epsilon?utm_term=.lm5AvNb35#.cp618g7qX.

146   **Halloween party at Yale's SAE chapter:** Jon Victor and Joey
Ye, "SAE Denies Charges of Racism," *Yale Daily News*, No-
vember 2, 2015. See also Susan Svrluga, "Students Accuse
Yale SAE Fraternity Brother of Saying 'White Girls Only' at
Party Door," *Washington Post*, November 2, 2015; and Mon-
ica Wang and Joe Ye, "Investigations Yield No Disciplinary
Action," *Yale Daily News*," December 9, 2015.

147   **two white SAE members at the University of Texas:** Cas-
sandra Jaramillo and Mikaela Cannizzo, "UT Students in
Racially Motivated Assault Appeal University Disciplinary
Process," *Daily Texan*, March 29, 2016.

147   **the University of Wisconsin at Madison suspended:** Results of a public-records request to the university. See also
"Timeline—Sigma Alpha Epsilon," The University of Wisconsin website, May 17, 2016 at http://news.wisc.edu
/timeline-sigma-alpha-epsilon.

147   **plotted to tie a noose:** Charlie Campbell, "Ole Miss Fraternity
Chapter Shuttered After Racist Prank," *Time*, April 18, 2014.

147   **spray-painted racial slurs:** Jacqueline Palochko, "Lehigh
Launches Survey Linked to Racist Graffiti," *Morning Call*,
October 13, 2015.

150   **the Bizzell Memorial Library stands:** Anne Barajas Harp,
The Sooner Story: The University of Oklahoma, 1890–2015
(Norman: University of Oklahoma Press, 2015), p. 77.

151   **$75 million dorm:** Jason Kersey, "Oklahoma Athletics: What's
It Like to Be a Non-athlete in Headington Hall?" *Oklahoman*,
July 12, 2014, at http://newsok.com/article/4988418.

151   **family of one of Rader's pledge brothers:** "OU President
David Boren Announces New Seed Sower Society Members
at Regent Meeting," *OU Daily*, March 9, 2016.

153   **pleaded guilty in 2014 to a misdemeanor:** Jake Trotter,
"Joe Mixon Reaches Plea Deal," *ESPN*, October 30, 2014,

at www.espn.com/college-football/story/_/id/11790146 /oklahoma-sooners-running-back-joe-mixon-reaches-plea -deal-case-punching-female-student.

154   **allowing them to withdraw:** Telephone interview with David Boren, March 2017.

156   **"Since we know we all have said things":** Maria Dixon Hall, "A Teachable Moment: How OU Failed Transformation 101," *Patheos*, March 10, 2015, at www.patheos.com/blogs /mariadixonhall/2015/03/a-teachable-moment-how-ou -failed-transformation-101.

156   **"All the apologies in the world":** Robert Wilonsky, "Highland Park's Levi Pettit Apologizes for Role in Racist SAE Video, Says It Was 'Disgusting,'" *Dallas Morning News*, March 24, 2015, at www.dallasnews.com/news/news/2015 /03/24/levi-pettit-the-highland-park-hs-grad-seen-on-racist -sae-video-to-publicly-apologize-wednesday.

156   **"I admit it likely was fueled by alcohol":** Bill Chappell, "Two Oklahoma Students Seen in Racist Fraternity Video Apologize," *NPR*, March 11, 2015, at www.npr.org/sections/ thetwo-way/2015/03/11/392279208/apologies-emerge- from-two-oklahoma-students-in-racist-sae-video.

157   **"It's sad that it's 2015 and stuff like this":** Sterling Shepard on Twitter, at http://twitter.com/sterl_shep3/status /574734237733023744.

157   **"shaking our hand, giving us hugs":** Maxwell Strachan, "Oklahoma Linebacker Eric Striker Shares 'His Thoughts on Fraternity's Racist Chant,'" *Huffington Post*, March 12, 2015, at www.huffingtonpost.com/2015/03/10/eric-striker -oklahoma-football-racism_n_6838804.html.

160   **University of Oklahoma's Student Affairs Office surveyed:** March 2017 interview with Clark Stroud, dean of students. At traditionally white fraternities, 2.56 percent of members were African American; 10.14 percent, American Indian; 4.42 percent, Asian American; and 7.78 percent, Latino. An additional fraternity with only four students had no black members.

164   **"hedonistic fantasy":** Will James blog post, "There Will Never Be Another Black S-A-E," at http://betweenthenotes .me/2015/03/09/there-will-never-be-another-black-s-a-e.

165   **"I wouldn't even hesitate for a split second":** CNN video, March 11, 2015, at www.cnn.com/videos/tv/2015/03/11/cnn -tonight-jonathan-davis-ou-sooners-racist-song-sae-fraternity william-bruce-james.cnn.

167   **More than a dozen universities:** Rachel L. Swarns, "Georgetown University Plans Steps to Atone for Slave Past," *New York Times*, September 1, 2016.

Chapter 6: Discriminating Gentlemen

I based the account of the 1951 Sigma Alpha Epsilon convention in Chicago on a transcript in the library of Sigma Alpha Epsilon's headquarters in the Levere Memorial Temple, Evanston, Illinois: "Ninety-Fifth Anniversary National Convention, Sigma Alpha Epsilon, Supplementary Proceedings," Chicago, Illinois, September 2–5, 1951.

169   **swayed to the Latin rhythms:** Don Gable, "Ninety-Fifth Anniversary Convention: Chicago Makes Historical Strides," SAE *Record*, November 1951, p. 118.

170   **"SAE's governing laws":** At the library, I reviewed copies of SAE laws dating back to the 1900s.

171   **lead financier of the fraternity's headquarters:** Joseph W. Walt, *The Era of Levere: A History of the Sigma Alpha Epsilon Fraternity, 1910–1930* (Evanston, IL: Sigma Alpha Epsilon Fraternity, 1972), p. 561.

171   **research on the Tuskegee syphilis experiment:** Donald H. Rockwell, Annie Roof Yobs, and M. Brittain Moore Jr., "The Tuskegee Study of Untreated Syphilis, the Thirtieth Year of Observation," *Archives of Internal Medicine* 114 (6) (1964): 792–798.

175   **"Who made it a bad word":** Interfraternity Conference Minutes, National Interfraternity Conference, 1947, University of Michigan, digitized October 12, 2007, p. 124.

176   **"The world was different then":** March 2017 telephone interview with G. Holmes Braddock. I also spoke with Samuel G. DeSimone, the Pennsylvania judge who was on the panel proposing the law change. "I don't remember any of that," he told me. The other members at the convention have since died.

177   **a descendant of French Protestants:** William C. Levere, "The Life of DeVotie," SAE *Record* 26 (3) (September 1906): 247–251.

177   **Staunch believers in slavery:** Ibid.

177   **"To the young white men of the South":** William C. Levere, *The History of the Sigma Alpha Epsilon Fraternity*, vol. 1 (Chicago: R. R. Donnelley and Sons, 1911), p. 108.

178   **"the best colleges and universities":** Ibid., vol. 2, p. 197.

178   **outsiders began to form their own organizations:** Craig LaRon Torbenson and Gregory Parks, eds., *Brothers and Sisters: Diversity in College Fraternities and Sororities* (Madison, NJ: Fairleigh Dickinson University Press, 2009), p. 39.

179   **wrote a novel set at his alma mater:** William Collin Levere, *Twixt Greek and Barb: A Story of University Life* (Evanston, IL: William S. Lord, 1900), pp. 97–112.

179   **Yale, and Princeton changed their admissions requirements:** Jerome Karabel, *The Chosen: The Hidden History of Admission and Exclusion at Harvard, Yale and Princeton* (Boston: Houghton Mifflin Harcourt, 2006), pp. 115, 133, 367.

180   **"alien and unwashed element":** Ibid., p. 112.

180   **Princeton admitted its first African American:** Ibid., p. 379.

180   **a 1936 Ohio State University catalog:** Ohio State University Archives.

181   **doubling of college enrollment:** Roger L. Geiger, ed., *The History of Higher Education Annual 2002* (Piscataway, NJ: Transaction Publishers, 2002), p. 95.

182   **incorporated racially tinged themes:** Anthony James, "College Social Fraternities, Manhood, and the Defense of Southern Traditionalism, 1945–1960," in *White Masculinity in the Recent South*, ed. Trent Watts (Baton Rouge: Louisiana State University Press, 2009).

182   **performed in blackface:** Charles Tucker, ed., *The History of Oklahoma Kappa of Sigma Alpha Epsilon* (Norman: University of Oklahoma, 1959), p. 263: Carroll L. Lurding Library of College Fraternity and Sorority Materials, 1834–2014, Lilly Library Manuscript Collections, Indiana University, Bloomington, Indiana, box 17.

182   **a 1949–1950 SAE scrapbook:** University of Oklahoma, Western History Collection.

182   **Amherst College in Massachusetts decided:** Nicholas L. Syrett, *The Company He Keeps: A History of White College*

Fraternities (Chapel Hill: University of North Carolina Press, 2009), pp. 248–250.

184 **"He was the first black man":** Daniel Sheehan, *The People's Advocate: The Life and Legal History of America's Most Fearless Public Interest Lawyer* (Berkeley: Counterpoint Press, 2013), chap. 5.

184 **Sigma Alpha Epsilon held its June 1969 convention:** SAE *Record* (February 1969): 5, Levere Library.

185 **Steve Walker, a consultant to the national SAE office:** Transcript, 1969 convention, Levere Library.

187 **One piece of news would have especially interested alumni:** Thomas M. Rigdon, letter to Eminent Supreme Recorder, April 23, 1970, Levere Library.

187 **a collection of oral histories:** Clarence G. Williams, ed., *Technology and the Dream: Reflections on the Black Experience at MIT, 1941–1999* (Cambridge: MIT Press, 2003), p. 377.

188 **became an emergency-room physician:** Tasneem Nashrulla, *BuzzFeed News*. The article, which alerted me to his account and Sheehan's, included an interview with Salih.

Chapter 7: Old Row

I reported at the University of Alabama in Tuscaloosa from October 20 to October 23, 2015, visiting the SAE chapter, interviewing students, and researching SAE's early history at the University of Alabama's W. S. Hoole Special Collections Library.

191 **onetime "segregation academy":** Gavin Wright, *Sharing the Prize: The Economics of the Civil Rights Revolution in the American South* (Cambridge: Harvard University Press, 2013), p. 168. John McWilliams, associate head of the school at Montgomery Academy, told me the school enrolled its first black student in 1972 and African Americans make up 7 percent of the student body. "One of our core values is we believe in sustaining a diverse school and community," he said.

191 **Goodwyn escorted his girlfriend:** "Southern Debutante Cotillion Holds Its Annual Ball," *Montgomery Advertiser*, July 26, 2014.

192 **A former Alpha Omicron Pi sister:** Interview with Yardena Wolf, who was a member of the sorority.

192 **fees can be competitive:** For on-campus room-and-board fees, see www.ua.edu/about/quickfacts. For average fees for members of the Interfraternity Council, see http://alabamaifc.com /financial-information.html. It's hard to make an exact comparison because fraternities also charge initiation fees.

193 **the "Machine":** The machine has long been an open secret at the University of Alabama. The *Crimson White*, the student newspaper, has done impressive reporting on its workings. See also Philip Weiss, "The Most Powerful Fraternity in America," *Esquire*, April 1992, pp. 102–106. A website, called WelcomeToTheMachine, keeps an archive on decades of reporting, at www.welcometothemachine.info/index.php.

193 **known on campus for his seersucker suits:** "Getting to Know the Man Behind the Bowtie: SGA President, Hamilton Bloom," *Odyssey*, April 20, 2014, at www.theodysseyonline .com/gettingto-know-the-man-behind-the-bowtie-sga -president-hamilton-bloom.

195 **An Alabama political science professor:** Interview with Norman Baldwin, professor at the University of Alabama.

197 **For a study published in 2012:** Rashawn Ray and Jason A. Rosow, "The Two Different Worlds of Black and White Fraternity Men," *Journal of Contemporary Ethnography* 41 (2012): 66–94. As is the practice in sociology studies, the authors decline to disclose the identity of the university, but it is clearly Indiana University based on their description, the institutions involved in funding, their location as scholars at the time, and a subject quoted who gives the street name of one row of fraternities.

197 **a rare glimpse of Greek demography:** Under a public-records request, the university provided only a chart, so I could make only broad estimates. Two small fraternities, including a new Lutheran sorority, had no minority members, and a large Jewish fraternity appeared to have less than 1 percent minority membership.

198 **"elitist social hierarchy":** "Vision for the Ideal Fraternity and Sorority Community," Indiana University, September 2016, at http://studentaffairs.indiana.edu/doc/sll/greek-vision/vifsc -strategic-plan-final-for-provost.pdf.

198   **"admirably suited to give large houses"**: "The Indiana Plan of Assistance to Fraternal Organizations at Indiana University," March 1962, Fraternity House Plans Committee, University Archives, Indiana University Libraries.

199   **45 percent of those elected:** Kallen Dimitroff, "Greek Students Are Overrepresented in UT's Student Government," *Daily Texan*, September 23, 2013.

200   **"a dynasty out of a democracy":** Suchi Sundaram, "This Year, Make Student Government Representative of All UT Students, Not Just the Greek Community," *Daily Texan*, February 11, 2014.

200   **"People like people who are like themselves":** Max Abelson and Zeke Faux, "Secret Handshakes Greet Frat Brothers on Wall Street," *Bloomberg News*, December 23, 2013, at www.bloomberg.com/news/articles/2013-12-23/secret -handshakes-greet-frat-brothers-on-wall-street.

200   **more likely to get higher-paying jobs:** David Marmaros and Bruce Sacerdote, "Peer and Social Networks in Job Search," *European Economic Review* 46 (May 2002): 870–879.

200   **received an e-mail:** Abelson and Faux, "Secret Handshakes."

201   **12 percent of undergraduates:** This figure and others in the paragraph are from the University of Alabama website, at www.ua.edu.

201   **have spent more than $200 million:** Jay Reeves, "'Bama Greeks in $202M Building Boom," *Associated Press*, November 9, 2013.

201   **"apologists for apartheid":** Ben Gose, "U. of Alabama Studies Why Its Fraternities and Sororities Remain Segregated by Race," *Chronicle of Higher Education*, December 5, 1997.

201   **"It is appropriate":** Stephen Nathaniel Dethrage, "Witt Defends Traditional Greek System," *Crimson White*, September 15, 2011.

202   **The *Crimson White* ran a story:** For the recounting of these events I relied on the student newspaper's extensive reporting.

202   **internal university documents:** I am including only members of the Interfraternity Council, which represents historically white fraternities.

203   **"Even in the age of Obama":** Lawrence Ross, *Blackballed: The Black and White Politics of Race on America's Campuses* (New York: St. Martin's Press, 2015), p. 13.

205 **"never gave up his quest to 'keep 'Bama White'":** E. Culpepper Clark, *The Schoolhouse Door: Segregation's Last Stand at the University of Alabama* (New York: Oxford University Press, 1995), p. 140.

206 **men in white sheets:** Chuck Whiting, "Crosses Burned After Election," *Crimson White*, February 10, 1976.

Chapter 8: The Phoenix

I attended SAE's biennial convention, held in Newport Beach, California, from June 18 to June 20, 2015. I based this account on observation and interviews, as well as a review of a transcript.

216 **he once suggested:** Cohen told undergraduates at a seminar held in his cabin aboard the leadership cruise in August 2015.

217 **He once brandished:** Cohen made these comments at a regional leadership conference held at the University of La Verne in California in March 2014. It was his first public appearance after announcing the fraternity ban.

218 **Its claims plunged 90 percent:** Phi Delta Theta statistics.

218 **"If your founders were in this room":** Transcript of SAE's 2013 convention at the Hotel InterContinental in Chicago, Levere Library.

220 **He was sixteen and a high school junior:** Part of this chapter is based on material that originally appeared in an earlier article: John Hechinger and David Glovin, "Fraternity Chief Feared for Son as Hazings Spurred JPMorgan Snub," *Bloomberg News*, March 27, 2014, at www.bloomberg .com/news/articles/2014-03-27/fraternity-chief-feared-for -son-as-hazings-spurred-jpmorgan-snub.

222 **"the deadliest fraternity":** John Hechinger and David Glovin, "Deadliest Frat's Icy 'Torture' of Pledges Evokes Tarantino Films," *Bloomberg News*, December 30, 2013.

222 **A drunk SAE member . . . a drunk freshman:** David Glovin and John Hechinger, "Fatalities in Michigan Spotlight Deadliest Fraternities," *Bloomberg News*, January 31, 2014. See also Laurence Hammack, "Drunken Driver in Crash That Killed W&L Classmate to Serve Three Years," *Roanoke Times*, January 15, 2015.

226   **Scarborough had nominated:** Transcript of the 2009 SAE convention at the New Orleans Marriott, Levere Library.

Chapter 9: The Lions

For this chapter, I traveled twice to Ohio State University in Columbus. I interviewed SAE members and attended the Monday night chapter meeting on November 2, 2015. I also watched the dedication of the lions on April 30, 2016.

232   **On the day of its installation:** William C. Levere, *The History of the Sigma Alpha Epsilon Fraternity,* vol. 2 (Chicago: R. R. Donnelley and Sons, 1911), pp. 159–162.

233   **best known for throwing beer bottles:** Ohio State University press release, November 2001, University Archives, Ohio State University.

233   **called its behavior "inexcusable":** Nick Proctor, SAE adviser, letter to Bill Hall, interim vice president of student affairs, January 9, 2001, University Archives.

233   **"Do not be an idiot":** Bowen speech at dedication ceremony for the lions.

235   **a member told Moore in a text:** Moore shared with me the written results of his internal investigation, which are the basis of this account. The accused student did not return messages.

236   **One student had suffered:** Early one morning on the leadership cruise in August 2015, members, requesting anonymity, shared these stories with me.

237   **the event raised a record $175,000:** See www.pghdonutdash .org.

237   **His SAE brothers helped him raise money:** Alexi Sciutto related this story to me during the March 2014 leadership conference at the University of La Verne in California.

238   **In the 1870s, chapters at the University of Vermont and Wesleyan:** "A Brief History of Phi Beta Kappa," at www .pbk.org/imis15/PBK_Member/About_PBK/PBK_History /PBK_Member/PBK_History.aspx?hkey=44391228-bb7c -4705-bd2e-c785f3c1d876.

238   **"Why discriminate because of sex?":** "Leadership, Friendship, Service: Pledge Manual 2015–2016," Alpha Phi Omega, p. 14.

239   **Phi Tau broke away from Phi Sigma Kappa:** Samantha
       Stern, "Greek Houses Adjust to New Concepts of Gender,"
       Dartmouth, May 19, 2016.
239   **Zeta Psi withdrew:** Julie Fei-Fan Balzer, "A Woman of
       Honor," *Brown Alumni Magazine* (May/June 1998). See also
       "Zeta Delta Psi: Our History" at www.zete.org/home.
239   **earliest and highest-profile campaigns:** For the history of
       Williams and its impact on other New England colleges, I
       relied on a comprehensive account by former Williams pres-
       ident John W. Chandler, *The Rise and Fall of Fraternities at
       Williams College: Clashing Cultures and the Transformation of a
       Liberal Arts College* (Williams College Museum of Art, 2014).
240   **"satisfied" or "very satisfied":** Joshua Miller, "A Decade After
       Frats, College Houses Evolve," *Bowdoin Orient*, October 12,
       2007, at http://bowdoinorient.com/bonus/article/2869.
241   **a lawyer and campus free-speech advocate:** Greg Lukianoff,
       *Unlearning Liberty: Campus Censorship and the End of Amer-
       ican Debate* (New York: Encounter Books, 2012), p. 19.
241   **one president, Robert Carothers, decided:** Carothers's
       efforts are chronicled in Henry Wechsler and Bernice Wue-
       thrich, *Dying to Drink: Confronting Binge Drinking on Col-
       lege Campuses* (New York: Rodale: 2002), pp. 228–231.
242   **A 2009 study:** Mark D. Wood et al., "Common Ground: An
       Investigation of Environmental Management Alcohol Pre-
       vention Initiatives in a College Community, *Journal of Studies
       on Alcohol and Drugs* 16 (July 2009): 96–105.
242   **"If in the next three to five years":** Matt Rocheleau, "Dart-
       mouth Bans Hard Alcohol, Forbids Greek Life Pledging,"
       Boston Globe, January 29, 2015.
243   **a group of more than one hundred college presidents:** John
       Hechinger, "Bid to Reconsider Drinking Age Taps Unlikely
       Supporters," *Wall Street Journal*, August 21, 2008.
243   **alcohol consumption has declined:** Anne T. McCartt,
       Laurie A. Hellinga, and Bevan B. Kirley, "The Effects of
       Minimum Legal Drinking Age Twenty-One Laws on Al-
       cohol-Related Driving in the United States," *Journal of Safety
       Research* 41 (April 2010): 173–181.

244   **fallen by half . . . saved more than 26,000 lives:** "Benefits of Higher Drinking Age Are Crystal Clear in Study After Study," Insurance Institute for Highway Safety, Highway Loss Data Institute, December 27, 2008.

244   **drink more than their peers who aren't enrolled:** "High-Risk Drinking in College: What We Know and What We Need to Learn: Final Report," Task Force of the National Advisory Council on Alcohol Abuse and Alcoholism, National Institutes of Health, at www.collegedrinkingprevention .gov/media/finalpanel1.pdf.

Conclusion

250   **and look to abolish them:** "Dean Wormer's Favorite Editorial," *Bloomberg View*, January 7, 2014, at www.bloomberg.com /view/articles/2014-01-07/dean-wormer-s-favorite-editorial.

250   **consider a proposal:** 161st Anniversary Convention, July 6–8, 2017, Boston, "Report to the Fraternity Convention, Permanent Committee on Fraternity Law," Proposal 13, at http:// data.sae.net/docs/LawProposals.pdf.

251   **A grand jury indicted:** First Centre County Investigating Grand Jury, Findings of Fact, May 5, 2017.

251   **Penn State's president demanded:** Eric Barron, "An Open Letter to Penn State's Greek Community," *Digging Deeper: A Blog by Dr. Eric Barron, President of Penn State University*, April 10, 2017, at http://diggingdeeper.psu.edu/2017/04/ an-open-letter-to-penn-states-greek-community/.

251   **Economists and public-health scholars agree:** Mark Goodchild, Anne-Marie Perucic, and Nigar Nargis, "Modelling the Impact of Raising Tobacco Taxes on Public Health and Finance," *Bulletin of the World Health Organization*, 943 (April 2016), 250–257.

252   **2017 convention:** I attended two plenary sessions of SAE's biennial convention, which was held at the Boston Marriott Copley Place. The first vote on the discrimination clause occurred Friday afternoon, July 7, 2017, and the second, the following morning.

INDEX

JOHN HECHINGER, a senior editor at *Bloomberg News,* was a 2011 finalist for the Pulitzer Prize in Public Service and a two-time winner of the George Polk Award for his reporting on education. Before joining *Bloomberg* in 2010, he was a senior special writer at the *Wall Street Journal,* where he focused on education and finance. A graduate of Yale University, he lives near Boston with his wife and daughter.

PublicAffairs is a publishing house founded in 1997. It is a tribute to the standards, values, and flair of three persons who have served as mentors to countless reporters, writers, editors, and book people of all kinds, including me.

I. F. STONE, proprietor of *I. F. Stone's Weekly*, combined a commitment to the First Amendment with entrepreneurial zeal and reporting skill and became one of the great independent journalists in American history. At the age of eighty, Izzy published *The Trial of Socrates*, which was a national bestseller. He wrote the book after he taught himself ancient Greek.

BENJAMIN C. BRADLEE was for nearly thirty years the charismatic editorial leader of *The Washington Post*. It was Ben who gave the *Post* the range and courage to pursue such historic issues as Watergate. He supported his reporters with a tenacity that made them fearless and it is no accident that so many became authors of influential, best-selling books.

ROBERT L. BERNSTEIN, the chief executive of Random House for more than a quarter century, guided one of the nation's premier publishing houses. Bob was personally responsible for many books of political dissent and argument that challenged tyranny around the globe. He is also the founder and longtime chair of Human Rights Watch, one of the most respected human rights organizations in the world.

• • •

For fifty years, the banner of Public Affairs Press was carried by its owner Morris B. Schnapper, who published Gandhi, Nasser, Toynbee, Truman, and about 1,500 other authors. In 1983, Schnapper was described by *The Washington Post* as "a redoubtable gadfly." His legacy will endure in the books to come.

Peter Osnos, *Founder*